Messiaen and the Tristan Myth

Jeremy P. Travell

Messiaen and the Trisan Myth

Jeremy P. Travell

Paperback Edition First Published in Great Britain in 2016
by aSys Publishing

eBook Edition First Published in Great Britain in 2016
by aSys Publishing

Copyright © Jeremy P. Travell

All rights reserved.

No part of this document may be reproduced or transmitted in any form or by any means, electronic, mechanical, photocopying, recording, or otherwise, without prior written permission of the Author or other copyright holders.

ISBN: 978-1-910757-03-1

aSys Publishing
http://www.asys-publishing.co.uk

Dedication

Dedicated to the memory of the Reverend Peter Travell
1923-1985

It is with great sadness that the author has learnt of the death of Pierre Boulez at the time of the publication of this book.

Boulez was a "Beethoven of the twentieth century."

He played a pivotal role in twentieth century music through the development of electronic music, controlled chance and integral serialism. He studied under Olivier Messiaen at the Paris Conservatoire and went on to promote Messiaen's music with great enthusiasm and energy.

January 2016

Contents

Dedication	iii
About The Author	vii
Abstract	ix
1 Introduction	1
2 Messiaen's Creative Practice	31
3 Wagnerism in Relation to Messiaen and Debussy	45
4 The Tristan Myth	63
5 Wagner's use of Myth	79
6 Messiaen's Tristan Trilogy Part 1: *Harawi*	95
7 Messiaen's Tristan trilogy Part 2: *Turangalila*	115
8 Messiaen's Tristan Trilogy Part 3: *Cinq Rechants*	139
9 Conclusion	151
Bibliography	155
Brochures	173
Periodicals	174
Dissertations	179
Documents	180
Scores	181
General Index	182

About The Author

At the age of 9 he won a choral scholarship to Exeter Cathedral Choir School to become a chorister. After graduating from university with honours he taught piano and has a particular interest in the performance practice and technique of Messiaen's piano music. The author studied for an MPhil and PhD as a mature student between 1998 and 2003. He is a fierce critic of of the current narrow empirical approach to the study of Messiaen's music which he considers ignores the value of its original meaning and philosophical significance for us today.

The author now lives in a small Hampshire town with his dog and writes about music.

Jeremy P. Travell

Abstract

The scope and content of this book examines the relation of the *Tristan* myth to Messiaen through the music of *Debussy and Wagner*. In literature, the notions of poetry and language found in the writings of Maeterlinck and Wagner have had a profound effect on Messiaen's compositional development, whilst the idea of myth has informed his aesthetic ideas and its expression in both his music and even in his meticulously written *Harawi* poem.

The importance of the *Tristan* myth is explored through the issues of nature, poetry and language which can be viewed as inspiration beyond music and the *Tristan* works are put into the context of Messiaen's output in terms of time and technique. Messiaen's fascination for Wagner is explored and discussed in relation to Debussy, who was also drawn to Wagner, but knew he somehow had to escape that influence. Messiaen's use of the myth avoids narrative whilst Wagner's employs narrative and is influenced by Schopenhauer and Buddhism.

Harawi is tonally and dramatically challenging and contains elements of Messiaen's style such as the Modes of limited transposition and rhythmic devices; *Tristan* connections are drawn out in *Turangalîla* and an explanation of how the myth is used is undertaken. In *Cinq Rechants* I examine new ideas including the use of non-pitched vocal cries found in all of Wagner's stage works and symbolic elements of the composition are explored and developed in new ways. I include analytical observations to complement the central issue of musical and literary sources relating to the *Tristan* trilogy.

Drawing on many different sources including Messiaen's own treatises, Samuel's interviews with the composer and an extensive literature survey, *Messiaen and the Tristan myth* provides an insight into this complex composer's musical world.

1

INTRODUCTION

The purpose of this book is to explore the importance of the *Tristan* myth to Messiaen and links with musical and literary sources. The origin of my interest in this topic lies in the idea of why a predominantly religious composer suddenly started to write secular music and why he chose the *Tristan* myth. My keen interest in contemporary music and my own reading fanned this enthusiasm, particularly in relation to Messiaen's own fascination with the East and the exotic. My curiosity in the above led me to the key research focus, Messiaen and the *Tristan* myth and from there to look at the inspiration behind his music.

The *Tristan* trilogy, Messiaen's trilogy on love and death, was completed in 1949.[1] This completion was the result of not only years, but decades of meditative thought on *Debussy's Pelléas et Mélisande* and Wagner's *Tristan und Isolde*; Messiaen was presented with the Score of *Pelléas* when he was only ten years old. A comparison of *Pelléas* and *Tristan und Isolde* reveals that those decades were not wasted, for Messiaen's *Tristan* trilogy is infinitely more than a musical version of Gottfried's poem. This purpose is achieved in nine chapters, which follow the outline below.

The aim of Chapter One is to present those themes and characters from other composers' *Tristan* myth compositions which, through Messiaen, have relevance to his *Tristan* trilogy. In order to identify the relevant themes and characters, it is necessary to look at the ways in which Wagner, Debussy, Stravinsky and Liszt inspire Messiaen musically. As I examine Wagner and Debussy's mediating role a synopsis of musical influences is compiled. These synopses describe much which has no direct association with Messiaen's *Tristan* trilogy; however, they place the observations of Chapter One Within their context.

The objective of Chapter Two is to compare Messiaen's creative practice and the place in which Messiaen's *Tristan* trilogy works occupy in his output. A selection of themes are considered, all of which are

---

1 Johnson, R.S., *Messiaen*, Dent, London, 1975. 77-98

pertinent to Messiaen's *Tristan* myth works. The comparison will show that Messiaen did not merely adapt Wagner's *Tristan*: he radically altered the fundamental structure of the musical language. It will be illustrated that Messiaen's harmonic and melodic style are central to the alterations.

In every sense, Chapter One is introductory to Chapter Two, which forms the first important focal point of the book. Messiaen's Creative Practice is concerned with putting the composer's *Tristan* trilogy into the context of his output. We will examine not only the development of his musical language but also how the *Tristan* trilogy made a radical break from purely religious subjects. However, many of the musical ideas contained in the religious works are developed in *Harawi*, *Turangalîla* and *Cinq Rechants*. The development of keys in relation to mystical love first used in theological Works are rediscovered in the *Tristan* trilogy. Circular, static writing that avoids modulation will be examined and its relevance to the *Tristan* works assessed. Timbre, rhythm, melody and figuration will be examined and their application in later compositions addressed. In Chapter Three, the effect of Wagnerism on Messiaen and Debussy is explored in depth, and many questions raised in the previous chapters are addressed. Chapter Three analyses a broad cross-section of matters relevant to Wagnerism's dramatic impact. This will then be compared to the influence of Wagner's *Tristan und Isolde* on Messiaen's *Tristan* trilogy works. A close examination of the extended references in *Harawi*, *Turangalîla* and *Cinq Rechants* may lead to a clearer understanding of Messiaen's musical and literary sources derived from Wagner's *Tristan*.

The aim of Chapter Four is to present those ideas and characters from the *Tristan* myth which, through Gottfried, have relevance to Messiaen's *Tristan* trilogy. In order to identify the relevant ideas and characters it was necessary to read all of Gottfried's poem. As I read Hatto's translation of *Tristan* (details of which are found in the bibliography), I compiled a synopsis of the tale, which is found in Chapter Four. This synopsis describes much which has no direct association with Messiaen's *Tristan* trilogy; however, it places the recorded facts of the origins of the myth within their context. It is important to look at Gottfried's *Tristan* to help understand Messiaen's reasons for using this literary source. Many episodes in Gottfried's *Tristan* have parallels to similar scenes in Messiaen's *Tristan* trilogy but carry an entirely different meaning and serve a different function.

The objective of Chapter Five is to compare Wagner and Gottfried's presentations of the mythological material. A selection of themes are examined, each of which are relevant to Wagner's use of myth. The comparison will display that Wagner did not just adapt Gottfried's *Tristan*, he fundamentally changed the structure of the medieval poem. It will be shown that concentration of the story is central to the changes. Chapter Five will also examine how Schopenhauer was to become the most important non-musical influence on Wagner's *Tristan*. It will show how Wagner's intense relationship with Nietzsche provided rich insights into the composer's ideas and personality.

In Chapters Six to Eight, Messiaen's reconstruction of *Tristan* and Isolde's roles are explored in depth. Isolde is a potent character; it is not possible, in these chapters, to look at all the issues which surround her. Nevertheless, Chapters Six to Eight analyse a broad spectrum of matters pertinent to her important role.

The purpose of Chapter Six is to present those themes and ideas from Gottfried's *Tristan* which, through Piroutcha, have relevance to Messiaen's *Harawi*. In order to identify the appropriate themes and ideas, it was necessary to translate and analyse Messiaen's poem. As I translated Messiaen's *Harawi* (the text of which can be found at the end of Chapter Six), I examined the connection between surrealism and the mythological character of Messiaen's *Harawi*. Both are concerned with the workings of the subconscious mind and employ allegory to portray their message; surrealism does this by invoking dreams or nightmares and mythology achieves this through narrative. Messiaen concentrates on surrealism for his account of the *Tristan* tale and includes ideas derived from Peruvian mythology.

The objective of Chapter Seven is to draw out connections between *Turangalîla* and the *Tristan* myth still further: A selection of ideas are considered, each of which are pertinent to how the *Tristan* myth is used. It will show that Messiaen did not merely adapt Gottfried's *Tristan*; he avoided the use of narrative and text altogether in this work. He concentrated instead on interiorising Wagner's *Tristan* and it will be illustrated that love and death are central to the alterations.

In *Cinq Rechants* Tristan and Isolde's restructured roles are explored in depth, and many questions in *Harawi* and *Turangalîla* resolved. The music is tonally and dramatically challenging. These chapters underline the importance of Wagner's music to Messiaen.

The significance of this study for Messiaen scholarship lies in the way that it builds on the work of Robert Sherlaw Johnson, particularly the work that he has devoted to the *Tristan* trilogy. It also extends the work of Robin Holloway's book *Debussy and Wagner* by developing some of the ideas connecting *Debussy and Wagner* to include Messiaen.[2] The thesis has drawn together many other areas of study, including Lucy Beckett's book on Richard Wagner and I have related them to Messiaen's own writings.[3] This book examines the relationship of Wagner and Debussy to Messiaen and the *Tristan* myth. I have shown that the notion of memory and time found in the writings of Wagner and Maeterlinck have had profound effects on Messiaen's compositional development, whilst the visual arts have informed his aesthetic ideas and their expression in both his music and even in his meticulously produced scores.

MESSIAEN'S SOURCES OF MUSICAL INSPIRATION
Messiaen and the Tristan Myth

When examining Messiaen's links with the *Tristan* myth the ways in which Debussy, Stravinsky, Liszt and Wagner inspired Messiaen musically are a useful way of organising the discussion. Debussy as the mediator between Wagner and Messiaen, in relation to the *Tristan* myth, will also be established.

Debussy

Throughout his interviews and writings Messiaen mentions Debussy and in his composition classes he analysed Debussy's works with the utmost skill. In spite of their technical devices Messiaen's compositions of the 1920s sound more like an imitation of Debussy. However, Ravel's *Oiseaux tristes* (1905), Liszt's St. François d'Assise: La *prédication aux oiseaux* (1863) and Bartok's *Musiques nocturnes* (1926), had an important effect on Messiaen's own works. Debussy's *Des pas sur la neige* starts like Bartok's

---

2 Holloway, R., *Debussy and Wagner*, Eulenburg, London, 1979
3 Beckett, L., *Richard Wagner: Parsifal*, Cambridge University Press, Cambridge, 1981

Musiques nocturnes. Messiaen's "Chants d'extase dans un paysage triste" is reminiscent of Debussy with an occasional element of surrealism.[4] In such works as *Harawi Turangalîla* and *Cinq Rechants*, the line between death and life is very narrow.

Debussy was the model for Messiaen's *Poèmes pour Mi* and Debussy's ideas affected Messiaen throughout his life, including his *Tristan* myth works. Messiaen admitted his indebtedness to Debussy, and he considered Debussy, along with the Catholic faith, to be among the most important influences on his art. In his interview with Claude Samuel, in 1967, Messiaen affirms that Debussy was instrumental in reawakening composers to new harmonies and to the possibilities of sound. As Messiaen states,

> *The sounds of wind and water are extraordinarily complex. On the other hand, they have long been listened to and captured by composers such as Berlioz, Wagner and, above all, Debussy, who was the great lover of wind and water.*[5]

Indeed, many similarities exist between the musical languages of Debussy and Messiaen including series of parallel triads or other parallel chords, the use of dissonance for the purpose of sonority, passages principally harmonised with seventh and ninth chords and the use of pentatonic whole-tone scales. Messiaen's use of major sevenths, elevenths and parallel fifths also resembles that of Debussy.

Debussy's static harmony, state of reverie and free form were compatible with Messiaen's character and use of form in the *Tristan* trilogy. Debussy's harmonic and colouristic experiments influenced Messiaen profoundly in the *Tristan* myth works. Debussy's discoveries affected Messiaen throughout his life. The connection between Debussy and Messiaen was most unusual. At the age of ten Messiaen was given the score of *Pelléas et Mélisande* and kept an admiration all his life for his musical predecessor and fellow countryman. They both emphasised the sensuous side of music and Debussy also had the ability to evoke mental pictures by sounds.

---

4 Johnson, R.S. *Messiaen* Dent, London, 1975. 26

5 Samuel, C. *Conversations with Olivier Messiaen*, original French edition: 1967 Editions Pierre Belfond, trans. Aprahamian, F., Stainer and Bell, London, 1976. 13

In formulating his ideas on opera, Debussy shows himself wholly aware that the cultural task performed by opera is to be psychological. As Bernard Williams states, "*Pelléas* offers a representation of its characters' inner life which is uniquely subtle in opera...."[6]

The essence of Maeterlinck's dialogue is that it embodies not only more than the outward appearance of dialogue but more than is spoken. Throughout the work Maeterlinck delineates the nuances of social psychology. In the showing-up of Golaud, the various discomfitures of Mélisande, and the embarrassments and uncertainties of the love between Pelléas and Mélisande, he puts on record the emotion of personal malaise in a social setting which is so important in modern life.

By developing a convention of dialogue which could represent not merely dialogue itself but the psychological relationships which issue in dialogue, Maeterlinck made himself able to express character through its relationships to other characters, an innovation and a great increase in dramatic power. For dramatic and narrative purposes, Wagner's music drama, like Debussy's drama, is not only infinitely rich in content but actually pithier in expression than operas where the dramatic line has to be supplemented by explanation and by descriptive summing up of character. Messiaen's creative impulse, which Debussy's influence helped in technical innovations, was pushed into a further innovation of form. Messiaen borrowed deeply from Debussy's device of capturing atmosphere and even character in the Preludes and songs; but Messiaen's own convention is so much more elastic that he can reveal his characters through twelve solo voices, through an orchestra of Wagnerian proportions, through reflexions or through cries and improvisations wrung from them by the dramatic action. For unrolling his dramatic action he invents his continuous musical fabric, which wraps not only different characters but different musical forms and themes into the integral mood of the whole. By musical means alone Messiaen subordinates even his rhythms to the *Tristan* trilogy. As early as *L'Ascension* (1933), itself a dramatic masterpiece, Messiaen was insisting that, "the essential element in music is rhythm".[7]

Claude *Debussy's Pelléas et Mélisande* developed its own convention for rendering dialogue, but before that properly happened, Wagner had

---

6 Williams, B., quoted in Orledge, R., *Debussy and the Theatre*, Cambridge University Press, Cambridge, 1982. 48

7 Johnson, R.S. *Messiaen*, Dent, London, 1989. 32

remoulded the rhetorical convention of opera. What Debussy's new convention allowed him to develop, through the weaving together of singing voices, was the exchange of tones of voice in dialogue. In the exchanges between *Mélisande* and Golaud, he captures, through the orchestra as much as through the singing voices, the very tone of a spoken, or almost shrieked, altercation between characters. Indeed, he goes further and captures the very gestures of anxiety and misery. He sketches the very outline of the situation, the relationship, which is suffused with eroticism and sexual imagery.

In Debussy's hands, *Pelléas et Mélisande* was carrying the psychologising burden of literature and one of the next times his themes of social discomfiture appears is in the *Tristan* trilogy of Olivier Messiaen.

Among grand themes that Debussy dabbled with as a successor to *Pelléas* was *Siddartha*, a play along Buddhist lines by Victor Segalen (1878-1919). As Orledge states;

> *Victor Segalen's Siddartha was begun during an enforced stay at Colombo in Ceylon in November 1904 and it was sent to Debussy early in August 1907, shortly after work had begun on Le roman de Tristan. The Buddhist drama tells the legendary Indian story of the young Siddartha's search for the secret of life, and the desires, visions and mental crises he undergoes during his long, troubled quest for Nirvana and incarnation as a Buddha.*
>
> (Orledge, R., Debussy and the Theatre, pp. 268-269)

Whether or not Debussy knew that, after *Parsifal*, his demon Wagner had also considered Buddhist themes is uncertain; the possible irony is compounded, though, by the fact that Debussy was, in his turn considering in some detail *Le Roman de Tristan*, a project construed by Gabriel Mourey (1865-1943) from texts written by Joseph Bédier (1864- 1938)[8] Mourey was an art critic as well as translator, who had known Debussy from before 1890 and who seems to have stolen the rights to the *Tristan* sketches from the vaudeville author Louis Artus (1870-1960).[9] Artus had obtained the rights from Bédier himself, to whom he was related.

---

8 Lockspeiser, E., *Debussy his Life and Mind*, Vol. 1, Cassell, London, 1962. 107 and Holloway, R. *Debussy and Wagner*, Eulenburg, London, 1979. 74

9 Orledge, R., *Debussy and the Theatre*, Cambridge University Press, Cambridge, 1982. 252

Artus declared that he was happy to collaborate but by then, Debussy was sufficiently self- important not to want to work with a man known as a hack playwright. He did want to work on a *Tristan* that drew from the French and specifically the old Breton, legends. Various meetings ensued. Unhappy with Mourey's text and appalled at the idea of association with Artus, Debussy saw Bédier himself but the latter had published his Histoire in a rather disinterested fashion. Bédier was surprised and unimpressed by his own success with the book and had indeed signed away the rights and could not obtain them back from Artus. As Orledge points out, "Bédier was willing for Debussy to write music for *Tristan*, but Artus remained adamant and even prevented him from collaborating direct with his cousin in April 1909."[10]

The negotiations continued with ever-diminishing energy until well into 1910, before abating altogether. Wrangling of this sort helps to demonstrate how easily an artist could become jaded and gloomy in this squabblesome French artistic world.

Victor Segalen was another important figure at this point in Debussy's life. Segalen was a character of some depth, who worked not only as a writer but also as a diplomat. He was fascinated by exotic culture and had written a study of Maori music.

Ravel was also interested in the exotic and imitated the sounds of wind and water in *Jeux d'eau*, *Ondine*, *Oiseaux tristes* and *Noctuelles* which all anticipate Messiaen's *Catalogue d'Oiseaux*. The assured tonality in Ravel is similar to Messiaen's tonal compositions. Ravel uses major sevenths and elevenths; successions of seconds, unresolved appoggiaturas; melodies built on seconds, fourths and fifths; pivotal notes joining unusual chords and folksong. Resembling Debussy, Ravel was intrigued by medieval and exotic scales; poetic titles; dance rhythms and the fantastic. Ravel's piano style is evident in the music of Messiaen. Although Messiaen suggests that Debussy is his main teacher, Messiaen's experimental and late periods are influenced by Ravel. It is a further paradox that Stravinsky, Liszt and Wagner, also had an effect on Messiaen's *Tristan* trilogy Works.

---

10 Orledge, R., *Debussy and the Theatre*, Cambridge University Press, Cambridge, 1982. 252

Stravinsky

In Stravinsky's *Le Sacre du Printemps*, Stravinsky, like Messiaen, broke down barriers between East and West. Stravinsky developed material from Russian folksongs. In *The Fire Bird* he employs the tritone which was Messiaen's preferred interval in the *Tristan* trilogy compositions. Messiaen and Stravinsky were both experts in diatonic music and rhythm. From Stravinsky, Messiaen obtained his interest in polyrhythmic layers, development of rhythmic cells and rhythmic characters. Messiaen like Stravinsky, preferred an unmeasured meter based on a short value. An interest in numbers and rhythms were common to both Stravinsky and Messiaen. As Messiaen states:

> *Stravinsky is of immense importance because he was the first to restore the emphasis on rhythm; through the use of exclusively rhythmic themes, superimposed rhythmic ostinatos, and especially by creating (consciously or not) the procedure of rhythmic characters. This last procedure pursues and amplifies the Beethoven type of development, or development by elimination. "The Glorification of the Chosen one" and, even more, "The Sacrificial Dance" in The Rite of Spring are striking examples of the juxtaposition of and manoeuvring through augmentation, diminution, or immobility of the rhythmic characters.*[11]

Messiaen's debt to Stravinsky lay in the rhythmic innovations of *Le Sacre*, which he first made use of in his orchestral work *Les Offrandes oubliées* (1930). Plainsong forms the basis of the melodic material, but the rhythm draws on Stravinsky's additive principle, and the way he expands and contracts rhythmic cells. As Robert Sherlaw Johnson says Messiaen's *Turangalîla* symphony is strongly influenced by the "Danse sacrale" from Stravinsky's *Le Sacre*, particularly the repetitive motivic ideas and contracting and expanding rhythmic cells.[12]

---

11 Samuel, C., *Olivier Messiaen Music and Colour Conversations with Claude Samuel*, trans. E. Thomas, Glasgow, Amadeus Press, Portland, Oregon, 1994. 193.

12 Johnson, R.S., *Messiaen*, Dent, London, 1975. 84

Stravinsky: *Le Sacre du Printemps*

Le Sacre du Printemps is both a landmark and a turning point in the history of music. Never before had an orchestra been made to unleash such barbaric violence. But the work marked the end of an older period rather than the beginning of a new one. Throughout the romantic era composers had demanded ever larger orchestral forces, and Stravinsky at first continued this tendency. Petrushka in its original version required a very large orchestra, but this was dwarfed by the composer's requirements for *Le Sacre*. The only department of the orchestra that is not large is the percussion.[13] This is surprising in view of the nature of the work. The timpani, however, are often very much to the fore, and in several places, the most notable being the finale, two players are required. Never again was Stravinsky to employ such a mammoth instrumental ensemble, and the general trend in the period following *Le Sacre* was to use orchestras of modest dimensions.[14] Economics played their part in this change, but there was also a strong reaction by composers against what they considered to be one of the excesses of romanticism. Stravinsky was not the only composer in the forefront of this reaction, but he was one of the most important and certainly most influential on Messiaen.

Although *Le Sacre du Printemps* has found its permanent home in the concert hall rather than in the theatre, it is essentially a non-symphonic composition which had an important influence on Messiaen. Its two parts each consist of a string of episodes, and occasionally a thematic idea stated in one episode is carried over to the next. For instance, the theme of the brief "Procession of the Sage" is already established in the previous "Games of the Rival Tribes", but these two scenes, both musically and choreographically, may to all intents and purposes be regarded as one. Again the principal thematic idea of "Mystical Circles of the Adolescents" has already become familiar during the Introduction to Part Two. Generally the only resemblances to classical forms or procedures are to be found in the manner in which certain episodes are themselves subdivided into smaller sections. In place of development in the normal sense there is tremendous rhythmic interest. As White and

---

13 *Stravinsky*, I., *Le Sacre du Printemps*, 1911-13, Boosey and Hawkes, London, 1969.
14 White, E.W., *Stravinsky*, in Hartog, H. (ed) *European Music in the Twentieth Century*, Routledge and Kegan Paul, London 1957. 52.

Noble state, "Rhythm, in fact the most strikingly original aspect of the score, is not a purely spontaneous manifestation, but is the product of quite as much intense creative effort as the harmony."[15]

Messiaen was highly influenced by this type of technique which can be found in Movement Six of the *Turangalîla Symphonie*. For the most part the thematic ideas in Stravinsky's *Le Sacre* are simple and brief. They are usually limited to very few notes and have a folk-like character. But the metric and rhythmic treatment of them is often highly complex. They are repeated over and over again, but with unpredictable changes in the accentuation occurring either within the motives themselves or, more often, in their accompaniment. Much of the counterpoint is the result of ostinati patterns being repeated, but in the Introduction to Part One a most complicated texture is built up from independent melodic strands. It is easy to imagine this section representing the germination of plant life trying to force its way through the still near-frozen soil after winter. Despite its starkness and the use of two keys simultaneously, the harmony is strongly allied to tonality. For all its splendour *Le Sacre* like Messiaen's *Turangalîla* is very much a sophisticated and impressionist work. As Boulez states of *Le Sacre*, "This ritual of "Pagan Russia" attains a dimension quite beyond its point of departure; it has become the ritual—and the myth—of modern music."[16]

Stravinsky: *L'oiseau de Feu*

Stravinsky's first ballet, *L'oiseau de feu* came into being partly because of Liadov's indolence and Diaghilev's boldness.[17] Liadov had been slow in responding to Diaghilev's original commission and it was transferred to Stravinsky, then a young man in his mid-twenties. He had already scored a success with his *Feu d'artifice* (Fireworks) with its strong resonances of Dukas and Rimsky-Korsakov, and Diaghilev had been impressed with it

---

15 White, W.E., and Noble, J., "*Igor Stravinsky*" *The New Grove Modern Masters Bartok, Stravinsky, Hindemith* ed. Sadie, S., Macmillan, London and Basingstoke, 1984. 128

16 Boulez, P., *Orientations*, ed. Jean-Jacques Nattiez, trans, Cooper, M., Faber and Faber, London, Boston, 1990. 363

17 White, E.W., and Noble, J., "*Igor Stravinsky*" *The New Grove Modern Masters, Bartok, Stravinsky, Hindemith*, ed. Sadie, S., Macmillan, London and Basingstoke, 1984. 111

when he heard it at a Siloti concert in February 1909.[18] Stravinsky had also scored a couple of numbers for the 1909 Paris production of *Les Sylphides*.[19] Setting aside his work on *Le Rossignol* (The Nightingale), he completed the score between November 1909 and the following Spring, working closely in collaboration with Fokine.[20]

The story of the ballet derives from Russian folk-legend and tells how the young Prince Ivan wanders into Kashchei's magic garden in search of the Firebird, whom he finds on a tree bearing golden apples. He captures it and exacts a feather as a forfeit before releasing the creature. Then he encounters a group of maidens and falls in love with one of them, only to find that they are still under the spell of Kashchei and have to return to his palace when morning breaks. The young prince follows them into the castle and is imprisoned by Kashchei's minions. However, he remembers the magic feather he took from the Firebird; he waves it and the Firebird re-enters and shows him the secret of Kashchei's immortality. Ivan seizes and smashes the vital egg and at one stroke destroys his power, thus releasing the captive princesses. Ivan and his chosen-one are then ceremoniously married.[21] The magic garden, morning breaking and the ceremonial marriage are all reminiscent of incidents in Messiaen's *Harawi* and *Turangalîla-Symphonie*.[22]

---

18 White, E.W., and Noble, J., "Igor *Stravinsky*" *The New Grove Modern Masters, Bartok, Stravinsky, Hindemith*, ed. Sadie, S., Macmillan, London and Basingstoke, 1984. 111

19 White, E.W., *Stravinsky*, in Hartog, H., (ed.) *European Music in the Twentieth Century*, Routledge and Kegan Paul, London, 1957. 43

20 White, E.W., *Stravinsky*, in Hartog, H., (ed.) *European Music in the Twentieth Century*, Routledge and Kegan Paul, London, 1957. 44 See also Fokine, M., (Mikhail, F. 1880-1942) *Russian ballet dancer and choreographer*. From 1909 he worked with Diaghilev's Ballets Russes in Paris, for which he choreographed such revolutionary ballets as *The Firebird* (1910) and *Petrushka* (1911). He went to New York in 1923 and became a naturalised US citizen in 1932. *The Macmillan Encyclopaedia*, Macmillan London Ltd., London and Basingstoke, 1981. 456

21 Boulez, P., *Orientations*, ed., Jean-Jacques Nattiez, trans, Cooper, M., Faber and Faber, London, Boston, 1990. 361. Boulez makes some further interesting comments on the story in this section of his book.

22 Messiaen, O., *Harawi*, Leduc, Paris, 1945. Messiaen, O., *Turangalîla-Symphonie*, Durand, Paris, 1946,

Liszt

There are many similarities between Messiaen and Liszt, not only in their religious thoughts but also in their compositional similarities. In the *Tristan* myth works these consist of rhythm, freedom of form, attraction to plainsong and use of modal scales in suspended tonality.[23] Liszt's compositions were admired by Messiaen and French piano works and technique would be different without Liszt and Chopin. In 1884, Debussy attended Liszt's concert in Rome in which ideas are built on a descending group of secondary sevenths, for example in *Les jeux d'eau à la Villa d'Este*.[24] Liszt and the young Debussy employed consecutive fifths and the augmented triad and Liszt was the first composer to significantly use the whole-tone scale; like Messiaen, throughout his compositional life Liszt was involved in harmonic experimentations.[25] It is difficult to conceive that Messiaen did not recognise Liszt's important contributions to musical technique, to French music and to his own *Tristan* Works. Several of Messiaen's compositions written before 1949 employ cyclic themes, which resemble Liszt, who wrote the cyclic B minor Sonata.[26] Messiaen employs cyclic themes in *Harawi*, and *Turangalîla*, some of which reappear in *Cinq Rechants*. For example, in Movement 1 of *Cinq Rechants*, bars 1-8 are derived from a cyclic theme in *Turangalîla*, Movement 3, bar 6, oboe part. There is also a cyclic connection between *Cinq Rechants* Movement 1, bars 10-12 and *Harawi*, "La ville qui dormait, toi", bars 5-6.

Liszt *Piano Concerto No. 1* in E Flat Major
Piano Concerto No. 2 in A Major.

These two piano concerti have strong elements of likeness but also sharp points of difference. Both are in single continuous movement with numerous tempo changes. Each embodies the principal of

---

23 Halbreich discusses this idea, see Halbreich, H. *Olivier Messiaen*, London, 1980, 98.

24 On the subject of *Les jeux d'eau à la Villa d'Este*, see Alan Walker, ed., *Franz Liszt: The Man and His Music*, Barrie and Jenkins, London, 1970. 351

25 Walker, A., (ed.) *Franz Liszt the Man and His Music*, Barrie and Jenkins, London, 1970. 354-355 and Footnote [1].

26 Johnson, R.S. *Messiaen*, Dent, London, 1975. 42.

"transformation of themes" which Liszt pioneered and from which Messiaen derived the flexibly varied form of motives to be found in *Turangalîla, Harawi* and *Cinq Rechants*.[27] Temperamentally, however, they are divergent, for the E flat tends to the dramatic tone, the narrative emphasis of the tone poems (Les Preludes, *Orpheus, Tasso*), whereas the A major looks back to the moody reveries of Chopin and that romantic era.[28]

Unlike the E flat, in which the piano is a proclamative protagonist from the start and never relinquishes its place of prominence, the A major begins quietly with a phrase for wood- winds (flutes, clarinets and bassoons) extended by the oboe. Its harmonic colouration as well as its melodic outline are alluded to frequently in the subdivisions that follow—it is, in effect, the seed from which the whole plant springs.

The first transformation in the A major is heard from the piano, first in a mood of reverie, then more aggressively. This portion culminates in a cadenza launching the piano on a new thought: "Scharf markiert" is the composer's specification.[29] Its possibilities absorb the attention till the Allegro assai is reached. This serves as a scherzo in the unbroken sequence and leads to a Tempo del Andante where after the piano arpeggiates the way into a quasi-slow movement. Though noted as "Allegro moderato", the dialogue of piano and solo violoncello has a slow movement feeling. Here the technique of "progress by transformation" is clearly audible in the rephrasing of the first idea.

In the miniature score, page 39 marks the end of what are, in capsule form, the first three Movements.[30] The work totals, in all, 108 pages, so the ensuing fantasy (old themes and new) is by much the largest division of the structure. Its first mood is Allegro deciso and it continues from there in swiftly changing, multi-mannered alteration of solo and orchestra passages. One has a suggestion of the Allegro marziale of the *E flat concerto*, though this time without the glamour of a triangle in the

---

27 Walker, A., (ed) *Franz Liszt The Man and His Music*, Barrie and Jenkins, London, 1970. For a fascinating discussion of Liszt's "transformation of themes" see Collet, R., "Works for Piano and Orchestra" p. 249.

28 Searle, H. *The Music of Liszt*, Dover Publications, New York, 1966. 83-85

29 Liszt, F., *Piano Concerto No. 2 in A Major*, for piano and orchestra, Eulenburg, London, 1966.

30 Liszt, F., *Piano Concerto No. 2 in A Major*, for piano and orchestra, Eulenburg, London, 1966.

orchestra. Other percussion instruments, however, including cymbals make up for any lapse in attention-commanding effects.

Liszt's *"Sonetti del Petrarca"* Nos. 104 and 123

The "Sonetti del Petrarca" Nos. 104 and 123 are from the second book, *Italie*, of the Années de Pèlerinage, published in 1858.³¹ Revised during the Weimar period, they date initially from the 1830's and were inspired by Liszt's visits—"the years of pilgrimage"—to Italy with the Comtesse d'Agoult, the mother of his children Blandine, Cosima and Daniel.³² Both "Sonetti" were originally conceived, in Rome, as songs and were later transcribed for the piano.³³ In the 104ᵗʰ of Petrach's sonnets the poet despairs of ever finding peace, so consuming is his ardour for his inamorata; in No. 123 he at last achieves that peace. The impassioned flight of the first "Sonetto" is perfectly balanced by the halcyon lyricism of the second, which inhabits the same world as the songs of Messiaen's *Harawi*. As Alan Walker states:

> *Ten years before Wagner had even begun Tristan (1857-59) Liszt had already anticipated its famous opening phrase. It comes from one of Liszt's love-songs Ich möchte hingehm (c.1845). Clearly, it became Tristan's love-motif ... It is impossible to say that Wagner knew Liszt's song; it is equally impossible to say that he didn't. Liszt, as he himself might have sardonically observed in later life, had a flair for robbing the future of some of its better ideas.³⁴*

The third of the six "Consolations" is another popular and beautiful piece that carries echoes of Chopin; this was written half-way between the death of the Polish master in 1849 and the publication of Liszt's

---

31 Kentner, L., "Solo Piano Music" (1827»61), in Walker, A., (ed) *Franz Liszt The Man and His Music*, Barrie and Jenkins, London, 1970. 120, 123, 124-5. See also "Complete Catalogue of Liszt's Works": Piano Solos (cont.), Catalogue Number 26. 397.

32 Walker, A., (ed) *Franz Liszt The Man and His Music*, Barrie and Jenkins, London, 1970. 366

33 Searle, H., *The Music of Liszt*, Dover Publications, New York, 1966. 29-31

34 Walker, A., (ed.) "Liszt's Musical Background", in *Franz Liszt the Man and His Music*, Barrie and Jenkins, London, 1970 70-71

book about him in 1852.[35] The title takes its name from poems by Sainte-Beuve.[36]

In 1860 Joachim, Brahms, Grimm and Scholz, signed the notorious manifesto deploring the so-called *"Music of the Future"* whose cause Liszt had so tirelessly espoused; its theories they thought were to the detriment of music. In the following year Liszt withdrew from Weimar.[37]

Liszt's Organ Music

Liszt enriched the organ repertoire with three masterpieces and, in so doing, revitalised an area of composition that had languished since the days of its Baroque splendour. The first of these great works, completed exactly a hundred years after the death of Bach, showed what the Romantic Age could achieve; the second and third pointed the way towards Messiaen and the twentieth century

Liszt's *Fantaisie and Fugue* on *"Ad nos, ad salutarem undam"*

This massive work was written at the beginning of 1850, when Liszt was 38 and had settled in Weimar after abandoning his career as a piano virtuoso.[38] Immediately prior to its composition, he produced his first three *Illustrations du Prophète*, which were piano transcriptions of extracts from Meyerbeer's *Le Prophète*, staged in Paris in 1849.[39] While immersed in the opera, he became fascinated by the chorale "Ad nos, ad salutarem undam", which the three Anabaptists sing during the first act, urging the people of Dordrecht to be rebaptised. He must have meditated at some length on this melody, for the *Fantaisie and Fugue* that it engendered is among the largest and most impressive single movements ever

---

35 Walker, A., (ed.) "Liszt's Musical Background", in *Franz Liszt The Man and His Music*, Barrie and Jenkins, London, 1970 64-65

36 Searle, H., *The Music of Liszt*, Dover Publications, New York, 1966. 61

37 Searle, H., *The Music of Liszt*, Dover Publications, New York, 1966. 98

38 Searle, H., *The Music of Liszt*, Dover Publications, New York, 1966. 86-87

39 Wilde, D., "Transcriptions for Piano", Walker, A., (ed) *Franz Liszt The Man and His Music*, Barrie and Jenkins, London, 1970. 169

conceived for the organ. Brilliantly utilising the full range of the instrument's capabilities, the work can create an awesome effect. Divided into three sections, it opens with a partial presentation of Meyerbeer's theme, which is developed in an extended fantasia. The complete melody is then unfolded in a beautiful adagio. There follows a thrilling, cadenza-like bridge passage that leads into the last section, the fugue.

This begins with a formal exposition, but gradually evolves into a free fugal fantasy, gathering tremendous momentum and culminating in a final, resplendent statement of the chorale. Dedicated to Meyerbeer, the *Fantaisie and Fugue* was published in 1852 as the fourth of the *Illustrations du Prophète* and provides a fascinating connection with nineteenth century French operatic music and Whose influence can be seen in Messiaen's *Tristan* trilogy.

Liszt's *Prelude and Fugue on BACH*

The *Prelude and Fugue* was composed at Weimar in 1855, published during the same year and revised in 1870; in our notation, BACH would be B flat, A, C, B.[40] Clearly laid out in two sections, the piece is remarkable for the use of a chromaticism that was much in advance of its time. To a certain degree this may have been prompted by the chromaticism inherent in the theme itself and by Bach's own harmonic adventurousness. As Messiaen says, "The music of Bach incorporates harmonic colours and extraordinary contrapuntal craftsmanship".[41] Nevertheless, Liszt's audaciously modem idiom is consistent with the innovations that he was carrying out in other compositions of this period. In many ways Liszt's adventurousness in the nineteenth century resembles Messiaen's in the twentieth century. As we have seen this was not just restricted to organ music but included songs, piano music and orchestral writing. During the opening part of Liszt's fugue, there are moments when we seem altogether to have slipped our tonal moorings, and in this respect, the *Prelude and Fugue* looks forward to Messiaen's *Tristan* trilogy and the twentieth century. The *Prelude and Fugue* is dedicated to the composer's pupil Alexander Winterberger, who was born in Weimar and became

---

40 Searle, H., *The Music of Liszt*, Dover Publications, New York, 1966. 87
41 Samuel, C., *Olivier Messiaen Music and Colour Conversations with Claude Samuel*, trans., E. Thomas Glasgow, Amadeus Press, Portland, Oregon, 1994. 68

one of the leading organists and pianists of his day.[42] He played the *Fantaisie and Fugue* on "Ad nos, ad salutarem undam" at the inauguration of the new organ in Merseburg Cathedral in the autumn of 1855, and Liszt travelled from Weimar to hear him.[43] A few months later, he gave the first performance of the *Prelude and Fugue* and, in the summer of 1856, successfully toured the Netherlands with both works.[44] As John Ogden states, "Later statements of the Fugue's subject presage Vaughan Williams and Messiaen in their alternations of gloom and bell- like brightness". (*Franz Liszt The Man and His Music* p. 147).

Liszt's Variations on "Weinen, Klagen, Sorgen, Zagen"

In 1861, after his hopes of building Weimar into a cultural centre were smothered by philistine opposition, Liszt moved to Rome.[45] The Variations were composed there in the Winter of 1862, following the death in St. Tropez of his daughter Blandine, aged 26.[46] It was a time of great sadness; he had now lost two of his three children, his son Daniel having died three years earlier. The Variations, initially written for the piano, were transcribed for the organ in 1863 and published in 1865.[47] They take as their motto-theme the ground bass of the chorale *Weeping, Wailing, Grieving, Quailing*, the second number in Bach's cantata BWV No. 12, composed in Weimar in 1714 to celebrate Jubilate

---

42 Collet, R., "Choral and Organ Music", Walker, A., (ed.) *Franz Liszt The Man and His Music*, Barrie and Jenkins, London, 1970. 348

43 Collet, R., "Choral and Organ Music", Walker, A., (ed.) *Franz Liszt The Man and His Music*, Barrie and Jenkins, London, 1970. 348

44 Collet, R., "Choral and Organ Music", Walker, A., (ed.) *Franz Liszt The Man and His Music*, Barrie and Jenkins, London, 1970. 348

45 Searle, H. *The Music of Liszt*, Dover Publications, New York, 1966. 143

46 Ogden, J., "Solo Piano Music" (1861-86), Walker, A., (ed.) *Franz Liszt The Man and His Music*, Barrie and Jenkins, London, 1970. 144. Searle, H. *The Music of Liszt*, Dover Publications, New York, 1966. 98, 143

47 Walker, A., (ed) *Franz Liszt The Man and His Music*, Barrie and Jenkins, London, 1970. "Complete Catalogue of Liszt's Works", Section II, Other keyboard Works (cont) Organ. Catalogue number 658

Sunday, the third Sunday after Easter.[48] The work opens in the style of a chaconne, but then proceeds more freely, introducing a number of startling time-changes. The chromaticism is again advanced, reinforcing the sense of desolation. This is reminiscent of the cries of Piroutcha in Messiaen's *Harawi*, sixth movement, "Répétition planétaire". Shortly after the Variations on "Weinen, Klagen, Sorgen, Zagen" has reached the climax of its anguish, consolation arrives with the chorale was Gott tut, das ist wohlgetan (Whate'er my God Ordains is Right), which concludes the cantata.

Wagner

Messiaen was intensely enthusiastic about Wagner. Debussy, on the other hand, ultimately reacted against Wagner, the musician and the man. Writing on the relationship between chords and melody in parallel motion, Debussy explained that his own exploration of the natural treasures of music was a reaction against the ultra-chromaticism of the Wagner-Strauss era.[49]

Considering Debussy's vigorous nationalistic sentiments toward his native France and his views against the tyrannical neighbour Germany, his reaction against Wagner was inevitable.

As a young man and as a mature composer, Messiaen particularly sought to discover the tetralogy to which he would devote a considerable portion of the rest of his life. Messiaen at no time discontinued his admiration of Wagner. Resembling Wagner, Messiaen was attracted to the mountains and the ancient Celtic medieval myths. Messiaen states,

> *Later, Wagner freely employed certain chords and black sonorities in scenes taking place at night, for dark characters like the Nibelung Alberich and his son Hagen; and in contradistinction, bright tonalities and chords with lightened, sharper instrumentation for events taking place on mountain heights or*

---

48 Searle, H. *The Music of Liszt*, Dover Publications, New York, 1966. 100

49 Messing, S., *Neoclassicism in Music*. UMI Research Press, Ann Arbor, London, 1992. 5-6; [footnote 21] page 157. Claude Debussy "Correspondence Ernest Chausson-Claude Debussy", *La revue musicale*, Ernest Chausson numéro special. 1 December, 1925: 120.

in water, like Siegfried discovering the happy mountains before encountering love in Brünnhilde, or the Rhinemaidens swimming in the Rhine.[50]

Messiaen and Wagner both appreciated the expressive nature of dissonance, connected to activity and incompleteness, contrasted with consonance, associated with rest and fulfilment.[51]

Périer states that in the composer's notes for *Meditations sur le Mystère de la Sainte Trinité*, Messiaen discusses his debt to Wagner. Preoccupied with a need for direct communication, Messiaen devised an alphabet for his young son. Messiaen's curiosity with language is reminiscent of Wagner's search for a new expression of his musical code of the leitmotiv.[52] Messiaen stated an enthusiastic admiration for Wagner's idea of the leitmotiv of nature in which each bird, stone and tree is given is own aesthetic quality and is characterised by its own theme. Messiaen considered Wagner's concept to be revolutionary particularly the integration of the elements of nature with elements of art and used these ideas in his *Tristan* trilogy works. For example, this can be seen in "La ville qui dormait, toi" in which "the grassy bank at midnight" represents the bank on which *Tristan* and Isolde recline in Act II, scene 2, of Wagner's *Tristan und Isolde* and "the double violet", the symbol of modesty.[53]

Wagner's conception of music-drama is essentially close to Messiaen's. For both Debussy and Messiaen, some of Wagner's attraction must have lain in the perverse element in both his music and his dramas. The brother-and-sister love of Siegmund and Sieglinde and the necrophilism of *Pelléas et Mélisande* both demonstrate perversity.

Opera could not portray the psychology of taboo until Wagner made splendid effects of mass and time by the literal method of deploying masses of singers and instrumentalists and keeping the audience in the theatre for great lengths of time. What opera excels in creating, by its nature (Wagner, though, was working against its nature) is, as Messiaen was to show, not a society but a nexus of characters on whom external

---

50 Samuel, C., *Conversations with Olivier Messiaen*, Original French edition: 1967 Editions Pierre Belfond, trans, Aprahamian, F., Stainer and Bell, London, 1976. 18

51 For an interesting discussion on this subject see Machlis J. *Introduction to Contemporary Music*, 1979, 18.

52 See Périer, A., *Messiaen*, Solfeges/Seuil, 1979, 156-157.

53 *Harawi*, Leduc, Paris, 1945, Movement 1, "Le plein minuit le banc" and "La Violette double". pp. 2-3

social forces impose nothing more constraining than good manners and who reflect society at large only in the freedom it has given them to form and express their personal inter-relationships.

When examining the themes and characters from Wagner's *Tristan und Isolde* it should be remembered that the writer and the musician both depend on unconscious motives to impel them into activity at all. They are also both dependent on the accessibility of fantasy- material from the unconscious. The Writer must have a supply of it if he is to create stories, and the composer if he is to create that different type of art which we call music. Wagner and Messiaen direct the fantasy-material to utterly different ends: Wagner works on the fantasy from outside, Messiaen from inside, the fantasy-illusion: yet not only is the source of the material the same in both cases, but in both cases what works on it is intelligence, though an intelligence specialised and temporarily narrowed down for a particular purpose.

The supreme artistic successes of Messiaen and Wagner rest on an intelligence which is of the same order of mental processes as Plato's or Jung's. As Donington states, "...Yet it is Jung's work that helps most in picking up the "inexhaustible" contents of mythology..."[54] We appreciate the *Turangalîla-Symphonie* through the same faculties as we acknowledge the truth of a syllogism or a theorem—but in appreciating *Turangalîla* we have agreed to suspend direct reference to the outside World. Our sense of the correctness of *Turangalîla*'s structure is an acquiescence in the internal logic of its structure and the same is true when we recognise a melody as correct: we admire its internal consistency. We acknowledge Messiaen's penetration of the form of his fantasy world, just as we acknowledge Newton's or Plato's seizing on the form, the essential principles, of the objective world.

Wagner's intelligence set to work to enlarge music. As Magee states, "The young Wagner believed that the primary function of art was to show people the true inner nature of the lives they lived as members of humanity."[55] The burden of carrying an implicit psychology usually falls to opera, which is flexible in conveying characters. It had been challenged by Wagner, whose blend of music-drama with poetry is the counterpart of Messiaen's blend of surrealism with music. Wagner transcends the

---

54 Donnington, R., *Wagner's Ring and its Symbols*, Faber and Faber, London, 1974. 33
55 Magee, B., *Wagner and Philosophy*, Penguin Books, London, 2000. 83

operatic conventions of his era, just as Messiaen transcends the musical ones of his time. As Boulez says, "What was novel and important was the way in which (Messiaen) was to amalgamate with limited Western tradition heterogeneous, if not heteroclite, elements that were profoundly to transform his musical point of view".[56]

When Wagner's music married itself to words and drama, and turned into music-drama, it acquired the imagery it lacks in its single state. In Wagner's essay On the Term Music- Drama published in 1872 he wrote: "I would almost like to call my dramas deeds (acts, actions) of music become visible".[57] Promptly it incurred the twentieth century's contempt. Wagnerian music-drama remained relatively fashionable even though many people threw intellectual criticism at it.

Gottfried von Strassburg lived in an age when story-telling was a competitive art. He kept the audience's attention with cliff-hangers, he showed the expected respect for his original sources and he fought the constant battle of keeping his listeners' goodwill. Both Wagner and Messiaen also lived in times of competitive art, but that is where the similarity ends. Messiaen did not remain true to his original source. The *Tristan* trilogy's intensity is enough to keep the audience's attention, without the aid of "cliff-hangers".

However, Wagner and Messiaen's imaginations were awakened by Gottfried's tale. They saw in it the beginnings of something powerful, and meditated upon it at considerable length. The integration of music and poetry was an important development of Messiaen during the writing of his *Tristan* trilogy. When the middle-ages filled the *Tristan* myth with homilies and moral points and squeezed the character out of the Arthurian hero, it was depriving the myth of the very qualities which eventually became the strength of the nineteenth century Wagnerian epic.

The development of myth telling had resulted from the first stirrings of the Celts and later in the progressive disuse of Latin in favour of the various national vernaculars. As Ferrante says, "The stories of *Tristan* and Isolt originated in Celtic sagas and folklore just as the Arthurian stories did..."[58] The *Tavola Ritonda* broke into Italian and Gottfried into German, as secular writers who have not thrown off Christianity but who

---

56 Boulez, P., *Orientations*, ed, Nattiez, I-I, trans, Cooper, M., Faber and Faber, London, 1990, 407

57 Quoted in Magee, B., *Wagner and Philosophy*, Penguin Books, London, 2000. 212

58 Ferrante, J.M., *The Conflict of Love and honour*, Mouton, The Hague, Paris, 1973. 12

are laymen and are neither appointed nor self-appointed as spokesmen of the church and its mythology. As Ferrante states, "... The Tavola (is) concerned only to establish *Tristan*'s relation to Mark and the feudal or chivalric world".⁵⁹ The *Tristan* myth was translated into German, English and Italian.

The convention from which Richard Wagner's opera developed was not in the Gounod, Bizet and Massenet mould. As Zuckerman states Wagner found Gounod, "good but not deeply gifted."⁶⁰ The Gounod opera, for all its deliberate and dispassionate touches of the fabulous, was imaginatively unrealised and stuck strictly to its intellectual, non-fiction thesis. Instead, Wagner took up the despised and often despicable German myth, which he became interested in as a young man. His persistent satire of Meyerbeer's opera does more than betray that it was the influence most continually present in his thoughts; the satire actually constitutes the process by which he refined and enlarged the form until its propensities for fantasy became capable of carrying imaginative psychological information. As Zuckerman observes, "Wagner himself ... criticised Meyerbeer for having relied too much on effects".⁶¹ There was disparagement for the extravagancies of Wagnerian opera; extravagancies which Claude Debussy diagnosed as thoroughly affected. It is as a Frenchman and on behalf of music that Debussy resents the supposition that affected feeling can substitute for talent, knowledge and work. As Lockspeiser states:

> *Debussy's anti-Wagnerism was to some extent a pose, designed to conceal both his admiration and his fear of Wagner. There is no evidence that Wagner's huge, sensuous philosophy left him indifferent. Very strong feelings were aroused. He is "the old poisoner", the "ghost of old Klingsor", language which indicates an obsession with a nature fundamentally too similar, and also too ruthless, to be ignored.*⁶²

---

59 Ferrante, J.M., *The Conflict of Love and honour*, Mouton, The Hague, Paris, 1973. 26

60 Zuckerman, E., *The First Hundred Years of Wagner's Tristan*, Columbia University Press, New York and London, 1964. 90

61 Zuckerman, E., *The First Hundred Years of Wagner's Tristan*, Columbia University Press, New York and London, 1964. 79

62 Lockspeiser, E., *Debussy: His Life and Mind*, Vol. 1, 1862-1902, Cassell, London, 1962. 91

The most fastidious of composers himself, Debussy was intensely irritated by the overblown symbolism of Wagnerian accomplishment, in drama as well as in music. Symbolism is, however, a significantly important part of the plot and music in *Pelléas et Mélisande*.

As a composer, Richard Wagner suffers from Claude Debussy's having developed his idiom to such immeasurably greater penetration and subtlety. Wagner's harping on Melot's treachery merely turns *Tristan* into a prig—of which the composer remains naively unaware. Sadly, this hardly matters, since in any case Melot does not possess the elements of a coherent character; it only forces us to notice that Wagner does not put forward so much as a germinal hint of that conscious and moral battle between priggishness and self-awareness which came into existence when Debussy created, in Mélisande, one of the most coherent characters in opera. In our eyes, therefore, Debussy is too kind to his predecessor when he unacknowledgingly chooses Wagner's operas as the planks on which to mount his love-hate defence of the opera as a genre.

Debussy as the Mediator between Wagner and Messiaen in relation to the Tristan myth

Debussy discovered the Japanese theatre at the Exposition Universelle, 1889, and its scenery and music intrigued him and may have contributed to his "detachment from the Wagnerian group".[63] Debussy's creation of a new type of lyric art contrasted with Wagner's ideas and vocal techniques.[64] Debussy had recognised the value of French vocal characteristics as well as French prose.[65] To favour music that lay beyond the West was to rebuff the Wagnerian music drama that was engulfing Europe. Messiaen's inconsistency, however, lies partially in his attraction to Wagner and Debussy simultaneously.

We would be more cognizant of Debussy's musical detachment from Wagner, in *Pelléas*, if Maeterlinck had not intentionally set out to elicit

---

63 Boulez, P., *Notes of an Apprenticeship*, trans. From the French by Herbert Weinstock, Alfred A, Knopf, New York, 1986. 342

64 For a discussion on this subject see Boulez, P., *Notes of an Apprenticeship*, trans. From the French by Herbert Weinstock, Alfred A. Knopf, New York, 1986. 348

65 Boulez, P., *Notes of an Apprenticeship*, trans. From the French by Herbert Weinstock, Alfred A. Knopf, New York, 1986. 348

the distant legendary realm of princes and kings, royal hunting-grounds and castles, complying with Wagnerian beliefs of the 1880's. The recurrent subject of envy and of an unlawfully obtained bride is similar to *Tristan und Isolde*. The succession of events is not limited by time and the symbolism is easy to see. A preference of deteriorating castles and ominous events of no obvious meaning came in any case to authors from Mallarmé, Baudelaire, Edgar Allan Poe, Maeterlinck and Debussy. In Poe they discovered a leader of their belief in allusion and representation whose toughness lay in the very opposite of the attempt to describe in art some fact as it actually is. In the French literary movement, aiming to suggest rather than depict reality, words no longer alluded simply to things and events. They were intentionally employed to elicit musical as well as linguistic reaction and to summon the images behind exact meaning. Partial stoppage of the breath, elaborate syllables, rules regulating the relationships of words in a sentence and suggestive poetic speech broadened artistic limits by conveying colours to music, as Messiaen did in the *Tristan* trilogy. Wagner's works consisted of antiquated language and words. Wagner had an enthusiasm for myth and powerful symbols such as spears, swans, poisonous drinks and all the devices of the music drama. He also believed that composer, poet and author in his own self became one. He discovered the foundation of an artistic belief that overpowered France and gave birth to Wagnerian verse, plays, symphonies, even fictional prose, in abundance.

Wagner said that the art of composition was the art of writing good transitions, but as Messiaen has proved, good transitions are not always necessary.[66] Messiaen has shown that music can be equally effective if blocks of apparently unrelated material are placed side by side and listeners have to make the connections themselves. These juxtapositions may be ambiguous in the *Tristan* trilogy works, but ambiguity is of the essence of poetry.

The orchestra Messiaen specified for *Turangalîla*, the work he composed immediately after *Harawi*, contains more or less the same instruments that Debussy might have used in 1900, the only difference being that Debussy would have employed fewer percussion instruments and would not have heard of the ondes martenot. The influence of Debussy also extends to Messiaen's use of parlando; vocal lines based

---

66 Wagner, R. *Three Wagner Essays*, trans. and ed. R. Jacobs, *Music of the Future*, Eulenburg, London, 1979. pp. 26-27

on the natural speech inflections of language, which can be observed in both *Harawi* and *Cinq Rechants*.

Debussy mediated between Wagner and Messiaen in relation to the *Tristan* myth by the creation of a new type of lyric art. This art consisted of a direction to sing in a conversational style built on natural speech inflections. *Pelléas* complied with Wagnerian stage representations, the ideas of envy and desire are similar to *Tristan und Isolde*. Debussy employed allusion in gag and suggestive poetic speech conveyed colour to his music. Messiaen then developed these speech techniques in *Harawi* and *Cinq Rechants*. Messiaen brought the scale and colour of Wagner's orchestral writing to *Turangalîla* coupled with a fascination for Debussy and Eastern music.[67]

Both Messiaen and Debussy were composers in the same mould; their music was one which demands a great deal of technical instruction. Debussy was the master of the apprentice. For Messiaen, however, music could not wholly express rebellion against Debussy, because Debussy, as composer, was likewise a rebel.

The great works of Messiaen's reactionary impulse, *Harawi*, *Turangalîla* and *Cinq Rechants*, express the reaction by casting back in time through the *Tristan* myth. With *Harawi* it is a case of casting back historically to Wagner. With *Cinq Rechants*, the archaism is stylistic—under the influence of Claude le Jeune.[68]

Cinq Rechants, is not entirely a work of reaction and neither is its counterpart, *Harawi*, wholly a Work of the twentieth century. In *Harawi* Messiaen achieved or suffered a certain fusion between the opposite poles of his ambivalence. In *Harawi*, whose message is so strongly against violence and in favour of reconciliation, Messiaen was certainly reaching out deliberately for fusion. The initiation is designed to set on rebellion a figure so reasonable and so disciplined as to make it acceptable. But the great love-figure in *Harawi*, Piroutcha, is seen by no means unambiguously.

Indeed, the song-cycle's presentation of Piroutcha illustrates how an unconscious impulse may take advantage of external and fortuitous

---

67 Drew, D., "*Modern French Music*", in Hartog, H. ed. *European Music in the Twentieth Century*, Routledge and Kegan Paul London, 1957. 286

68 Freeman, R., "Trompette d'un Ange Secret: Olivier Messiaen and the Culture of Ecstasy", *Contemporary Music Review*, Vol.14, Parts 3-4, Overseas Publishers Association, Amsterdam, 1996. 66

circumstances If it is correct to deduce that the plot of the *Tristan* myth was altered, then it is this quite external fact which made the opening for the doubts we cannot help feeling about Piroutcha. The final intention may be to make her ultra-virtuous but Messiaen has not given himself quite time to shake off his first plan, in which she was to be the villain. The poem as a whole obliges us to conclude, despite the accepted ideas of Johnson that she does appear, after all, to have really stolen the youth.[69]

In this first breach in the image of a virtuous Piroutcha, Messiaen's responsibility does not go beyond passive complicity. He has merely failed to insist that the two versions of the *Tristan* myth be more adroitly patched and the image of Piroutcha properly established. However, having once found the crack in Piroutcha's virtue, Messiaen has not resisted its being enlarged. Having stolen the youth, Piroutcha exposes him to the insults of love, allows him to be tortured by the thought that she no longer loves him and herself preaches at him—both about her wickedness and, most unfairly, as the poem finally shows, about the shortcomings of the female sex. The total impression of Piroutcha could, arguably, be considered not very far short of a charming bully.

The reconciliation towards which *Cinq Rechants* reaches out is, once again, to be achieved by Messiaen's identification of himself with Wagner. Yet Wagner's music cannot manifest itself in Messiaen's dramatic work except in an ambiguous way through Messiaen's ambivalence towards him.

In *Turangalîla*, on the other hand, the coalescence between Wagner's opposite point of view has been agonisingly forced on Messiaen. Messiaen's intention in *Turangalîla* is to retreat from his own ecclesiastical manner to the philosophical assurance of Wagner. For Messiaen this retreat into Wagner is itself dangerous, because it carries him away from the Catholic Church. From there he is carried, by way of the greater emphasis placed on Schopenhauer back almost beyond Christianity into

---

69 Johnson, R.S. *Messiaen*, Dent, London. 1989. 79

the ancient Buddhist world with its bleak uncertainties about life after death.[70]

Once again in *Turangalîla* Messiaen employs the trombones to announce supernatural and deadly terror. Messiaen cannot decide whether the ghostly influence of Wagner is *sacre*d or profane. *Turangalîla* is Messiaen's most convulsive attempt to remove himself from the Catholic Church and not accept the consolation and terror of heaven and hell. Yet the music of *Turangalîla*, according to Robert Sherlaw Johnson, contains religious allusions, "As in *Trois petites liturgies*, the pitched percussion and piano are grouped together to form the gamelan, which, in this case, also includes the metal percussion—the triangle, cymbals, tam-tam and bells".[71]

The effect the *Tristan* trilogy makes is quite beyond Christianity and almost beyond art. The music is very nearly too naked to be judged as art; Messiaen's retreat into the solid conventions of Claude le Jeune in *Cinq Rechants* has nearly burst the conventions of art itself. It is impossible to say whether the *Tristan* trilogy is good art; it is certainly great art.

In this chapter it has been shown how themes and ideas from other composers' *Tristan* myth works have relevance to Messiaen's *Tristan* trilogy. We have also examined other sources of musical inspiration and their effect on Messiaen. The way in which Debussy, Liszt, Stravinsky and Wagner inspired Messiaen has been established. We have seen that Stravinsky's *Le Sacre du Printemps* was an important influence on Messiaen and how the Work helped break down barriers between East and West. The "Danse sacrale" from Stravinsky's *Le Sacre* exerted a strong influence on Messiaen's *Turangalîla-Symphonie*. There are also compositional and

---

[70] Parrinder, G., *Worship in the World's Religions*, Sheldon Press, London, 1961. 96. As Parrinder states, "European scholars have dated the death of Gautama the Buddha about 480BC or even 370 BC. Mahayana dating's go back to 1000 BC or earlier. The dates now affirmed by Theravada Buddhists are 624 BC for his birth and 544 BC for his death. It is declared that Gautama was born on the full moon day of the month of Kason (May), the first month of the Buddhist year, and that he attained both Enlightenment (bodhi) and entered final Nirvana on the same day of the month". See also Macmillan Encyclopaedia, London, 1981. 197. Buddhism, "the nontheistic religion and philosophical system founded in NE India in the 6th century BC by Gautama Siddhartha (the Buddha). His followers seek to emulate his example of perfect morality, wisdom and compassion, culminating in a transformation of consciousness known as enlightenment".

[71] Johnson, R.S. *Messiaen*, Dent, London, 1989. 84

religious similarities between Messiaen and Liszt which have been explored through Liszt's piano and organ music. We have also noted how enthusiastic Messiaen was about Wagner's music. Both composers appreciated the expressive nature of dissonance connected with activity, contrasted with consonance associated with rest and fulfilment. This chapter has also shown how Debussy acted as the mediator between Wagner and Messiaen in the creation of his *Tristan* trilogy. This chapter has explored the importance of the *Tristan* myth to Messiaen.

2

MESSIAEN'S CREATIVE PRACTICE

This introduction to Messiaen's creative practice is a way of putting the *Tristan* Works into the context of his output with regard to historical time and technique. Subheadings have been used to clarify the ideas of rhythmic characters and melody. An argument has been created surrounding Messiaen's musical language and the place which the *Tristan* trilogy Works occupy in Messiaen's output. It will be shown how the *Tristan* trilogy has not only developed from his musical language but also made a radical break, for the first time, from purely theological subjects.

To understand Messiaen's musical language we must remember that although his training at the Paris Conservatory was complete in its study of traditional harmonic forms, his natural inclination was not in the nineteenth-century symphonic tradition.

Whilst at the Conservatory he studied under a variety of teachers: Paul Dukas, composition and orchestration; Joseph Baggers, tympani and percussion; Maurice Emmanuel, history of music and Greek metre; Marcel Dupré, organ improvisation and plain-chant; George Caussade, fugue; C.A. Estyle, piano accompaniment and Noël Gallon, counterpoint.

He made creative decisions about his *Tristan* myth works with a confidence taken from a highly disciplined technique and from his own musical inspirations. Prior to these compositions, Messiaen endeavoured to express in sound the symbol and conceptions inspired by his devout faith in God and in the Roman Catholic Church. The music developed from the images Messiaen often conveyed with regard to each work. Messiaen's musical structures usually described miracles, or holy images important in Roman Catholicism, for example, *Les Corps Glorieux* and *Vingt Regards sur l'Enfant Jésus*.

In many works he makes use of cyclic themes that have a symbolic function within the context of the work in which they appear. *Vingt Regards sur l'Enfant Jésus* means more than the literal translation of "twenty gazes upon the infant Jesus". A better definition for the Word "regards" is "contemplation"; the twenty movements in this work involve the contemplation of the child of God by God the Father, the church, the Holy Spirit, the Virgin, angels, Wise men, and immaterial or symbolic entities that include Time, the Star, the Cross and Silence. This idea of contemplation is also important in the *Tristan* trilogy but, for the first time, in a non-theological way.

Certain keys in association with specific modes of limited transposition are also associated with symbolic ideas, For example, the key of F-sharp major, together With mode 2 has been associated by Sherlaw Johnson with expressing the mystical experience of superhuman love, it is used in several of Messiaen's works in slow ecstatic movements.[1] The key of E major, in slow movements, has been symbolically associated with the praise of the Blessed Trinity.[2] The "Louange è l'Eternité de Jésus" and "Louange è l'Immortalité de Jesus" from *Quatuor* would be examples of this. The key of G major is associated with desire in *Harawi* in "L'amour de Piroutcha" and the key of F-sharp major is also heard in "Amour, oiseau d'étoile". Messiaen's most significant contribution to harmony were the modes of limited transposition He said that, "They are at once in the atmosphere of several tonalities, without polytonality, the composer being free to give predominance to one of the tonalities or to leave the tonal impression unsettled".[3] In Le Banquet céleste (1928) the added sixth chords can be heard as a first inversion triad of the relative minor or as a root position major triad with added note. The initial chord of Le Banquet céleste inclines, because of the 3 beats, to look for a C sharp root as much as it implies an F sharp resolution. It has a first inversion A sharp rather than C sharp triad and B. The work makes more sense in terms of modes and the tension between the two is very interesting.[4]

The mathematical divisions of the number 12 are paralleled in musical terms by Messiaen's modes. These modes equal the number of semitones in the equally tempered octave. The "charm of impossibilities" inevitably leads to a harmony that is able to move in a circular, static way instead

---

[1] Johnson, R.S. *Messiaen*, Dent, London, 1989. 42.

[2] Johnson, R.S. *Messiaen*, Dent, London, 1989. 43.

[3] Messiaen, O., *Technique de mon language musical*, trans. Satterfield, 1., Vol. 1, Text, Leduc, Paris, 1956. 58

[4] Messiaen, O. *Le banquet céleste*, Leduc, Paris, 1928

of in a progressive movement, as in the diatonic system.[5] As Messiaen states, "modes which cannot be transposed more than a limited number of times without reproducing the original scale, and their counterpart in rhythm-rhythmic patterns which cannot be reversed because they are the same both forwards and backwards.[6] The idea of writing that is circular, static and that avoids modulation is important. There is a tendency for music built on these modes to persist in one place, and then possibly move to another, without developing through modulation.[7]

For the most part the modes contain nothing resembling a dominant; with the exception of one, they all have F sharp as their central notes. The augmented fourth was considered by Messiaen to be his favourite interval. The rejection of conventional cadence and progression was the implication held within Messiaen's modal system.

The formal structure of his works needs to be based on some other parameter, for example, figuration, melody, rhythm, timbre or a combination of these factors. In Claude Samuel's book, *Conversations with Olivier Messiaen*, Messiaen says that rhythmic music is, "inspired by the movements in nature, movements of free and unequal durations".[8] Based on the argument that rhythmic music scorns equal divisions, Messiaen selected Stravinsky's *Le Sacre du Printemps* as an example of rhythmic writing. Later, when he became a professor of harmony at the Paris Conservatory, his analysis of that work was so detailed that it required a full year of study to complete. This is probably the most significant study of Stravinsky's rhythmic practices. Pierre Boulez's analysis of *Sacre*, derived from the analytical study in Messiaen's classes may be found in Notes of an Apprenticeship.[9]

For Messiaen, discipline was made to interact with freedom; in Poèmes pour Mi, for example, the right-hand piano part is in mode 3, a series of six chords, the initial five are then repeated; mode 2 harmonies

---

5 Johnson, R.S. *Messiaen*, Dent, London, 1939. 36

6 Johnson, R.S. *Messiaen*, Dent, London, 1989. 36

7 Messiaen, O. *Technique de mon language musical*, trans, Satterfield, 1., Vol 1, Leduc, Paris, 1956. 58-63; Vol. 2, 52-56

8 Samuel, C. *Conversations with Olivier Messiaen*, Original French edition: 1967 Editions Pierre Belfond, trans. Aprahamian, F., Stainer and Bell, London, 1976. 33

9 Boulez, P., *Notes of an Apprenticeship*, trans. Herbert Weinstock, Alfred A. Knopf, New York, 1968. 72-145

are in the left-hand, in a series of five chords, repeated unbroken. The two parts move in a rhythmic canon a crotchet apart in the first part.[10]

The number of the precipitating chords in the build-up to the second recitative is increased from three to six and in the third the organisation of the rhythm is fully realized. The group of six chords is repeated five times in the right-hand while in the left-hand the group of five chords is repeated six times, the two hands maintaining the rhythmic canon throughout this cycle. The number of chords is then increased to nine. Messiaen was just creating a different system which bounded his freedom and creative order. Messiaen's harmonic and melodic style reached new heights with *Trois Mélodies* (1930), *Poèmes pour Mi* and *Chants de terre et de ciel* (1938). *Chants de terre et de ciel* does, however, present particularly difficult problems for the singer. If the modes began as entities of harmonic colour for Messiaen, they frequently gave rise to recurring germane melodic formulae, from composition to composition; Messiaen tells us that one is derived from *Boris Godunov*.[11] This derivation remains fragmentary in Messiaen's Work but transformed into his own characteristic modality and style.[12]

Dieu parmi nous, the largest piece of the cycle, crowns *La Nativité;* it begins with an invocation in mode 4. By using all four of the notes excluded from the first transposition of the mode (E flat, E natural, A natural, B flat) the pedal theme, in mode 2, gains contrast. This is written a major 3rd higher than mode 4, and is the ending of the last of the Poèmes pour Mi. In the final minim chord, the E natural and C# are foreign to mode 4. In my view this use of foreign notes halts the natural downward thrust of the music.

Les Corps Glorieux (1939) consists of seven pieces in which extreme contrasts are contained. Monody, absent from La Nativité but present in the second movement of *L'Ascension* reappears in the first, third and fifth pieces; the second and third contain mixed chromatic 'modes; there is much organ colour in the sixth and the central piece "*Combat de la Mort et de la Vie*" is monumental through the expansion of the block contrasts of the early Dyptyque. The cycle has a quiet ending referring back to *L'Ascension* but there are new techniques and perspectives hidden in this

---

10 Messiaen, O, *Poèmes pour Mi*, Durand, Paris, 1- Action de graces, 1936. 2

11 Messiaen, O. *Technique de mon language musical*, Vol 1, trans., Satterfield, J., Leduc, Paris, 1956. 31; Vol, 2, Example 75 pp.4 13

12 Johnson, R.S. *Messiaen*, Dent, Loudon, 1989. 20

portrait of the Holy Trinity. The piece is both horizontally and vertically tripartite in honour of the Trinity.

The overall plan is that of a nine-fold Kyrie, each third is divided into three, as the melody in the middle part shows. The right-hand arabesques are almost atonal. However, the melody is firmly centred on D minor and uses it as a pivot/anchor note. Messiaen uses a version of râgavardhana rhythm in the pedal line. From 1939 onwards Hindu rhythms were a constant feature of his music; (4, 4, 4, 2, 3, 2) and the initial series of six values was one of his most frequent rhythmic patterns. The pedal line is repeated five times but small differences and the unregulated length of pauses is included in each repetition. Messiaen arranged the D naturals in the bass to coincide no fewer than ten times with those of the melody, either actually or by implication. Râgavardhana is also a particular feature of the *Turangalîla-Symphonie*.

The field of sonority is closest to the realisation of harmony; chord building was Messiaen's first concert, the listeners' interest within the chord needed to be retained. In order to achieve this two specific categories of chord were developed. The chord of "superimposition"; this chord is usually a major or minor triad and is formed by adding notes of the high harmonics of the fundamental.

Alternatively, another chord can be superimposed on it, or a specific intervallic relationship, for example the "chord of fourths" consisting of all the notes of mode 5. The second category is that of the added note or appoggiatura chord. Only one or two notes are added to the basic chord, for example, an added augmented fourth or added sixth.

The first device, that of added resonance is the one with the most far reaching implications not only for Messiaen but also for other younger composers. Most notably when a louder chord or principal note is played and an added chord or note is played quietly above.

An alternative use, that of "inferior resonance", is where other material is played against a loud sounding chord in the bass register of the piano.[13] The principal notes should absorb as much as possible of the resonance notes; this device is basically a modification of timbre. This unity of timbre and harmony is utilised by some post-War composers, for example Stockhausen. It is also of special importance in electronic music. Intervallic relationships are emphasised in Messiaen's melodies as

---

13 Messiaen, O., *Technique de mon language musical*, Vol. 1 trans. Satterfield, J., V01. 2 examples 218, 219, 220, p.38, Leduc, Paris, 1956

a result of his harmonic ideas; this tendency is at the expense of implied harmony. Extended melodies are frequently monodic. Birdsong, Hindu music and plainsong are three of the most fundamental influences on his melodic writing. Plainsong and birdsong are monodic, and no account of tertiary harmony is taken by any of them but the influence of these three elements are essentially different as are their effects on Messiaen's melodic style. The effect of rhythm on Messiaen's melodies is the main influence of Hindu music; it also adds to his use of timbre. He does, however, use some Hindu melodies. The melody of the coda of Île de Feu II is derived from the melodic shape of various jâtis quoted in Lavignac's *Encyclopédia de la Musique*.[14] The particular jâtis used are "nandayantî", "ândhrî" and "naishâdi".

It was Marcel Dupré and Maurice Emmanuel, at the Paris Conservatory in the twenties, who first introduced Messiaen to Greek rhythms. At about the same time, he discovered the table of 120 Indian "decî-tâlas"—that is, rhythms of the Indian provinces—listed by Sharngadeva in his treatise "Samgîta-ratnâkara" and reproduced in Lavignac's Encyclopédie de la Musique. Johnson has argued that as a source of structural principles and for expressive melodic contours Messiaen has used plainsong, though he does not quote from it directly.[15]

In chapter 12 of *Technique de mon langage musical* Messiaen discusses the influence of antiphon melodies, psalmody, Alleluias and Kyries on particular melodies of his own. Some are striking examples of the transformation of actual plainsong into his own melodic style. The initial movement of *Les Corps Glorieux* is taken from the solemn Salve Regina melody and the last movement from Kyrie IX in the Roman Gradual. *Regard de l'Esprit de joie* is based on the Gradual Haec dies for Easter Sunday.

Messiaen literally quotes and modifies birdsong in a more stylised way to create melody. Fundamental problems of authenticity are posed by the use of birdsong, as birdsong is usually high-pitched and very fast and can incorporate microtonal intervals. The songs are therefore transcribed as accurately as possible in a way that human beings can understand and

---

14 Lavignac, A., *Encyclopédia de la Musique et Dictionnaire du Conservatoire*, Vol. 1, Albert Lavignac and Lionel de la Laurencie, (eds), Delagrave, Paris, 1924 - articles on Greek and Indian music are also quoted in Johnson, R.S., Messiaen Dent, London, 1989. 109-110, 115 and 225.

15 Johnson, R.S. *Messiaen*, Dent, London, 1989. 110

perform. For example, it would be based on a melodic interval, Written slower and at a lower register. At this point different but complementary paths involve the concept of polyrhythm. Messiaen experimented with rhythmic ostinati because he had no compulsion for his music to lead anywhere, He realised, however, that within ostinato there was a need for greater integration; as an alternative means towards polyrhythm be began to use rhythmic canons. A complex rhythmic canon can be seen in the last movement of *Visions de l'Amen*.[16]

When examining the differences the bass pitch ostinato 2 is a simplification of pitch ostinato 1. It is also a reordering (3, 1, 2). The two-part canon recurs in three forms at a quaver, a crotchet and a minim apart. The fifth movement of the same work reveals another complex rhythmic canon.[17]

Two further aspects of this line of thought are revealed in this latter example. Firstly, the later mathematical rhythmic complications which Messiaen added to his repertoire and secondly palindromic rhythms. In Messiaen's compositions palindromic rhythms appear outside rhythmic canons, for example in t *Quatour pour la fin du Temps*.[18]

Messiaen sees these as the rhythmic counterparts of the modes of limited transposition; this is literally total limited transposition, in this case limited by reversal.

There were further mathematical ideas developed from this point onwards. Rhythmic negatives are one of these developments and one of the few instances of this occurs in the sixth movement of the *Turangalîla-Symphonie*. There are two rhythmic tâlas in the percussion at the start of the middle section. The second of these tâlas, on glockenspiel and celesta, substitutes, in its rhythmic cells, silences for sounds and vice versa.[19]

The values are augmented to three times their length and the process is repeated, firstly in the original form, and then brought to an end, by a concluding motive on the glockenspiel. The post-War generation of serialists, notably Boulez and Pousseur, found this an important technique in their Work. In *Second Improvisation* on Mallarmé (1958) Boulez

---

16 Johnson, R.S. *Messiaen*, Dent, London, 1989. P.21

17 Messiaen, O., *Visions de l'Amen*, 1st Piano Pan, Durand, Paris, 1943

18 Messiaen, O., *Quatour pour la fin du Temps*, Durand, Paris, 1941

19 Johnson, R.S. *Messiaen*, Dent, London, 1989. p.91

alternates between two vocal styles, one melismatic, and the other syllabic. The melismatic sections are based on additive rhythms: each note is preceded and often terminated by grace notes, which are unmeasured and therefore rhythmically free. The material comes from a succession of carefully spaced chords, each note being fixed in its octave. In the syllabic sections, all the grace notes are removed. The rhythm consists of a succession of semibreves, each with a pause marked over it. The first two phrases contain eight semibreves each and the singer is requested to sing each phrase in one breath.

Symmetrical permutations/inversions are first discovered in Messiaen's Île de Feu II; the Work comprises the permutation of a chromatic series of rhythmic durations which are in a wedge shape.[20]

In *La Messe de la Pentecôte* the technique is used in a less complex way, only five durations, but reappears with more complexity in *Chronochromie*; in this instance Messiaen employs a slightly different system. Note lengths are taken in an arbitrary order, for example ♪ = 5, 4, 2, 8, 3 1, 6, 7; then each number refers to the position within this order. The first duration 5 gives the fifth position 3, which in turn becomes the first duration of the next permutation.

In *Chronochromie* 36 possible inversions are given employing 32 note values; using only 16 of these inversions Messiaen handles them singly and simultaneously in groups of three. Post-War avant-garde composers have adopted this technique, particularly Boulez in his works *Kontakte* and *Répons*.

RHYTHMIC CHARACTERS

The second group of developments is Messiaen's use of Hindu and Greek rhythms and "rhythmic characters". The latter consists of three rhythmic ideas. The first one becomes augmented or extended and "attacks"; the second is diminished or contracts and is therefore "attached"; the third remains unchanged and takes on the role of an "observer".

Messiaen developed this technique after studying Stravinsky's Rite of Spring. The technique of "rhythmic characters" is derived from the expansion and contraction of rhythmic cells in Stravinsky's *Sacre*, especially the "Danse sacrale" and "Glorification de l'ilue". Messiaen

---

20 Johnson, R.S. *Messiaen*, Dent, London, 1989 109

illustrates this in Volume 2 of Technique with a fragment from "Danse sacrale" and subsequently with the Hindu rhythm "simhavikridita".²¹

"Rhythmic characters" are found in Messiaen's "*Turangalîla 1*", and other compositions. The form of "*Turangalîla 1*" is episodic. The first theme alternating between clarinet and ondes martenot is followed by a contrasting theme in trombones, bassoon and double basses. The first theme returns on the strings with additional material superimposed on it and is followed by the third theme on the oboe. The complex rhythm of this oboe theme not only supplies, in its retrograde form, the rhythm of the counter-melody in clarinet and oboe, but also forms part of a longer tâlas other parts of which are used in the first and last movements of *Cinq Rechants* and in *Cantéyodjayâ* (p, 15, bar 13.)²²

The last main section of the movement superimposes the first theme on the second and is followed by a coda which resumes fragments of the third theme. The independent rhythmic structure takes the form of "rhythmic characters" extending throughout the fourth and fifth sections of the movement. These "characters" are played on the bass-drum (values increasing from one to eight semiquavers, then decreasing), maracas (values decreasing from eight to one semiquavers, then increasing) and wood-block (non- retrogradable rhythm of five semiquavers, remaining unchanged). A fragment of this rhythm is resumed in the coda.

Messiaen was at first attracted to Hindu and later to Greek rhythms because of their irregular character. He first came across the word "*Turangalîla*" in 1935, when, in a French encyclopaedia, he found it in a list of 120 Indian rhythms compiled in the thirteenth century by an Indian scholar called Cârngadeva.²³ Most of the rhythms are ametric, some are non-retrogradable, and others contain units that expand or contract. The list was of importance to Messiaen for two reasons: firstly because it placed at his disposal an invaluable reservoir of additive rhythms, a fact that immediately became apparent in his nine meditations for organ, *La Nativité du Seigneur* (1935), and the nine *Poèmes pour Mi* for soprano and piano or orchestra (1936-7); and secondly because all 120 rhythms have

---

21 Johnson, R.S. *Messiaen*, Dent, London, 1989. 36
22 Johnson, R.S. *Messiaen*, Dent, London, 1989. 208
23 Burkat, L., "*Turangalîla-Symphonie*" Musical Quarterly, XXXVI, April, 1950. 262

Sanskrit names, and some of the titles have cosmic overtones, which were of significance to him.

Messiaen uses a version of the tâlas" rhythm known as 'râgavardhana" in *Combat de la Mort et de la Vie* which has almost become a stereotype of his work.

The second section of the first movement of the *Turangalîla-Symphonie* sums up Messiaen's whole attitude to rhythmic organisation, with the superimposition of five separate rhythmic ideas upon each other.

MELODY

Up to the time of *Technique* Messiaen considered melody as the most important element in his music. It is therefore not surprising that most of the forms in his compositions up to the *Turangalîla-Symphonie* arise from melodic considerations and not from harmonic ones. Even more complex forms derived from sonata form and other sources are melodically orientated. Other forms derived from the sonata are not as important as they are only used once. The most important form is described as "Variations of the First Theme separated by Developments of the Second."[24] Criticism has been levelled at Messiaen because of his use of sectional forms. There is some justification for this because sectionalisation was a weakness in a number of early works. Messiaen has also been accused of harmonic inconsistency because of the way in which he uses harsh or complicated dissonances in the same work as constant sounding harmonies. This criticism is not borne out because, however dissonant or consonant the harmony, Messiaen always considers it in terms of colour or timbre.[25]

Melodic considerations are behind three of Messiaen's early formal developments. Sherlaw Johnson explains this firstly through "Binary Sentence", which consists of "Theme" and "Commentary", comprising a melodic realisation in which fragments are varied rhythmically, harmonically and melodically; they are repeated on different degrees. The introduction and expansion of foreign elements may occur but these will be stylistically similar to the theme; the last element is "Open Cadence".

---

[24] Messiaen, O., *Technique de mon language musical*, Vol.1, trans, Satterfield, L, Leduc, Paris, 1956. 42

[25] Johnson, R.S., *Messiaen*, Dent, London, 1985. 22

The other subdivision of Binary Sentence is Theme, Commentary and Closed Cadence. The second formal process is Ternary Sentence comprising, (a) Theme and Consequent, (b) Commentary on Theme and Consequent and (c) Repetition of Theme and Consequent. The third and final element, at this stage, is Song Sentence made up from Theme and Consequent, at a later stage inclining more towards the dominant and finally, arising from the Theme but not an exact repetition of it. Another important factor is the variations of the first theme which are separated by developments of the second theme.[26]

In some of Messiaen's larger Works there are even more interesting formal constructions. In *Visions de l'Amen*, II "Amen des étoiles", the movement begins with an octave monodic theme, written in all A^1, A^2, B, A^3, C construction; three increasingly complex stages are then developed. In the first, the notes are changed by registrational and rhythmic variation. Secondly, the notes are altered by sequence and inversion. Thirdly, there is a fulfilment of the ostinato implications of the original theme. This is achieved by the derivation of the melodic ostinato from the first and second bars remaining static throughout. At each repetition another melodic ostinato descends a semitone, and across both these ideas a melodic rhythm derived from bar 5 of the original is developed. This is followed by a complex polyharmonic accompaniment to the original theme while it is recapitulated.

In *Vingt Regards*, IX "Regard du temps", a conflict between the "head and the heart" is symbolised in the internal structure, "Time sees, born into itself, he who is eternal".[27]

B^1 has the semiquaver values of 8, 4, 8; B^2 consists of semiquaver = 6, 3, 6 but with the expansion and contraction of some material; B^3 has the initial semiquaver values of 10, 5, 10. Theme A consists of A^1, A^2, A^3 and is in three distinct parts. Theme B is a three part rhythmic canon, the second part is a vertical and horizontal pitch inversion of the first part; the third, lower part consists entirely of tritones and is "free".

In the *Turangalîla-Symphonie* Movement VII, "*Turangalîla* 2", there is an interesting sectional character and a formal episodic construction.

This introduction to Messiaen's musical language has placed the *Tristan* trilogy works into context. It has been shown that there is an

---

26 Johnson, R.S., *Messiaen*, Dent, London, 1985. 22
27 Johnson, R.S., *Messiaen*, Dent, London, 1985. 72

important connection with the idea of theological and non-theological contemplation. This is clearly evident in the purely religious contemplation of Vingt Regards, contrasted with the *Tristan* trilogy's earthly contemplation. For example, when Piroutcha becomes the object of the youth's intent desire in *Harawi*.

An argument has been created surrounding Messiaen's creative practice and the place which the *Tristan* trilogy works occupy in Messiaen's output. Keys and modes first used as symbolic ideas in religious works are now used in the *Tristan* trilogy. Rhythmic negatives were employed in *Quatour pour la fin du temps* and then extended and developed in the *Turangalîla-Symphonie*. This begins to show how the *Tristan* works have been put into the context of Messiaen's technique. Rhythmic characters are another important development in Messiaen's musical language which are used to great effect in "*Turangalîla 1*". The first movement of the *Turangalîla-Symphonie* shows the extent of Messiaen's attitude to rhythmic organisation, in 1946, with the superimposition of five separate rhythmic ideas upon each other.

Up until 1942, when Messiaen wrote *Technique de mon language musical*, the composer had always considered melody as the most important element in his music. The *Turangalîla-Symphonie* marked an important turning point in this way of thinking; harmony and form, from then on, played a much more important role in Messiaen's compositional thinking. This shows the extent to which the *Tristan* music spawned other ideas and its importance to twentieth-century music in opening up the possibility of making a completely fresh start in music. The *Tristan* works have not only developed naturally from Messiaen's musical language but also made a complete break, from purely religious subjects.

In this chapter we have placed the *Tristan* works in the context of Messiaen's output and Technique. This has been achieved through an understanding of Messiaen's musical language. We have seen that particular keys in connection with specific modes of limited transposition are associated with symbolic ideas and that this technique has been employed in the *Tristan* trilogy works. Melody and rhythm are also important aspects of Messiaen's ideas through his use and development of Hindu melodies and rhythms. Mathematical division and palindromic rhythms also play an important part in his compositional procedures. This chapter can be linked to the main argument of the thesis through the second section of the first movement of the *Turangalîla-Symphonie* where Messiaen's whole attitude to rhythmic organisation can be summed up with the superimposition of five separate rhythmic ideas upon each other. We have also shown that Messiaen's technique has thoroughly permeated his *Tristan* trilogy works.

It is important to note the connection between Messiaen's creative practice and Wagnerism in relation to Messiaen and Debussy. This will help develop the argument surrounding the exploration of Messiaen and the *Tristan* myth; having examined the musical connections we will now turn our attention in Chapter Three to literary and philosophical ideas.

3

Wagnerism in Relation to Messiaen and Debussy

Further to the thoughts conveyed in Chapter Two, Chapter Three will now look into the literary and philosophical ideas that have influenced Messiaen's *Tristan* trilogy works.

To understand the importance of the effect of Wagnerism on Debussy and Messiaen it is first necessary to consider Wagner's importance on the cultural milieu of the nineteenth century. This will ultimately help place the literary impact of the *Tristan* myth in context.

As Large, Weber and Sessa state, "The music, texts, and ideas of Richard Wagner stimulated a cultural movement that attracted dedicated adherents throughout the world, especially in Europe and the United States. This movement was by no means confined to music lovers, though they, of course, constituted an important group among Wagner's supporters."[1]

Wagner repeatedly returned to the inheritance of the Middle Ages, comprehended in the nineteenth-century, fairly widely, as comprising of the Norse *Volsunga Saga* and poems of the *Edda*, and gallant verses such as *Tristan* and *Parzival*. Wagner understood and altered this material through a refined awareness that reflected the aesthetic and cultural interests of his own time and society. The Romantic generation had perceived the Middle Ages as a time of intense mythological and philosophical importance. Novalis, possibly the greatest of the German Romantic poets, set down a renowned essay commemorating the Christian medieval period. He also compiled a number of brief, rapturous poems in prose and verse, the *Hymns* to Night (1799), in which his desire for union with his betrothed beyond the grave gives rise to an amorous and mystical commemoration of Night as the sphere of the most important experience and truth. The ideas taken from Romantic medievalism and from

---

1 Large, D.C., Weber, W. and Sessa, A.D., *Wagnerism in European Culture and Politics*, eds. Large and Weber, Cornell University Press, Ithaca and London, 1984. 7

Novalis's *Hymns* can be perceived clearly in Wagner's *Tristan und Isolde*, Debussy's *Pelléas et Mélisande* and Messiaen's *Tristan* trilogy.

Debussy's Reaction to Wagner

Debussy was far too good a composer and innovator to ignore Wagner's impact. The seamlessness and atmospheric resonance of Wagner's compositions were also suited to Debussy's music. On the other hand, Wagner was seen as an oppressor and his music was so overwhelming. The admirers and his detractors all agreed on one thing, that Wagner's compositions demand an extreme response. Both sides of this love-hate means that although in his Writings and reported opinions Debussy became quite emphatically anti- Wagner, the homage to and exploitation of Wagner's music was often discernible in his own work.

Debussy possibly first heard Wagner at the Conservatoire in 1876, although he could have heard some of his music on the Côte-d'Azur even a few years before that. Act I of Lohengrin was heard in Paris in 1879, and in 1880 Debussy attended a performance of orchestral excerpts in Vienna, on his expeditions with the von Meck family. In his adolescence, he and Lavignac, his teacher, went through the overture to Tannhäuser, they ended up by being locked in the college building, so intense was their absorption with the effect of this music.[2] By the mid-1880's Debussy was writing to M. Vasnier in a famous expression of self-deprecation: "Wagner could be of use to me, but I needn't tell you how absurd it would be even to try."[3]

The French were not unanimous in their rejection of Wagner, far from it: by 1885 there was even a Paris based newspaper, entitled the *Revue wagnérienne*. Lohengrin in its entirety was given its initial Paris performance in 1887, a performance, delayed several days because of objections and demonstrations against it.[4] In 1888 and 1889 Debussy actually journeyed to Bayreuth, home of the Wagner festival and shrine to the admirers of Wagner's compositions.[5] There he attended *Die Meistersinger* and *Parsifal*,

---

2 Holloway, R., *Debussy and Wagner*, Eulenburg Books, London, 1979. 18

3 Lockspeiser, E., *Debussy: His Life and Mind*, Vol.1. Cassell, London, 1962. 76

4 Lockspeiser, E., *Debussy: His Life and Mind*, Vol. 1. Cassell, London, 1962. 90

5 Orledge, R., *Debussy and the Theatre*, Cambridge University Press, Cambridge, 1982. 5

in both years, and *Tristan und Isolde* in the second year.[6] As late as 1894 he earned 1,000 franc for performing and even singing Act I of *Parsifal*, not yet heard in France, at a private party.[7]

It was in the 1890's, during the writing of *Pelléas et Mélisande*, that Debussy's outward attitude to Wagner changed to hostility. In many respects, given the extraordinary influence of the music of *Parsifal* on the *Tristan* inspired plot of *Pelléas*, it was almost inevitable that Debussy should create a smoke screen, if only for his own benefit. Moreover, the influence of this composition in particular lingers in orchestral compositions such as Le Martyre de Saint Sébastien (1911) as well as in Q (1912-13). Both, interestingly, were written in a hurry; it is as though he could not help himself, Debussy discovered in Wagner a lexicon of scraps with which he could write most easily.[8] It is also true of the orchestral interludes that he was still Writing, during the first performances of *Pelléas*.

In spite of the similarities of plot and title between *Tristan und Isolde* and *Pelléas et Mélisande*, it was the more shimmering, nebulous, later music of Wagner's final opera *Parsifal* that influenced Debussy more. Debussy himself referred to the work as being "illuminated from behind" and it is true that in this work Wagner achieves a world of subtlety and sound, of finish and flow completely different from that of early operas such as Tannhäuser or Lohengrin, and even from the Ring cycle.[9] Debussy was aware of this. In a review of a production of a production of *Parsifal*, and despite his usual public anti-Wagnerian Stance here expressed by a need to give something of a parody of the plot, he could write that "(the music) is incomparable and bewildering, splendid and strong".[10] *Parsifal* "is one of the loveliest monuments of sound ever raised to the serene glory of music".[11]

The composer Robin Holloway has written a technical and musicological account of the relationship between *Debussy and Wagner*. One of his most interesting observations is in the Way Debussy's attitude not

---

6 Orledge, R., *Debussy and the Theatre*, Cambridge University Press, Cambridge, 1982, 49

7 Holloway, R., *Debussy and Wagner*, Eulenburg Books, London, 1979. 19

8 Holloway, R., *Debussy and Wagner*, Eulenburg Books, London, 1979. 18

9 Orledge, R., *Debussy and the Theatre*, Cambridge University Press, Cambridge, 1982. 123

10 Holloway, R., *Debussy and Wagner*, Eulenburg Books, London, 1979. 20

11 Lockspeiser, E., *Debussy: His Life and Mind*, Vol.1, Cassell, London, 1962. 96

only resembles that of the philosopher Nietzsche, moving from love to hate, but also of many of the things Nietzsche stated, and which he intended as the worst barbs with which to attack Wagner, become true, and flatteringly so, of Debussy. To Nietzsche, French culture was an urbane and spent weak force, and in one of his tirades he described his former friend Wagner as, "our greatest musical miniaturist", a comment as full of insight as it was intended to be full of disparagemeiit.[12] Nietzsche provokingly described Wagner as, "a master of the first rank who compresses an infinity of meaning and sweetness into the smallest space"—an intendedly venomous description that can nevertheless describe the special genius of Debussy.[13]

Together with Mussorgsky's *Boris Godunov* the strongest influence on *Pelléas* was Wagner, or more particularly *Tristan* and *Parsifal*. The complicated background of Wagner's effect in France has been interpreted by Lucy Beckett, and the matter of *Tristan*'s and *Parsifal*'s influence on *Pelléas* carefully examined by Holloway in his book *Debussy and Wagner*.[14] Debussy underwent the inconsistent pressures of praise and rejection and accordingly always spoke of Wagner with some caution, being aware of both his debt and his impatient wish to escape it. As Debussy states,

After several years of passionate pilgrimages to Bayreuth, I began to have doubts about the Wagnerian formula; or rather it seemed to me that it could only serve Wagner's particular genius One should therefore seek to be "post (après) Wagner" rather than a Wagner imitator (d'après Wagner).[15]

The prevailing musical action dwells in the orchestra as it does in Wagner, where the motifs are introduced, argued and woven together in a Wagnerian way. It should be remembered that Berlioz and Verdi had already been writing in this Way as well. The orchestral writing in *Pelléas* is treated with far more restraint than Wagner ever displayed, even in *Tristan*, and moves forward prominently only in the interludes written at a later date to make scene changes easier. However, the harmonic colour

---

12 Holloway, R., *Debussy and Wagner*, Eulenburg Books, London, 1979. 17
13 Holloway, R., *Debussy and Wagner*, Eulenburg Books, London, 1979. 18
14 Holloway, R., *Debussy and Wagner*, Eulenburg Books, London, 1979; Beckett, L, Richard Wagner: *Parsifal*, Cambridge University Press, Cambridge, 1981
15 Orledge, R., *Debussy and the Theatre*, Cambridge University Press, Cambridge, 1982. 51

is unmistakably Wagnerian, in spite of the shifting triads and extended chords which Wagner had not risked.

Maeterlinck filled his drama with abstract ideas, in many cases to the point of naïveté, creatures of different kinds, gateways, the fortress, hair, the well, the clock and particularly blindness. Maeterlinck intentionally refrained from whimsical prose and wrote in the plainest language. The dissimilarity between the apparent clearness of every sentence and its obscure meaning is thereby stressed to great effect and the terrifying directness of the play is strengthened. To Debussy this unelaborated language was perfect because he specifically aimed at understatement as an escape from Wagnerian rhetorical exaggeration and as a powerful dramatic tool. Regarding the symbolism, he refrained from the orderly act of applying motifs to thoughts and representations. There is, for instance, no motif for being blind. He made no effort to mark references forward or back and employed a considerably more frank and open plan of motifs which comprise of the most important actors and a small number of abstract ideas for example, "the announcement of love", all free enough to subject Debussy to no inconvenient restraints. Arkel does not have a motif, however, his music has more strength and solidity than the other characters, possibly because he observes (in spite of his blindness), or supposes he observes, how events will prove to be. Arkel's joyful expectations for a new era are painfully betrayed by occurrences, and his own misfortune is at any rate as intense as that of the others. Arkel's observations are deceptive when everything has been said and done; he is as without sight as everybody else.

Difficulties with fitting language to music and the continuing matter of verse competing with music for the control of opera had been forcefully discussed for the last three hundred years. Debussy had no desire to increase heaps of theory to the amassed mound as Wagner had. Debussy merely left the serious representations of Maeterlink's play as he discovered them and employed music for its long respected goal as a producer of emotional impression, suspense, memory and colour. By avoiding lyrical tunes he placed upon himself a harsh but forcefully effective limitation. This could have condemned him to being forgotten forever, had he not pulled from within himself at the most favourable time of his compositional life, resembling Mussorgsky, a source of creative faculties and notions that controls the audience's consideration and esteem.

In *Pelléas et Mélisande* there is a more relevant relationship with the music of Fauré, whose freely modal vocal modulations influenced Debussy's move away from strict tonal movement. As composers of song Debussy and Fauré had much in common: an appreciation of Verlaine, an elegant feeling for vocal melody and a liking for moving inner parts. Fauré, with Debussy's knowledge, supplied music for a London performance of *Pelléas et Mélisande* in 1898.[16] In *Debussy's Pelléas et Mélisande* one perceives Fauré in the composition's persistent avoidance of firm diatonic cadences and in the unsettled orchestral figures in Golaud's scene with Yniold.

The aim of this section on Wagner and Debussy is explained through Debussy's knowledge of Oriental music which deepened partly through the various concerts and exhibitions staged at the "Exposition Universelle" of 1889. Technically, he was attracted to the harmonies of Oriental music, which, he knew, could be made to work within the context of European harmony. He was also attracted to the fact that Oriental music is less of a concert phenomenon, with all the superficial and competitive elements that that implies, and more of a spiritual, or meditative, inner expression. Two things in particular occurred to him: the way in which Oriental music relates closely to physical expression such as dance, much more so than European concert music, and its mood of avoidance of resolution. None of these aspects of Oriental music is alien to the true aims of Wagner's music; Wagner wished to suppress the usual conventions of "performance" (in Bayreuth, the theatre created by Wagner himself for the Wagner festivals only the on-stage action was to be seen, the orchestra and conductor being out of sight) to bring together all art forms, including dance and drama, within "music-drama", and, in *Tristan* most spectacularly, to evade harmonic resolution in an apparently never-ending ebb and flow of music.

The Music of Debussy's *Pelléas et Mélisande*

At the time of its first appearance, *Pelléas et Mélisande* was hailed as a violent reaction against Wagner. The composer himself confirmed that view, and France's musical avant-garde, dominated by the Wagnerites for more than three decades, from now on consisted of Debussysts.

---

16 Orledge, R., *Debussy and the Theatre*, Cambridge University Press, Cambridge, 1982. 58

Today this judgement has changed and we recognise the way in which this music differs from Wagner as well as the way in which it takes over from him and provides continuity. From the outset, Debussy felt no attraction whatsoever either for the *Ring of the Nibelungen* or for the Mastersingers.[17] The heavy Germanic nature of the subjects, the heavy symphonic nature of the musical elaboration, and the systematic nature in the use of the leitmotiv all necessarily repelled him. But very early he fell in love with *Tristan* and *Parsifal*, and he remained faithful to both.[18] *Pelléas* is unthinkable without either. Debussy creates a wholly novel and original work, that has nothing in common with the productions of the post-Wagnerians. Here the music of Mussorgsky has played a decisive part in freeing Debussy from Wagner's fetters.[19] He fortunately discovered it (namely *Boris Godunov* and the Song cycles) just at the right moment: towards 1892-93, when he abandoned the all too Wagnerian *Rodrigue de Chimène* and began serious work on *Pelléas*.[20] In Mussorgsky's music, Debussy found above all a vocal style and a word-setting totally different from Wagner's—a supple and endlessly shaded melodic recitative with mainly narrow, diatonic intervals.[21] Mussorgsky's peculiar harmony, his striking freedom in the handling of dissonance, his blending of modal turns into an enlarged tonality.[22] This eschews classical laws, his fresh diatonicism and partiality for the secondary degrees (11, VI, also Ill, VII) all exerted a powerful influence on the young Debussy. Returning to Wagner's music dramas, it could be thought that owing to the subject Debussy would stand closest to *Tristan*; a *Tristan* in which the traitor Melot would be missing but in which King Marke would split his personality into two halves, Golaud and Arkel.[23] Debussy himself knew that nobody would be able to write another *Tristan*, and as well harmonically as orchestrally his work stands much closer to *Parsifal*, which he adored, and the influence of which can be followed much later, right

---

17 Lockspeiser, E., *Debussy: His Life and Mind*, Vol. 1, Cassell, London, 1962. 91

18 Lockspeiser, E., *Debussy: His Life and Mind*, Vol. 1, Cassell, London, 1962. 95

19 Holloway, R., *Debussy and Wagner*, Eulenburg Books, London, 1979. 138

20 Abbate, C., "*Tristan* in the Composition of *Pelléas*", 19th Century Music, Vol. V., No. Z. University of California, Fall 1981. 118

21 Lockspeiser, E., *Debussy: His Life and Mind*, Vol. 1, Cassell, London, 1962. 48-49

22 Lockspeiser, I-5., *Debussy: His Life and Mind*, Vol. 1, Cassell, London, 1962. 49

23 Holloway, R., *Debussy and Wagner*, Eulenburg Books, London, 1979. 63

up to Le Martyre de Saint Sebastien.[24] The treatment of the orchestra is far more subtle and transparent than with Wagner, even though the scoring of *Pelléas* includes exactly the same forces as that of *Tristan*, with the sole exception of a bass clarinet.[25] Debussy uses his complete forces rarely and actual tutti are to be found only in the orchestral interludes added at the last moment, so that the voices are never covered.[26] The orchestra hardly takes any part in the action, as it did with Wagner. It has a wonderful, ever-present background, like a landscape changing at any moment. The relationship between the orchestra and the singers with its recitative-like declamation, sometimes even reminiscent of Gregorian plain-song.

It has been a matter open to much discussion, whether *Pelléas et Mélisande* contains any leitmotiv in the Wagnerian sense.[27] Just as Debussy's language remains tonal, but tonal functions are no longer perceived as such, Debussy drowns the keys.[28] He also drowns and veils the theme, or leitmotiv even though they remain present. Thus amongst those leitmotiv only very few are important to the listener, namely the two themes of Golaud (hovering between the notes D and E, but rhythmically strongly defined with its triplets and dotted notes) and of *Mélisande* (at its first appearance, a supple melodic arabesque on the oboe), both to be heard in the short orchestral "Prelucle".[29] The theme of *Pelléas*, of modal, pentatonic structure, is first heard when the character appears, in Act 1, Scene 2. The remaining motives do not fulfil any clearly defined leitmotivic function. They are mainly motives of atmosphere, or landscape, which are part of the continuous refined Web of the orchestral background.

We do not know where the landscape is situated or where the action takes place. The author and composer willingly leave us in the dark about these matters. Yet the old venerable castle and its inhabitants suggest some remote middle ages, just as the thick, dark forests near the sea call up that Celtic landscape far in the West, in which *Tristan* also takes

---

24 Lockspeiser, E., *Debussy: His Life and Mind*, Vol. 1, Cassell, London, 1962. 95-96

25 Lockspeiser, E., *Debussy: His Life and Mind*, Vol. 1, Cassell, London, 1962. 199

26 Holloway, R., *Debussy and Wagner*, Eulenburg Books, London, 1979. 76

27 Holloway, R., *Debussy and Wagner*, Eulenburg Books, London, 1979. 55-56

28 Lockspeiser, E., *Debussy: His Life and Mind*, Vol. 1, Cassell, London, 1962. 192

29 Lockspeiser, E., *Debussy: His Life and Mind*, Vol. 1, Cassell, London, 1962. 199

place. Allemonde cannot be too far from Tintagel or Kareol and the sea, whose hollow, quietly threatening noise we perceive towards the end of Act One. This is unmistakably the same dark-green Celtic sea which Debussy was to portray much more powerfully in *La Mer* a few years later.[30]

The composer also wished for characters that do not argue, but submit to life and fate. Indeed, in *Pelléas* the characters hardly act, rather are they being acted by the only active protagonist: blind, merciless Fate. The hard-tried Golaud suffers most from it and something of Anifortas lives again in him. Of *Mélisande* he knows nothing when he marries her, and hardly more when she dies. His brutality towards the frail young woman, his blind murderous instinct are nothing but weakness in front of almighty and undecipherable fate. After the catastrophe he is just like a child. As Parks states, "His anguished declaration "I have killed without reason! It is enough to make the stones weep!" is set very sparsely in the middle and lower registers of horns and cellos.[31] *Pelléas* is also weak and submissive to fate. He is unable ever to fulfil his project of a journey far away, unable to escape the fatal, deadly atmosphere of the old castle. He is at the same time stronger and frailer than his half-brother. Requited love strengthens him and he is younger by some twenty years. The loving wisdom and impotence of old age are embodied by the venerable Arkel. He, however, is not only physically near-blind, for in his mild goodness he is equally unable to prevent the blows of Destiny, which he suspects from time to time. Ultimately everything circles around Mélisande.[32] She is for Debussy the ideal woman as Isolde had been for Wagner and Piroutcha for Messiaen

The Influence of Wagner on Messiaen

Messiaen says little about Wagner or his music, nevertheless, Wagner did have a strong, powerful effect on Messiaen's ideas, it is difficult to make actual musical connections but influences are there, particularly in form

---

30 Howat, R., *Debussy in Proportion*, Cambridge University Press, Cambridge, 1981. 178

31 Parks, R.S., *The Music of Claude Debussy*, Yale University Press, New Haven and London, 1989. 272

32 Abbate, C., "*Tristan* in the Composition of *Pelléas*", *Nineteenth Century Music*, Vol. V. No.2, University of California, fall, 1981. 134

and orchestration. It is the notion and symbolism in *Tristan und Isolde* which influence Messiaen, who was clearly very familiar with the opera.

Each work of Messiaen's *Tristan* trilogy has a unique musical atmosphere. Death hovers over *Harawi*, *Turangalîla* takes place amidst the scents of a summer night and the warning of approaching dawn; the bleakness in *Cinq Rechants* highlights *Tristan*'s inner suffering. In Wagner's *Tristan und Isolde* an analogy may be drawn: Death hangs over the first act; the second act takes place amidst the scents of a summer night; the bleak sea and burning sun of the third act lead into *Tristan*'s inner suffering. In each composer's interpretation of the *Tristan* myth there is an elemental climax: the drinking of atonement, the extinguishing of a flaming torch, the final embrace and the third climax contains the music of both the others. This sequence suggests that Messiaen modelled his *Tristan* myth closely on Wagner's opera, and more closely than Debussy; the synopsis of *Debussy's Pelléas et Mélisande* reinforces this argument.

The musical essence of the drama—the love idea-lies in *Harawi* in "La ville qui dormait, toi". In Wagner's work the musical essence lies in the prelude. Wagner described this as the "love-death" and the end of the opera as "love's transfiguration". Messiaen in his *Tristan* trilogy repeatedly draws on these ideas in their entirety and in fragments. In Messiaen's *Harawi* the silences between the phrases are significant; the famous first line will develop "the town which sleeps, you": here it aspires towards the last line of "Dans le noir", "the town that sleeps..." which has come to symbolize the workings of fate.[33] Of the other themes, death and eternity are particularly important. Wagner's prelude forms a great arch and begins a recapitulation before one is fully aware of it; the climax, which foreshadows that of Act One, dies away in an ominous cello and double-bass phrase while preparing the way for the young sailor's song.

The night plays a central part in Messiaen's *Harawi*, as "Repetition planétaire" clearly shows. The stars are particularly important: the cosmos in *Harawi*, the "Joie du sang des étoiles" in *Turangalîla* and the dark in *Cinq Rechants*. When "La ville qui dormait, toi" begins, the youth is gazing intently, while Piroutcha is motionless and does not respond. "Bonjour toi, colombe verte" provokes her into telling her story. In Wagner's opera, when the curtain rises, *Tristan* is at the stern of a ship sailing from Ireland to Cornwall, while Isolde is seated motionless on

---

[33] Messiaen, O., *Harawi*, Leduc, Paris, 1945, Movement 1, "La ville qui dormait, toi" p.2; Movement 12, "La ville qui domiait..." 100

the deck. The song of the Cornish sail sailor of sight) provokes her into telling her story to Brangäne. Messiaen has replaced the sailors with the green dove who is also symbolically out of sight.

Resembling Wagner the ambiguity of the words find their true expression in the music. When Piroutcha sings, "Hello you limpid pearl" or "shared shadow", there can be no doubt that she is in love with the youth.[34] Likewise in Wagner's opera when Isolde sings, "who from mine eyes averts his own" or "shrinking shame my gaze he shuns" there can be no question that she is in love with *Tristan*.[35] Piroutcha also confesses it to herself and later sees death as the only solution.

In a stormy outburst Piroutcha calls upon the mountains to destroy their love the turbulence continues through "Doundou tchil" the fourth song's attempt to soothe her. The phrase "the dance of the stars doundou tchil" will underlie the lovers' suffering in *Cinq Rechants*.[36] In Act 1 of *Tristan und Isolde*, Isolde in an angry outburst calls upon her mother's arts to destroy the ship. The turbulence continues through Brangäne's attempt to soothe her. The phrase at "pale and speechless, on the way, food rejecting, without sleep" will underlie *Tristan*'s suffering in Act 3.[37] Once more an analogy is apparent between Act 1 of Wagner's *Tristan* and Messiaen's I-*Harawi*; Act 3 of Wagner's opera and Messiaen's *Cinq Rechants*. Though Brangäne sings above it, this music belongs to Isolde, and returns whenever Isolde recalls how she let the sword drop—it suggests that this memory is a traumatic abyss which she must somehow bridge. This traumatic abyss is symbolically represented by Messiaen in "Montagnes" with the words "in their tight cowls the firs rush towards the darkness.[38] On the first occasion Piroutcha describes her love "My

---

34 Messiaen, O., *Harawi*, Leduc, Paris, 1945. Movement 2 "Bonjour toi, perle limpide" p.6; "Ombre partagé" p.9

35 Wagner, R., *Tristan und Isolde*, trans, H. and F. Corder, Breitkopf and Härtel, Wiesbaden, Eulenburg London, 1865. "der meinem Blick den seinen birgt" p.47 and "Scham und Scheue abwärts schaut7 p 48

36 Messiaen, O., *Harawi*, Leduc, Paris, 1945, Movement 4., p.22. "la danse des étoiles doundou tchil"

37 Wagner, R., *Tristan und Isolde* trans, H. and F. Corder, Breitkopf and Härtel, Wiesbaden, Eulenburg London, 1865. p.40 "bleich und schweigend auf der Fahrt, ohne Nahrung, ohne Schlaf"

38 Messiaen, O., *Harawi*, Leduc, Paris, 1945, Movement 3, p.16, "En capuchons serrés les sapins se hatentvers le noir".

fruit lightweight in the light, doundou tchil"; on the second the words "Cut my head off doundou tchil" expresses her sense of shame; on the third, when she addresses the youth she demands that he atone with the words "My hands, your eye, your neck, the sky".[39] There is another connection here with Wagner's *Tristan und Isolde*, on the first occasion Isolde describes healing the wound; on the second the orchestra expresses her sense of shame; on the third, when she addresses *Tristan*, she demands that he atone with the death drink. The healing of the wound has been replaced, or is possibly seen, by Messiaen as the act of falling in love.

Turangalîla could be said to represent the pull of the day upon lovers dedicated to the night. Before the lovers can fully lose themselves in their love for one another, Isolde has to express her pent-up reproaches. As they relive the time when *Tristan* ignored and repressed his love for her, the music appears in different guises: poetic, heroic and violent. In the quick music it undergoes rapid transformations and in the slow music it binds the whole fabric together. This is also true of Act 2 of Wagner's *Tristan und Isolde* when at the start a chord of the seventh carries a motif which will be of primary importance to this act.

Turangalîla opens with what is, in a sense, an interlude between two long scenes for Tristan and Isolde. The "Introduction" speaks in a complex rhythmic language where the semiquaver string patterns show Isolde's impatient expectancy, the night sounds (from figure 1 woodwind) and the "flower theme" (violins echoed by wind) grow into a welter of rhythmic complexity.[40] It avoids a tonal resting place. The music of the first section contains the "statue theme" and "flower theme". As the second section grows more rhythmically complex it is as though Isolde ceases to believe in reality and the rhythms increase in intensity.

In "Chant d'amour 1" Isolde still believes in Tristan's love for her. The music here is in Couplet-refrain form with poetic use of the horn calls played loudly by the woodwind and looks back to Act 2 of Wagner's *Tristan*, where the horn calls build up as Isolde beseeches Brangäne to extinguish the torch. The movement contains a rhythmic motif

---

39 Messiaen, O., *Harawi*, Leduc, Paris, 1945, Movement 4, p.23, "mon fruit léger dans la lumiere, doundou tchil"; Movement 5., p.30 "Coupe moi la téte, doundou tchil"; Movement 10, p.87, "Mes mains, ton oeil ton cou, le ciel".
40 Messiaen, O., *Turangalîla-Symphonie*, Durand, Paris, 1948. 2-3

exchanged between cellos and violins suggesting Isolde's excitement and an invocation to the night. (Figure 1).[41]

In *"Turangalîla* 1" the music is more abandoned still and reaches a momentous climax which is analogous with the extinguishing of the torch, which Isolde identifies with the light of day itself, at the start of the final episode (Figure .12).[42] Although the music of "Chant d'amour 2" is overwhelming it is not at all loud: the mezzoforte markings are notable (Figure 4).[43] The "statue theme" and "flower theme" with their hyperactive string figuration gives the "Chant d'amour 2" movement a full texture.

The music of the "Joie du sang des étoiles" draws us in to the mysteries of the night. It is fascinating to see how Messiaen repeats and transforms the "Chant d'amour 1" music in this movement in a totally different character.[44] There it was brilliant and glamorous here it is full of passionate night colours. We sense that we pass through the door of the night; the chromatic harmony is in keeping with the more intricate style of the musical language that has developed. A poetic transition calms the music with just a hint of the danger in the background.

"Jardin du sommeil d'amour" ("Garden of the sleep of love") is an invocation to the night to envelop them and release them from the world. This is Messiaen's response to the Act 2 music of Wagner's *Tristan* "O sink hernieder Nacht der Liebe" ("Oh sink around us Night of loving"). The "love theme" is spun into a legato line; the clarinets and cellos intertwine with each other over two-bar phrases.[45] The "flower theme" appears transformed into violent agitation in *Cinq Rechants*, here breathes warmth and peace. There is a further connection with Wagner, the melody, sung by *Tristan*, is none other than the notes of the *"Tristan"* chord spun into a legato line; the voices intertwine with each other over two-bar phases, and with the resolving chords from the song "Traume" in the Wesendonck Lieder. Isolde's theme "Barg im Busen uns sich die Sonne" ("In my breast, the sun is declining"), which Will appear transformed into violent agitation in Act 3, here breathes warmth and peace.

---

41 Messiaen, O., *Turangalîla-Symphonie*, Durand, Paris, 1948. 35»36
42 Messiaen, O., *Turangalîla-Symphonie*, Durand, Paris, 1948. 108
43 Messiaen, O., *Turangalîla-Symphonie*, Durand, Paris, 1948. 119-121
44 Messiaen, O., *Turangalîla-Symphonie*, Durand, Paris, 1948. 163
45 Messiaen, O., *Turangalîla-Symphonie*, Durand, Paris, 1948. 248-250

With bass clarinets and double-basses added to the cellos and violas, the music of "*Turangalîla* 2" sounds garish. A phrase (at figure 1) punctuated by two stabbing figures in the piano, states that catastrophe is foreshadowed.[46] This would fit in with Act 2 of Wagner's score when King Mark cannot comprehend how *Tristan* could betray him. Bass clarinets and double-basses are also added to the violas and cellos by Wagner and the music sounds gaudy.[47]

The third episode of "*Turangalîla* 2" can be seen as Tristan's tribute to Isolde, and his sense that she was untouchable. Messiaell's phrases are legato arches, at first with the flutes, then with the tubas and trombones.

The music of the "Développement de l'amour" evokes a sense of the primal mystery of nature, and includes all the cyclic themes. The languorous music of the "love theme" dominates and Tristan's love is illustrated by the way that he is unable to resist Isolde's beauty. There are parallels again with Act 2 of Wagner's *Tristan* when Tristan's nobility is illustrated by the way he excuses Melot's treachery by supposing he was, as any man would be, unable to resist Isolde's beauty, and that he only acted out of jealousy. Messiaen has stripped the essence of the story to its barest emotional essentials and concentrates on the psychological aspects of Tristan's love with a symbolic representation of nature.

In "*Turangalîla* 3" the celesta and cellos play an agitated rising phrase (Figure 6) in variations on the opening theme, which expresses despair.[48] In the third section of Act 2 of Wagner's *Tristan* the cellos and double-basses play an agitated rising phrase which expresses Tristan's despair.[49] This movement calls up the essence of the *Turangalîla* music—its first theme and the simultaneous resolution of the four variations go a step further than before.

In "Final" love is seen as the redeeming solution. Messiaen vividly portrays this in sonata form, ignoring Wagner's narrative which concentrates on the world between life and death. Messiaen replaces Wagner's "King Mark" theme, which resounds tragically in the trumpets, with the more optimistic "love theme" which concludes *Turangalîla* with a

---

46 Messiaen, O., *Turangalîla-Symphonie*, Durand, Paris, 1948. 265

47 Wagner, R., *Tristan und Isolde*, trans. H. and F. Corder, Breitkopf and Härtel, Wiesbaden, Eulenburg, London, 1865. 674

48 Messiaen, O., *Turangalîla-Symphonie*, Durand, Paris, 1948. 342-350

49 Wagner, R., *Tristan und Isolde*, trans. H. and F. Corder, Breitkopf and Härtel, Wiesbaden, Eulenburg, London, 1865. 678-679

complex rhythmic coda. Messiaen departs from Wagner's ideas in this movement and *Turangalîla* ends with a celebration of the playful irresistible love of its title.

One of the wonders of *Cinq Rechants* is its form; even without a thorough knowledge of it, one may sense its indebtedness to Claude le Jeune—above all in its couplets and refrains. If the first movement belongs to the lovers, then the last is fundamentally concerned with the *Tristan* myth and magic. We experience with Tristan the pain he feels, deprived of his beloved, his great longing for death to unite them both, and the agony of returning to consciousness, with all the renewed pain and longing which that involves. In Act 3 of Wagner's *Tristan* the melody heard at the outset returns to evoke his earliest memories of his parents' death. Messiaen takes this further, in *Cinq Rechants* the past and present constantly intermingle: recalling the evocation of birth and death.

The first movement is not so much an entity in itself, like the "Introduction" of *Turangalîla*, but a part of the entire work. The twelve lone voices set a tone of foreboding that is sustained through the desolation of the words and the violence of the movements that follow.

In the second movement the Words are a mixture of the sophisticated and the natural. Different symbolic ideas are developed during the course of the movement, the most significant being the opening of the fan and then its closing.[50] In Wagner's Act 3 different episodes are developed during the course of the act, the most important being its opening fifth, a direct inversion of the "day" motif. It is as though Messiaen has taken this musical idea and transformed it into a symbol of the fan, which, with its closing represents night, and with its opening symbolises day.

The third movement is something of a shock, for there is more symbolism here than in the whole work. The singers announce the first fulfilment of love and a new landscape comes forth from Tristan and Isolde. The words wild and paradoxical as they are, are the key to the Work. Isolde is the light: although Tristan cannot see her, he can hear her voice.[51]

In the fourth movement the contralto and bass voices are heard singing a long drawn out incantation, "ro-ma ta-ma ta-ma", like a lost

---

50 Messiaen, O., *Cinq Rechants*, Salabert, Paris, 1949. pp.1 1-12

51 Messiaen, O., *Cinq Rechants*, Salabert, Paris, 1949. Movement3, 26-27

soul in the night.⁵² The intervening lines in the voices of the refrains surrounding the repeated couplet renews the first experience of love.

In the fifth movement although the music contains repetitions of the first refrain's music, in extended form, the new vocal bass line (tk tk tk tk) creates the impression of a new composition.⁵³ The brutality evoked here by the singers is all revealing; it can be understood to represent Isolde's lament for Tristan in a triumphant apotheosis, as in Wagner's version of the myth, she sinks lifeless on to Tristan's body.

It is apparent that Messiaen based his *Tristan* trilogy works on Acts 1, 2 and 3 of Wagner's opera, respectively. *Harawi* is Messiaen's response to Act 1 of *Tristan und Isolde*, *Turangalîla* is inspired by Act 2 and *Cinq Rechants*, like Wagner's *Tristan* before it, incorporates and develops the ideas of the previous two Acts within it. It is possible to chart Messiaen's symbolic response to the action within each act, whether he did this consciously we shall never know. But the connections are there and can be teased out with careful analysis of each score.

In Messiaen the musical connections are so strong that it is possible to plot the development of Wagner's *Tristan und Isolde* in Messiaen's *Tristan* trilogy works, step by step.

This chapter has examined the effect of Wagnerism on Messiaen and has placed the literary impact of the *Tristan* myth in context. We have seen that Wagner repeatedly turned to the Middle Ages and the poems of *Tristan* and *Parzival*. We have concluded from this that ideas taken from Romantic medievalism had an important effect on Messiaen's *Tristan* trilogy, Debussy's *Pelléas et Mélisande* and Wangle's *Tristan und Isolde*. We have demonstrated that the seamlessness and atmospheric resonance of Wagner's music suited Debussy's music; yet Debussy became anti-Wagner. Debussy's outward hostility to Wagner became apparent during the composition of *Pelléas et Mélisande*. It has been shown how the influence of Wagner's *Parsifal* permeated *Pelléas*.

The key argument of this chapter is, however, the influence of Wagner on Messiaen. Although it is difficult to make actual musical connections Wagner's influence is apparent on Messiaen. This has been demonstrated through the unique musical atmosphere in each of the works that comprise Messiaen's *Tristan* trilogy. It is, therefore, important in the next

---

52 Messiaen, O., *Cinq Rechants*, Salabert, Paris, 1949. Movement 4, pp. 31, 32, 34 and 35

53 Messiaen, O. *Cinq Rechants*, Salabert, Paris, 1949. Movement 1, p.2 and Movement 5, p. 36. "tk tk tk tk".

chapter to examine the historical, philosophical and literary importance of the *Tristan* myth itself to demonstrate how, as a prime literary source, it relates to the book as a whole.

4

THE TRISTAN MYTH

INTRODUCTION

Gottfried's *Tristan* is the main literary source for Messiaen, who was extremely influenced by it. This, in itself, should justify this chapter and the detail which is contained within it.

'When examining the theory of the *Tristan* myth, the origins and sources of the stories and poems that have been handed down throughout the generations will be looked at. It is interesting to see how the tales have changed with retelling and how the different emphases on social and moral ideas have developed. A brief synopsis of the *Tristan* myth will be included and the way in which Wagner interpreted it will be discussed in Chapter Five. It will then be valuable to look at the way in which Messiaen treated the subject matter and interpreted various aspects of the myth. This chapter will then examine how Messiaen changed the emphasis of the myth and in doing so reinterpreted it avoiding narrative.

Origins of the Myth

It is of great interest, when examining the origin of the *Tristan* myth, to observe that the familiar versions of the story are no older than the most important Arthurian tales. Such tales include those by Chrétien de Troyes, Geoffrey of Monmouth and other twelfth- century poets. However, the seeds of the *Tristan* myth are considerably older than any known Arthurian legend and there is little doubt that the material was already known, orally, through Breton minstrels.[1]

An examination of the evidence of three twelfth-century poets, who wrote about the *Tristan* romance, throws light on the origin of the story. It is apparent that a Norman, named Béroul, at the end of

---

[1] For further evidence of Breton influence on the *Tristan* myth see Eisner, S., *The Tristan Legend, a Study in Sources*, Illinois University Press, 1969. pp. 14, 18 and 154

the twelfth-century wrote a *Tristan* which is considerably shorter than the two other versions.² Béroul's verse is a tale of courtly intrigues and revenge. The hero is a flatterer and lover who is neither courageous as a knight nor distressed as a lover.

A German named Eilhart von Oberge possibly translated a lost French account of the tale. Eilhart's story is more of a nobly courageous epic tale of failure than a romance. The hero is more of a fighter than a lover, who is broken by the love which a pitiless fate pushes upon him.³

Thomas of Britain also prepared an interpretation, in French, at the Court of Henry II of England, circa 1150.⁴ Much of this poem has not survived but rather has been reconstructed from poems that were derived from Thomas's original. The poems that were reconstructed from Thomas's original include the Tristian und Isolt of Gottfried von Strassburg and the Norse version of Tristram's Saga which was derived from Thomas's poem in 1225 by Brother Robert.

The Tale of *Tristan* and Isolt came into existence in Celtic narratives and traditional legends just as the Arthurian tales did, and resembling them, it was reshaped and recounted in the twelfth-century, when the romance Works dominated vernacular literature. The lifespan of Arthurian verse as an important poetic type dealing with individual ethical difficulties was short. After the period of Hartmann and Chrétien, the ideas kept their popularity but the handling changed. The prose poems are more clumsy in their moral rightness and, at the same time, careless in the addition and reproduction of events; they are more pedantic and less perceptive. Most significantly, they are all-encompassing; they bring all the obtainable material into one loosely constructed united story. When they placed the *Tristan* myth in the Arthurian sphere, they could no longer escape from the inferences of a love that is obviously of the body and adulterous, or keep the results of such a love unmistakable, and they must permit it to do away with that world.

The *Tristan* works have already caused much learned activity as well as providing an important literary source for Messiaen. The greatest

---

2 Ferrante, J.M. *The Conflict of Love and Honour*, Columbia University, Mouton, The Hague, Paris, 1973. 60

3 Ferrante, J.M. *The Conflict of Love and Honour*, Columbia University, Mouton, The Hague, Paris, 1973. 63

4 Gottfried von Strassburg. *Tristan, with the Tristan of Thomas*, Penguin Books, London, 1967. 356

amount of it, however, has been concentrated on the consideration of sources, Celtic or classic, and what degree of similarity has been made between existing verses has been undertaken mostly to demonstrate effect, importance or superiority. The only serious efforts to understand a distinct outlook beyond unsophisticated or courtly opinions have been made in relation to Gottfried.

Careful examination of Gottfried's version of the romance has given rise to mostly theological and philosophical understandings extracted from the verse alone, devoid of careful thought of its connection to the complete tradition. There has been much reasoned argument but scant agreement regarding the real nature of the poem. Agreement cannot be reached on how Gottfried imagines human love; it is not apparent if he sees it as a struggle between body and soul, or as a route to the highest good, and it is not clear whether or not he opposes carnal desire to Christian love. Gottfried's treatment of significant events show that he establishes a religious love which adopts its metaphors and its basic ideas from Christian beliefs and which exists independently from, but not opposed, to the Christian faith.

The French prose custom is considerably more complex. It depends on Grail and Arthurian stories as Well as on the verse tradition of *Tristan*, and comprises of wildly dissimilar ideas often only tenuously linked to the principal tale. The knightly exploits are given more consideration than the circumstances of the love story. There are forty-eight French documents from the twelfth-century onwards and nine in printed form, however, not one that can be understood as whole in itself, but Löseth has endeavoured to produce a complete account of the tale, prepared from what he thinks the most fitting documents. There are various other Italian accounts of the *Tristan* story, some Written without rhyme (the *Codice Ponciatichiano*, the *Tristano Riccardiano*), and episodic verses, but not one so complete as the *Tavola Ritonda*.

The theme of Gottfried's *Tristan* will be used as it is written, free from allusion either to its assumed model or to other accounts of the story, unless such connection is required by the direct concerns of the argument. It is easy to understand that the poet selected his tale, and this specific account, with its particular events, and with its omissions and inclusions, to fit his own purposes.

In conclusion, the earliest interpretations of the *Tristan* myth in France and Germany are the poems of Béroul, Eilhart, Gottfried and

Thomas. Although they all incorporate the main elements of the myth, the result of each of their own retellings is quite different. Close scrutiny by Bromwich, Loomis, Löseth, Polidori and Zimmer of these four writers and the prose editions including the *Tavola Ritonda* has led to a more complete appreciation of the tales and to some understanding of medieval story-telling techniques. The *Tristan* myth, arguably, offers one of the finest examples of the medieval skill to use a well-known story for a multitude of different purposes. The *Tristan* myth was ultimately used by Wagner in his quest for a neo-Hellenic Gesamtkunstwerk, "the summum bonum of art".[5] This will be examined later in Wagner's interpretation of the *Tristan* myth.

The *Tristan* of Gottfried

The *Tristan* of Gottfried is a poem of barbaric splendour and artistry; an eloquent celebration of a heroic life and death; an "action" of epic sweep and scope. As the attempt to imitate the local triumphs of verse and syntax was prolonged, something of the deeper pattern and the real substance and significance of *Tristan* began to reveal itself.

Much of the characteristic power and beauty comes from the traditional poetic and narrative forms. It is written after the unmistakable style of oral poetry, a highly- developed medium evolved in and for oral composition and performance, which here can be seen in the first stage of its long adaptation to writing.[6] *Tristan* is a very important poem. Its historical position at the beginning of literature has, however, proved something of a mixed blessing so far as its reputation is concerned. It is a document of prime philological, cultural and historical, as well as literary interest.

The emphasis of this section is upon *Tristan* as an epic poem. Specific aspects of the poem are also addressed.

Tristan is a heroic poem in the simple sense that it celebrates the actions of its protagonist. *Tristan*, son of Rivalin, is the very type of hero whose eagerness to seek out and meet every challenge alone and unarmed makes him glorious in life and brings him to his tragic death

---

5 Jacobs, R.L. trans., *Three Wagner Essays*, Eulenburg Books, London, 1979. ix

6 Ferrante, J.M. *The Conflict of Love and Honour*, Columbia University, Mouton, The Hague, Paris, 1973. 12

He also has a hero's delight in his own prowess and a hero's magnanimity to lesser men.

Tristan is a typical heroic poem not only in its central figure but also in its world and in its values. The knights are either feasting or fighting; they are devoted to glee in hall or glory in the field.

Hero-tales or heroic poems do not usually remain at the level of simple adventure stories. Even in later medieval romances the heroic code is usually complicated and its values tested by a clash of loyalties. Most of the northern heroic tales involve a conflict between an absolute obligation such as the revenge of a slain kinsman, and other obligations such as oaths of allegiance or of marriage.[7] Most of these themes are raised in *Tristan*, but usually in the interrelated set of stories which support the central action; these stories are alluded to rather than related fully.[8]

These outside episodes set the story of *Tristan*'s life in a much larger context. The development of the foreground story is slow and simple; the episodes are arranged around and behind it, and lend a depth and complexity to the whole.

This chapter is concerned with the reader's and Messiaen's imaginative experience of *Tristan* as a work of art. This experience is not adequately accounted for by a discussion of literary sources. While the opportunities for fantasy in myth-criticism are apparent, it seems pointless to ignore the evidently superhuman powers attributed to *Tristan*.

An epic should be universal, taking in all of life and representing it in such a way that the general truth of the presentation is universally recognised. Its scope should embrace war and peace, men and gods, life and death in a comprehensive and encyclopaedic way. Its presentation should be objective: its scenes, events and characters should form an inter- connected and solid reality, being presented from a consistent and impartial viewpoint. *Tristan* is inclusive in that it comprehends life and death, peace and War, man and God.

The inclusive of is picture of human life may be doubted on the grounds that it is too aristocratic. The whole life of the people and of mankind is involved in the struggle of the hero. Gottfried's *Tristan* is not

---

7 Goldschmidt Kunzer, R., *The Tristan of Gottfried Von Strassburg. An Ironic Perspective*, University of California Press, London 1973. 135-137

8 Ferrante, I.M., *The Conflict of Love and Honour*, Columbia University, Mouton, The Hague, Paris, 1973. 23

an irresponsible single-hero romance—it is very much concerned, like Messiaen's, with social ethics.

Another criterion offered for epic was objectivity. Every one of the individual human deaths in the poem is given its full weight and significance. The death of Tristan himself has a full and tragic ending. Death, irrespective of nationality or merit, is always given due space and honour. The human concern is moral, emotional, and even anxious. Much of the objectivity comes from the traditional presentation of life in the heroic world.

Each action in Gottfried's and Messiaen's *Tristan* has a full spatial and temporal dimension, and the cosmic envelope of space and time is always assumed and usually felt to be there, immutable. The metaphysical, ethical and moral universe of the poem is also fixed and unalterable in its operations of cause and consequence, origin and end.

The operations of nature, time and cosmos are inescapable, and the consequences of evil human actions scarcely less so. In fact, to speak of nature as an inert stage upon which the human drama is played out is to undervalue nature and overvalue human motive. In epic, human and non-human actions are felt to be part of a larger impersonal process, the authority of which is not questioned, but accepted and respected. Messiaen may feel that the hand of God is so frequently visible in the world of the poem that it is misleading to regard the cosmic process as truly impersonal.

If Gottfried voices the communal view, it is not an undifferentiated or a primitive view. The sensibility through which Gottfried's *Tristan* is filtered is not entirely at one with the world id discloses. Gottfried admires, idealizes and identifies with the epic synthesis. He works within its conventions but is more reflective and more analytical.[9]

A typical moralist, Gottfried's traditional wryness is modified in places by a Christian note of moral and spiritual concern. Where his voice is heard, Gottfried makes *Tristan* more of a lament than a celebration of heroic life. But if Gottfried, in making the *Tristan*—story into the poem that it is, has deepened it, shaped it and softened it, his consciousness still operates quite naturally in the categories and procedures of the epic tradition. The significance and weight of *Tristan* lies primarily in the logic of the story and the nature of the style, both traditional, and

---

9 Goldschmidt Kunzer, R., *The Tristan of Gottfried von Strassburg. An Ironic Perspective*, University of California Press, London, 1973. 3

not in the comments of Gottfried. To a literate consciousness deepened by Christianity, the heroic world of these heathen ancestors must have seemed doubly admirable and the limitations of heroic life doubly tragic. The mythic unity of consciousness is supplemented rather than supplanted by the moral and thematic concerns of Gottfried.

The greatness of the story to Messiaen does not depend on its theme—man against death—nor on certain important moments. The actual story must dramatize the forms of a particular and important human problem. In *Harawi* and *Turangalîla* as in *Cinq Rechants*, the theme of guilt and expiation is prominent. In these works Messiaen fuses his primitive pagan ritualism with his Christian sense of guilt, thereby creating an art immemorially ancient and yet immediately contemporary. The climax of the drama is again a death—Tristan's own—but here no hope is held out to blunt the force of an overwhelming pessimistic tragedy

The epic, as opposed to the merely heroic, potentialities of this story are activated by its relation to the wider theme of human social order. Even in his *Tristan* trilogy Messiaen remains Catholic enough to remember that marriage is a sacrament. The new birth which ensues from the initiation is the new unit of husband-plus-wife. When Tristan and Isolde emerge from the ordeals of *Cinq Rechants*, the chorus greets them not as two but as one. But if at the back of Messiaen's mind is a Catholic turn of thought, it is certainly not Catholic doctrine he is enunciating. He has pointedly made the marriage in the *Tristan* trilogy a secular sacrament.

A secular sacrament is, indeed, just what the *Tristan* trilogy initiation was. Its purpose was to activate in the members those virtues by which they could be bound into a brotherhood, its implication that if everyone practised them society at large would become a brotherhood—or, as depicted in *Turangalîla*, a heaven-state on earth.

These virtues are, of course, social; and they can be liberated in man's nature only by overcoming the fear of hell. So long as man fears hell, he will devote his attention to scrambling into heaven; he will waste no energy in social love or in improving the state of society either now or for future generations; he will spread fear and superstition in place of friendship and education; he may even quit society and fail to contribute children towards its perpetuation, shutting himself up in a celibate's cell in order to make himself worthy of heaven after his death. The two qualities, erotic love, which alone can make society continue forwards through time, and social love, which alone can widen society outwards into a universal brotherhood, are the themes of Messiaen's *Tristan* trilogy.

It is perhaps not surprising that the values of *Tristan* should turn out to be those of the classic heroic ethic. But the stress is more upon mutual obligation than on individual glory. *Tristan* was perhaps to Messiaen a semi-divine representative of humanity but unless the hero is also a champion, mere heroism is an adolescent ideal—arrogant and irresponsible. The heroic ideal of unflinching individual courage, of a glorious personal transcendence of human limitations, is always being stalked in *Tristan* by a complementary ideal of responsibility towards kindred. This second ideal of mutual sen/ice between a lord and his people is more honoured in the breach than the observance as the poem progresses.[10]

It has been shown that if the characteristics of epic are inclusiveness of range, objectivity of treatment, unity of ethos and a significant action, then *Tristan* may fairly be called an epic. One could express the poem's apprehension of a deeper reality by saying that the life and death of Tristan recapitulates the life-cycle of the race: the heroic generation is born, flourishes and dies. Onto the elemental power of the original tale (or myth) Gottfried, like Messiaen, has grafted a set of human and social themes, so that the single-handed adventure comes to express the struggle of the forces of life and death in human society.[11]

Opposition and dualism work throughout the poem: the attraction and repulsion between Tristan and Iseult can be felt in its every part. Such violent oppositions, contrasts and comparisons can be found at every stage of the poem. In places the paralleling and pairing can seem a little schematic, as in the elaborate exclamations over the double death of Tristan and Iseult. But this elaboration and orchestration of the primitive conflict of Tristan and Iseult into an epic conflict between life and death, harmony and chaos, good and evil, is Gottfried's chief work. The murderous hatred of individuals and of people, takes on the pattern of an apparently inextinguishable and tragic blood-feud. The duty to avenge a slain kinsman is absolute; even Iseult seems to receive some sympathy for her vengeance when Tristan kills Morold.

---

10 Ferrante, J.M. *The Conflict of Love and Honour*, Columbia University, Mouton, The Hague, Paris. 1973.
11 Gottfried von Strassburg, ints. Hallo, A.T., *Tristan*, Penguin Books, London, 1967. 16

Gottfried constantly connects the nightmare of the love potion with the distinctiveness of the blood-feud, and in his critique of heroic society there is a Christian element, shown in the ideal of a more god-fearing, responsible and civilized hero.

Literary, rhetoric and oral composition have in common many techniques designed to aid extempore improvisation and declamation; they both use procedures of amplification and variation upon a typical theme.[12] If Gottfried is anything like he is commonly conceived to be, he, like Messiaen, had heard and even read sermons and saints' lives, and had learned from their techniques.[13] But Gottfried could never have begun to compose unless he had had an oral vernacular poetic tradition of totally different origin from rhymed Latin.[14] It was the Germanic tradition of oral heroic verse composition that supplied him with his repertoire of themes and narrative devices and verbal formulae.[15] *Tristan* is now a written poem, not an oral one. But a written oral poem tends only to make sense when the conventions of the original are understood. *Tristan* shows many signs of oral narrative composition: it has type-scenes which are themselves narrative formulae and its whole structure conforms to the typologies of folk-lore.[16]

The habit of regarding everything in the narrative as if it had already happened and the results were only too well known is typical of traditional poetry. The directness and allusiveness of Gottfried's style are chiefly created by diction.[17] The nouns and adjectives which make up most of the epic formulae are highly poetical—not only imaginative and beautiful but far-fetched and peculiar to poetry. The tradition and stylised quality of the poetic diction is difficult to convey in translation without recourse to archaism.[18] The diction is special and archaic and

---

12 Goldschmidt Kunzer, R., *The Tristan of Gottfried von Strassburg. An Ironic Perspective*, University of California Press, Berkeley, London, 1973. 18-19

13 Ferrante, J.M., *The Conflict of Love and Honour*, Columbia University, Mouton, The Hague, Paris, 1973. 20

14 Goldschmidt Kunzer, R., *The Tristan of Gottfried von Strassburg. An Ironic Perspective*, University of California Press, Berkeley, London, 1973. 10

15 Gottfried von Strassburg, *Tristan*, Penguin Books, London 1967. 11

16 Goldschmidt Kunzer, R., *The Tristan of Gottfried von Strassburg. An Ironic Perspective*, University of California Press, Berkeley, London, 1973. 6

17 Gottfried von Strassburg, *Tristan*, Penguin Books, London 1967. 32

18 Gottfried von Strassburg, *Tristan*, Penguin Books, London 1967. 32

the effect is of an untiring eloquence rather than of a sweetly flowing rhetoric.

Synopsis of the Tristan Myth

The story of Tristram and Yseult, to give them their English names, took place at a time when England and France were politically closer to one another than at present. Tristram was son to Rivalin, the King of Lyonesse, a region West of Cornwall incorporating what are now the Scilly Isles: but his ancestral home was Kareol in Brittany. The old Cornish and Breton languages, like Welsh, are still mutually intelligible, and the regions were then even more closely linked, since the terms Breton and Briton were interchangeable. Tristram's mother, Blanchefleur, was sister to King Marke of Cornwall whose palace was at Castle Dor, inland of Fowey.[19] Tristan, reverting to Wagner's spellings, was so-named because he was born in tristesse, or sadness: his father was killed in battle before his birth, during which his mother died.[20] He was brought up by Rivalin's squire Kurwenal and later taken to King Marke's court. Isolde was the daughter of the King of Ireland.

Ireland was a hostile power which had defeated Cornwall in war and now exacted an annual human tribute. When the Irish emissary, Morold, arrived at Castle Dor to collect his tally of slaves, Tristan slew him in single combat and sent his head back to Dublin in lieu of tribute. But he himself had been mortally wounded by Morold's sword.[21] Assuming the name of Tantris, Tristan sailed to Ireland to seek the miraculous healing skills of Isolde.[22] He was unaware that Isolde was Morold's betrothed, but she recognised him and vowed revenge. As Eisner states, "Tristan acknowledged his own identity and soothed her by explaining that he wooed her not in his own name but in King Mark's".[23] Tristan did not

---

19 Goldschmidt Kunzer, R., *The Tristan of Gottfried von Strassburg, An Ironic Perspective*, University of California Press, Berkeley, London, 1973. 118 and 144
20 Gottfried von Strassburg, *Tristan*, Penguin Books, London, 1967. 64-65
21 Gottfried von Strassburg, *Tristan*, Penguin Books, London, 1967. 133
22 Ferrante, J.M., *The Conflict of Love and Honour*, Columbia University, Mouton, The Hague, Paris, 1973. 35
23 Eisner, S., *The Tristan Legend, A Study in Sources*, North-western University Press, Evanston, Illinois. 1969. 25

want Isolde for himself, but for his uncle King Marke, so that Ireland and Cornwall would then be at peace. Marke sent Tristan back to Ireland, with a suitable retinue, to win Isolde for his bride. Solemn treaties were sworn, and Isolde set off, with her servant Brangaene, to Cornwall on Tristan's boat. Though she could not refuse, she took with her a chest of potions, supplied by her mother and vowed to kill Tristan.

During the voyage her vow is turned upside-down by Brangaene's disobedience in substituting a love-potion for the cup of poison demanded by Isolde. Brangaene is motivated by an awareness of the unspoken love that has grown between Isolde and Tristan. When the ship arrives, Isolde and Marke are married. Isolde takes her place at court, and is installed with Brangaene in apartments of her own. The lovers can only meet after dark, when the King has retired. It was essential that they never consummate their passion, even when Isolde's warning torchlight is extinguished outside her garden-house. Brangaene, realising that her charges are menaced by Melot, Tristan's false Friend, greedy for power at court, enamoured of Isolde and jealous of her love for Tristan, warns Isolde of this danger. Persuaded by Melot to hunt by night, King Marke returns early to Isolde's summer-house and having ignored Brangaene's warning cries, Isolde and Tristan are duly found in a compromising situation. Tristan challenges the traitor Melot to a duel, then lets fall his sword and is gravely wounded.

Kurwenal carries away the dying Tristan to his Kareol home, and tends him as best he can. But he also sends for Isolde, hoping her miraculous powers will save Tristan. Unbeknown to Isolde, she is followed, in another boat, by King Marke, Brangaene having revealed to him the truth behind Tristan and Isolde's love. Tristan in his excitement at her arrival, undoes all Kurwenal's good work, and expires upon her embrace. Kurwenal, out of his mind with grief, slaughters Melot, but is himself mortally wounded and dies. As Marke mourns these deaths, Isolde rises from her swoon to explain how she and Tristan are at last united in a loftier sphere of spiritual existence. For her Tristan is only now truly alive, as she is for him, for now she is to forsake her body for eternal happiness with him in another life.

Messiaen's Treatment of the Tristan Myth

The influence of the *Tristan* myth proved a turning point for Messiaen because as Johnson states, "*Messiaen abandons Christian symbols in these works...*"[24]. He had known about the myth since his youth, and was inspired by it to temporarily move away from the forms of his religious works up to Vingt Regards (1944). Like Wagner in his *Tristan und Isolde*, Messiaen has never set the words of Gottfried's *Tristan* to music, nor has he based a piece on a particular narrative text. Rather, there are aesthetic links with Gottfried's *Tristan* and several significant connections.

Gottfried's vast *Tristan* is so long and complex that any attempt to summarise it is bound to appear trite, but thankfully its influence on Messiaen is easier to quantify. The legendary romance's central and interconnected concepts of time and memory are of fundamental importance to Messiaen, and there are even parallels between one of the important characters Isolde, the heroine, and Piroutcha. Piroutcha has been the object of more critical attention than any of the other characters. The musical model for Messiaen's *Harawi*, especially its recurring cyclic themes, continues to intrigue Messiaen researchers, and Messiaen himself provided contradictory information about the models for Piroutcha's tragic love. Robert Sherlaw Johnson has pointed out the similarities between, "the town which was sleeping—as yet unawakened to a life of love; she is the grassy bank at midnight and the bank on which Tristan and Isolde recline in Act II (Scene 2) of Wagner's *Tristan und Isolde*."[25] The recurrence of this extramusical idea is an intriguing feature of Messiaen's music. The youth possibly views Piroutcha as a compensation for the disappointments of his private life, and this is one of the main factors that leads him to believe that the only authentic and unclouded, therefore the only true form of love, is to be found in death. Love in life, according to the youth, appears unordered and people are not constant, whereas in death love is transfigured and has an eternal value.

Messiaen's interest in the *Tristan* myth could be paralleled with the belief of Proust, Baudelaire and Gide that the human personality is a series of successive states. In *Cinq Rechants*, the lovers are constantly

---

24 Johnson, R.S., *Messiaen*, Dent, London, 1989. 77
25 Johnson, R.S., *Messiaen*, Dent, London, 1989. 79

frustrated because Isolde seems to be several different women. Tristan appears convinced that she lies to him and suspects her of being involved in a plot with Brangäne. This idea is symbolically developed further in *Cinq Rechants* and his inability to pin her down either physically, mentally or sexually fuels his obsessive jealousy and results in her being a virtual prisoner, "my robe of love, my love, my prison of love."[26] In Messiaen's compositions, there are often striking similarities between one piece and the other works which are chronologically closest to it. Thus, *Turangalîla* and *Cinq Rechants* share some features, and the cyclic themes not only look forward to *Cantéyodjayâ* (1949), but also backwards to the songs of *Harawi*.

This reinforces the notion that the idea of memory is equally valid between different pieces as within the same work. This is a manifestation of unintentional memory, and this type of unity is exhibited in the pieces of every important composer.

Turangalîla is perhaps the most Wagnerian of Messiaen's Works, and he tends to mention this piece whenever he discusses the concepts of memory and time and the influence of Wagner on his music. The title is Messiaen's own—he has described the symphony as "a song of love".[27] There are echoes of Wagers *Tristan und Isolde*, especially in the movements entitled "Chants d'amour". Most obviously Wagnerian in the dream-like atmosphere of the "Jardin du sommeil d'amour", which ties in with the multiple plays on time. The world of dreams is one in which chronology has no meaning; even if the events of the past day are often relived in dreams, they recur in a jumbled, often fragmentary form, interspersed with other memories and seemingly unconnected events. As the boundaries between past, present and future are constantly blurred in a dream world over which we have no control, dreams can be considered to be the supreme manifestation of involuntary memory. Proust wrote to Louis de Robert that, "Dreams have always fascinated me because of

---

26 Messiaen, O., *Cinq Rechants*, Salabert, Paris, 1949, 3"! Movement, "ma robe d'amour, mon amour, ma prison d'amour". 15

27 Messiaen, O., *Traité de Rythme de Couleur, et d'Ornithologie*, Book 2, Leduc, Paris, 1995. 15 l. "La *Turangalîla*-Symphonie est un chant d'amour'".

the astonishing game they play with time".²⁸ *Turangalîla* reveals Messiaen's shared fascination for this dream world.

In his *Tristan* trilogy works Messiaen's concept of memory has extended to embrace the allusion to music by Wagner. One example of this can be found in the "love theme" of his "Développement de l'amour" which features a reference to *Tristan und Isolde*. Messiaen possibly included this short allusion because the Wagner piece was also dedicated to "Transfigured love" and the "Love death". Messiaen shares Wagner's obsession with the idea of eternal spiritual love and redemption.²⁹

It is correct to assert that we at all times listen to music in relation to what we have already heard, whether in an individual composition or in a wider historical setting. Therefore, it is legitimate to consider that Messiaen's reference to Wagner's music should be viewed as another manifestation of the centrality of the role of memory in his music. Wagner's concept of the *Tristan* myth possibly stimulated Messiaen because his desire to write large- scale works accentuated his concern for symbolic coherence within a piece, a unity which would be perceptible without being immediately obvious.

It is noteworthy that in the *Tristan* trilogy works Messiaen is using redemption as a metaphor for the restoration of freedom to those who have been deprived of it: freedom is so precious, that its restoration can be likened to life being restored to the dead. Certainly, we feel, the music Messiaen poured into his *Tristan* trilogy works is capable of sustaining such an interpretation of it as this. In his treatment of topics such as death and redemption, sin and atonement in *Harawi*, *Turangalîla* and *Cinq Rechants*, a novel light is cast upon these profoundly theological concepts.

This chapter has looked at the theory of the *Tristan* myth and the sources of the stories and poems examined. We have explored the *Tristan* of Gottfried and concluded that it is a celebration of a heroic life and death. To Messiaen, however, the actual story dramatizes the forms of a particular and important human problem and the influence of the myth proved a turning point for the composer. We have concluded that *Turangalîla* is the most Wagnerian of Messiaen's works and

---

28 Cited in Mein, M., *Proust's Challenge to Time*, Manchester University Press, The University Press, Manchester. 1962. 66 "Les Rêves m'avaient toujours fasciné par le jeu formidable qu'ils font avec le Temps."

29 Samuel, C., *Olivier Messiaen Music and Colour Conversations with Claude Samuel*, trans. E. Thomas Glasgow, Amadeus Press, Portland, Oregon, 1994. 30-31

we have examined the influence of Wagner on his music. Chapter Five will deal with the important issue of Wagner's use of myth which will help us to understand the implications of the *Tristan* myth's musical and literary sources on Messiaen's works.

5

WAGNER'S USE OF MYTH

The purpose of this chapter is to place Wagner's interpretation of the *Tristan* myth in a philosophical and historical context. This will give us a better understanding of the background and its effect on Messiaen's *Tristan* myth works.

Wagner's drama is set in the mythical Celtic world of the early Middle Ages. Many important events have taken place before it starts and are retold at different points in the drama. These events comprising half the knightly poem *Tristan*, by Gottfried von Strassburg, circa. 1210, are Wagner's prime source. When writing his text, Wagner concentrated the story by expanding upon particular episodes and reducing the number of people involved.

Colourful and improbable sentiment overtakes Wagner's libretto with Isolde sparing Tristan from immediate death by the look of abject misery in his eyes, but of course the rest of the story relies heavily on this. If Isolde had killed Tristan at this stage there would be no need for the subsequent drama.

It is quite clear that Wagner has taken Gottfried's text and adapted it to a considerable extent. In the original story Tristan and Isolde were found sleeping together with a sword between them in the shack in Morrois wood. In Wagner's version there is no subsequent trial of ordeal by a scalding iron for Isolde. The resentful and scornful barons are not included and their role is taken by Melot who, in Gottfried's original account, was an evil little dwarf. Wagner may well have been attracted to certain expansions that Gottfried made to the minor characters such as Melot. According to Ferrante, "Gottfried expands the parts of minor characters mainly to keep his major figures free from worldly intrigue." [1]

Kurwenal's role is also amplified by Wagner and a large part of Gottfried's text is simply ignored, such as the two Isolts, the little dog

---

[1] Ferrante, J.M. *The Conflict of Love and Honour*, Mouton, The Hague, Paris, 1973. 60

Petit Crû, Kaherdin, Tristan's exploits in Wales and the episode of the white and black sails.

In Wagner's version the death of Tristan has a significant effect on Kurwenal. He is overwhelmed with grief and viciously attacks and kills Melot. Kurwenal is fatally wounded in the fight and quickly dies. As King Marke grieves over their deaths, Isolde recovers from her loss of consciousness to describe how she and Tristan are now joined together in a higher spiritual sphere. Pure Wagnerian melodrama ensues: Isolde states that Tristan is for the first time really alive, a state reflected in her own ecstasy. She forsakes her body for immortal happiness with him in a different life. In a letter to Mathilde Wesendonck (1864) Wagner talks of Schopenhauer and reincarnation: death, life and transfiguration, Day's illusion and Night's redemption. All the old esoteric ideas with which, in days of trial now past, he had constructed for himself a golden bridge to his own soul in the understanding that he was building one to hers. Wagner states:

> *When all has withdrawn inwards, unsatisfied, the life within grows warmer and brighter. This is the night of Tristan: "Barg im Busen uns sich die Sonne, leuchten lachend Sterne der Wonne!..." A life-course such as mine must always be illusory to the onlooker; he sees me engaged in acts and undertakings he imagines to be my own, whereas at bottom they are utterly alien to me; who perceives the repugnance that often fills my soul? All this will remain uncomprehended until the day comes when the sum is cast and the balance struck.*[2]

Schopenhauer's philosophy that the true aim of life was negation of living, the death-wish, found a welcome response in Wagner's mind: the idea had been behind many of his earlier operas, as even more did the Schopenhauer doctrine that music was the superior art, infinitely superior to any words that might clarify its meaning to uncultivated audiences. *Tristan* is the direct result of Wagner's response: it proclaims love, in more or less unintelligible words, which is given comprehensibility by music, as an ideal unattainable except after death. It further contrasts Night as the world in which lovers thrive and die with Day as the world of worthless bourgeois pseudo-morality. Shakespeare regularly used death as a poetic image of orgasm. As the score directions indicate: "Isolde sinks as if

---

2 Newman, Ernest, *The Life of Richard Wagner 1859-1866*. "En Route to Tannhäuser", Vol. 3, Alfred A. Knopf, New York, 1966. 80

transfigured, in Brangaene's arms, upon Tristan's body. There is great emotion and grief of the bystanders and Marke invokes a benediction of the dead. The curtain falls slowly during the last pause" (Richard Wagner, *Tristan und Isolde*, 1865, p. 1025). Isolde sings with her dying breath: "ertrinken versinken unbewußt höchste Lust!" ("and sinking, be drinking, in a kiss, highest bliss!")[3]

Wagner was clearly attracted to the idea of the *Tristan* myth as the perfect topic and theme. As he states in *Music of the Future*:

(I) felt bound to single out "myth", that original, anonymously created poem of the people which throughout the ages, in one cultural period after another, great poets have treated in ever fresh ways. For here all that smacks of convention and all that pertains to abstract reason is completely missing: all we have is the eternally comprehensible, the purely human, albeit presented in that inimitably individual concrete form which is immediately recognisable in every genuine myth.[4]

He chose the myth for its lack of abstract reason and lack of convention because it allowed him a previously unknown freedom whilst at the same time binding him to the unchanging ideas inherent in folklore.[5]

Nietzsche continued to praise *Tristan* after he had turned his soul against Wagner. As Magee states, "Even after his friendship with Wagner had broken up ... he never ceased to voice a unique sense of indebtedness to him."[6] In a letter to Liszt of 16 December 1854, Wagner wrote about a music-drama of lasting value dedicated to ideal love which was to be a "monument to this most beautiful of all dreams, in which for once this love shall Well and truly gorge itself from beginning to end: I have sketched a *Tristan und Isolde* in my head, the simplest but most

---

3 Wagner, R. *Tristan und Isolde*, Wiesbaden, Breitkopf and Härtel 1865. English translation H. and F. Corder. 1021-1025.

4 Jacobs, R.L., (trans) *Three Wagner Essays*, Eulenburg Books, London, 1979. 24. "That *Music of the Future* is succinct, attractively written and comparatively balanced is largely due to the circumstances of its composition. It was written in 1860. After his long sojourn in Switzerland, where he had written megalomaniacal theoretical treatises, two-thirds of the *Ring* and *Tristan*, Wagner settled in Paris in the autumn of 1859 in order to bring about a production of *Tannhäuser* and create interest in *Tristan*." P. viii

5 Zuckerman, E., *The First Hundred Years of Wagner's Tristan*, Columbia University Press, New York, 1964. 14

6 Magee, B., *Wagner and Philosophy* Harmondsworth, Penguin Books, London, 2000. 81

full-blooded musical conception..."[7] The Work became one of the turning points in musical history; its singular importance is recorded by Nietzsche in *Ecce Homo* (*Behold the Man*), the autobiographical book written at the same time as *The Wagner Case* and *Nietzsche Contra Wagner*. As Zuckerman wryly observes, this was: "the last productive year of Nietzsche's life".[8] As Nietzsche stated:

> *All things considered, I could never have stood my youth without Wagner's music...When one wants to rid oneself of an intolerable pressure, one needs hashish. Well, I needed Wagner...From the very moment when there was a piano score for Tristan—my compliments, Herr von Bülow—I was a Wagnerian. I considered Wagner's previous works beneath me—they were too common too "German". But to this day I am still looking for a work of equally dangerous fascination, of an equally silvery and sweet infinity, as Tristan—and I look in all the arts, in vain...This work is by all means the "non plus ultra" ("there can be nothing beyond") of Wagner; the Meistersinger and the Ring were merely relaxation to him...I regard it as a particular good fortune to have lived at the right time and to have lived precisely among Germans, in order to be ripe for this work. The world is poor for those who have never been sick enough for this "voluptuousness of hell": it is permissible, it is almost imperative, to have recourse to a formulation of the mystics.*[9]

It was quite soon after these comments that Nietzsche started writing the attack on Wagner that developed into his famous anti-Wagnerian essays—the ills of Wagnerism itself were interpreted as the signs of an overall cultural decadence. He thought that to immerse oneself to the exclusion of all else in this timelessness was immoral.

The myth on which *Tristan und Isolde* was based had been well known as far back as the medieval era: Dante alludes to *Tristan* in *The Divine Comedy* ("Inferno Canto V") Shakespeare, in an equally renowned love drama, examines the poetic ideas of tragic youthful infatuation in *Romeo*

---

[7] Barth, Mack and Voss, *Wagner a Documentary Study*, Dent, London, 1875. 185

[8] Zuckerman, E., *The First Hundred Years of Wagner's Tristan*, Columbia University Press, New York, 1964. 63

[9] Nietzsche, F. Ecce Homo ii, 6 (Werke, ed. Karl Schlechta (Munich Mauser 1956) 11, 1091-92). Most of the translation is from Kaufmann, Nietzsche, 38, in Zuckerman, E., *The First Hundred Years of Wagner's Tristan*, Columbia University Press, New York, 1964. 63, 201

and Juliet. In contrast, Wagner investigates the conscious and unconscious elements of fully developed adult love. Through the exclusion of all minor episodes in the myth, he fixes his attention on the souls of the lovers, throwing light, like Messiaen, on metaphysical as well as sexual ideas of love. In Messiaen's *Tristan* trilogy the works wear that unmistakable but delicate mist of eroticism which suffuses so much of Wagner's *Tristan und Isolde*.

Nietzsche, however, detects a defect in Wagner's rhythm and melody: he expresses these defects firstly in general terms as "German" and compares them with the rhythmic and melodic inventiveness of French music.[10] His second accusation is that Wagner was principally an actor who relied on the elaborate use of language for his message. Nietzsche's third contention comprises several different objections to Wagner's indulgence in sensual pleasure.

As a young man, Wagner became infatuated with an attractive actress, Minna Planner, who already had a daughter from one of her earlier relationships. Their subsequent marriage was based on weak foundations; within two or three months she had left him for another man, but then came back to Wagner. For most of their married life Minna appealed to Wagner physically—he perhaps considered her the Venus to his Tannhäuser. She rarely had faith in his more difficult creative undertakings, often rebuking him for wasting time in writing unperformable operas. She complained that other less talented composers who lacked Wagner's remarkable conducting ability led, apparently, more successful careers. The writer Malvida von Meysenburg commented on Wagner's marriage with Minna (Paris, 1860) that, "She tried to mediate by demanding concessions towards the world from the genius, which the latter could not and must not make".[11]

The flowering of the musical characteristics of the love drama of *Tristan und Isolde* was a crucial part of Wagner's swift stylistic development. The opera also underwent a stimulus from a passionate affair with Mathilde Wesendonck. Wagner became acquainted with her and her husband Otto in Zurich, Switzerland in 1852. She became his dedicated follower and firm friend. Intensely delighted by his Tannhäuser music, Mathilde was starting to fall in love with him and Wagner quickly

---

10 Zuckerman, E., *The First Hundred Years of Wagner's Tristan*, Columbia University Press, New York,1964. 75

11 Barth, Mack and Voss, *Wagner a Documentary Study*, Dent, London, 1975. 188

found himself deeply involved. He was captivated by the beautiful Mathilde and an intimate friendship grew up between them; this mutual sympathy, suspected by Minna Wagner as well as Otto Wesendonck, has often been cited as the motivating force for the poem and musical composition of *Tristan und Isolde*. Although no such direct cause and effect can be established, a clear connection does exist.[12] Biographers of Mathilde Wesendonck like to suggest that she was the main source of inspiration of *Tristan*. That *Tristan* inspired the Wesendonck affair is closer to the truth, in the sense that Wagner allowed notions related to the opera to affect his behaviour.[13] The Wesendonck house quickly attracted numerous intellectuals and artists with Wagner as its prevailing star. Surrounded by this artistic elite, Minna felt inferior and excluded. Mathilde, however, believed absolutely in Wagner's genius and supplied a sympathetic vitality that was his genuine refuge. As Zuckerman ironically observes:

> *In this way the "bourgeois drama" enacted by the Wagners and the Wesendoncks is converted into an idyll about a romantic genius and his Platonic love. The amount of falsifying this requires is evident when one considers the banal and sordid details that must be glossed over in order to make the affair resemble the myth: Wagner's sponging on Otto Wesendonck, the compromising letters and unheroic indiscretions. And throughout the story sounds the basso ostinato of Wagner's egotism.*[14]

Wagner's letters to Mathilde are striking for their examination of philosophy as it related to his composition of *Tristan*. In Act Two, the love scene involving Tristan and Isolde turns into a philosophical argument—a quest for a metaphysical answer, as opposed to physical gratification. In a letter to Mathilde Wesendonck, Paris 29 October 1859, Wagner wrote:

---

12 For an interesting account of this matter see Barth, Mack and Voss, *Wagner a Documentary Study*, Dent, London, 1975. 186-187. Wagner's "Morning Confession" to Mathilde Wesendonck. 7 April 1858; Millington, 13., (ed.) The Wagner Compendium, Schirmer Books, New York, 1992. 33

13 Zuckerman, E., *The First Hundred Years of Wagner's Tristan*, Columbia University Press, New York,1964. 35-36

14 Zuckerman, E., *The First Hundred Years of Wagner's Tristan*, Columbia University Press, New York,1964. 38

> *My greatest masterpiece of the art of the most subtle, most gradual transition is certainly the big scene of the second act of Tristan und Isolde. This scene begins with pulsating life at its most passionate—and ends with the most mystical, innermost longing for death...*[15]

When Wagner had finished the last preparations for Act One and the initial stage for Act Two, his infatuation with Mathilde had ended. She was not prepared to leave her husband and her children and Wagner was not prepared to abandon his sick wife.

In 1854 Wagner described to Liszt his new regard for the philosophy of Arthur Schopenhauer:

> *His central thought, the final denial of the will to live, is of frightful seriousness, but the only salvation. Of course this idea was not new to me and no one can think it at all in whom it did not already exist. But it was this philosopher who first showed it to me with such clarity. If I think back to the storms of my heart and the terrible cramp with which it clutched—against my will—at the hope of living, indeed when these storms even now still rise in tempestuous strength—now at last I have found a palliative, which alone helps me to sleep in sleepless nights; it is the deep and innermost yearning for death: total unconsciousness, absolute non-being, the extinction of all dreams—unique and final salvation.*[16]

Wagner continues to discuss, in this context, the score of *Der fliegende Holländer*, despite the fact that, as in his other compositions relating to redemption, there is no actual "total non-existence" but a new type of continuity after death.

Schopenhauer's philosophy is interwoven with Indian teachings on the ultimate nature of existence derived mainly from the Upanishads and from Buddhism. The cause of mankind's suffering is born as a consequence of never ceasing "Desire", represented in *Tristan* by the second theme which is persistently developed, from the first to last bars.

Schopenhauer's main contribution to philosophy is contained in the emphasis that he placed upon the human Will. According to

---

15 Barth, Mack and Voss, *Wagner a Documentary Study* Dent, London, 1975. 189

16 Barth, Mack and Voss, *Wagner a Documentary Study*, Dent, London, 1975. 185. From a letter by Wagner to Liszt, December 1854, about Arthur Schopenhauer, whose philosophy he had discovered that autumn. *Briefwechsel zwischen Wagner und Liszt*, Leipzig 1910, Vol. 2, pp. 42—3

Schopenhauer the Will was the means by which all other things were understood.[17]

> *He is one of the first in a long line of philosophers who, in an age of Hegelianism, adopted the slogan "Back to Kant!" as a protest against prevailing tendencies.*[18]

He proposed that the "Ding an Sich" ("the thing in itself"), which Kant postulated as the ultimate reality, was a universal cosmic Will. The world is the expression of blind striving or Will. We know our own inner nature as Will in direct experience; thought is but one of the outward forms or disguises taken by Will. Life is blind, cruel, meaningless, but we disguise this fact in our theorizing; and in our actions we cling to life through extremes of pain and suffering. As Schopenhauer states, "Life presents itself as a problem, a task to be worked out, and therefore, as a rule, as a constant conflict with necessity."[19] The natural world bears witness to the continuous reproduction of the species and the continuous destruction of the individual. The forms remain the same; the individuals who exemplify them continually perish. In this we get a hint of Schopenhauer's relation to Plato and Kant.

This was in contrast to rationalism which was a philosophical movement derived from seventeenth-century attempts to study the universe using reason, in the form of deductive and mathematical methods, rather than sense-experience. Descartes tried to deduce what God's world was like from the axioms of divine existence and goodness. The scientific interests of the early rationalists made use of their religious views but conflict between the new sciences and religion emerged and is shown in the writings of Spinoza, Arnauld and Leibniz. By the nineteenth century a compromise developed allocating science and religion to their

---

17 Schopenhauer, A. *The World as Will and Idea*, 1818, sets out his principal ideas and conclusions.

18 Aiken, H.D., *The Age of Ideology*, The New American Library of World Literature, New York, 1962. 100

19 Schopenhauer, A., The World as Will and Idea, Vol. III (trans. Haldane, R.B. and Kemp, J) Routledge and Kegan Paul Ltd, London, 1948. 377

individual spheres. lntuitionism comprises any doctrine in which what appears to be self—evident is regarded as the basis of knowledge.[20]

ln the nineteenth century Schopenhauer was distrustful of rationalism and the scientific method and was instead concerned with intuitive cognition; he saw the ideal state of man as one of contemplative freedom, achieved through art.[21] He was a lifelong misanthropist, a man well aware of his exceptional intelligence and extremely susceptible to music and literature.[22]

Schopenhauer's study of the East included Buddhism, a nontheistic religion and philosophical system founded in North East India in the sixth century BC. by Guatama Siddhartha, the Buddha (c.563-0486), an Indian prince Whose teachings formed the basis of Buddhism. He was the son of Suddhodama and his queen, Maya. Gautama was reputed to have been a child of exceptional intelligence and beauty about whom many stories and legends have been told. At the age of 16 he married his cousin, princess Yasodhara, who 13 years later bore him a son called Radhula. Soon alter this event Gautama, renouncing his life of indolence and luxury, abandoned his family and set out to seek solutions to the problems of the transience and suffering of human existence. After six years of emaciating asceticism he reluctantly concluded that austerity was unlikely to provide the solution he sought. Abandoned by his five companions because of his rejection of mortification, he determined to seek enlightenment alone, within himself. According to legend, this he achieved while seated under a banyan tree, in what is now called Buddh Gaya, in Bihar. His title, Buddha, is Sanskrit for the "Awakened One". He devoted the rest of his life to teaching the principles or "dharma" of his enlightenment, first moving to Benares Where he Founded the Buddhist order of monks and afterwards teaching in various places in Northern India, "Dharma" is a Sanskrit term with various religious and philosophical meanings. In Buddhism it signifies truth, the teachings of the Buddha in whole or in part. It also denotes the law regarding the

---

20 Aiken, H.D. *The Age of Ideology*, The New American Library of World Literature, New York, 1962. 34

21 Schopenhauer, A., *The World as Will and Idea*, Vol. III, (trans. Haldane, RB. and Kemp, I.) Routledge
and Kegan Paul Ltd., London, 1948. I76

22 Zuckerman, E., [he First Hundred Years of Wagner's *Tristan*, Columbia University press, New York,1964. 4

ultimate nature of things. In Hinduism, it refers to social law or caste duty. Gautama died at Kusinagara in Uttar Pradesh c.486 BC.[23]

The followers of the Buddha seek to emulate his example of perfect morality, wisdom and compassion culminating in a transformation of consciousness known as enlightenment. Buddhism teaches that greed, hatred and delusion separate the individual from the true perception of the nature of things, causing him to remain tied to the "bhavachakra" or "wheel of becoming". This is an important element in Wagner's Rem particularly in relation to Kundry. In Buddhism, an image of the cyclical nature of earthy existence is in the form of a Wheel held by the demon Impermanence. Its segments represent the six possible states into which beings are reborn: the realms of gods, titans, hungry ghosts, humans, animals and demons. At the centre, turning the wheel are greed, hatred and delusion. These are depicted as a cockerel, snake and pig biting each others' tails. Around the rim, the twelve stages in the cycle of life are symbolically expressed. The apparent substantiality of all objects, including the self, is illusion; everything mundane is impermanent and ultimately unsatisfying.[24]

The central beliefs of Buddhism are based on the Buddha's "Four Noble Truths", the last of which is the "Eightfold Path" by which enlightenment may be attained and the individual self annihilated in nirvana. The "Four Noble Truths" are the fundamental doctrine of Buddhism, set out by Gautama in his first discourse at Benares. The Truths are: "existence is characterised by suffering"; "the cause of suffering is craving"; "to end craving is to end suffering"; "the way to achieve this is the Eightfold Path". This consists of the eight ways that lead the Buddhist to enlightenment. They are: right understanding; right resolve; right speech; right action; right livelihood; right effort; right mindfulness; and right meditation. The Path is not a series of successive steps but an integrated number of spiritual attitudes.[25]

Nirvana is the supreme goal of Buddhism, in which liberation from the limitations of existence and rebirth are attained through the extinction of desire. Whereas the "Theravada" (old conservative school of Buddhism) sees nirvana as the negation of the mundane, the "Mahayana"

---

23 Tastard, T., *World Religions*, Pitkin U11lCll1'0fl18, Hampshire. 2002. 24

24 Happold, F.C., *Mysticism and an Anthology*, Penguin Books, Middlesex, 1963. 78

25 Happold, F.C., *Mysticism and an Anthology*, Penguin Books, Middlesex, 1963. 78-79

or "Great Vehicle" (school of Buddhism dominant in Tibet, Mongolia, China, Korea and Japan) regards it as man's essential Buddha-nature. In Hinduism nirvana also means spiritual release in the sense of freedom from reincarnation or union with God or the Absolute. Wagner, who was reading the *Ramayana* as well as Schopenhauer, thought of Day and Night in Act Two of *Tristan* as essentially an oriental antithesis, For years he contemplated a Buddhist opera called *The Victors*, but he did not see *Tristan* in this way at all.[26] He wanted audiences to surrender to his music in order to detach themselves from life. Some of these ideas are, however, portrayed in *Tristan* when the lovers' immortal spirits try to discover release from the ceaseless cycle of reincarnation. What is enacted in one life, whether praiseworthy or damaging, is considered a consequence of the Will. Mystical higher hopes or plans, a tranquil renouncing of Desire and a willing symbolic death to insatiable longing and to the life of the senses were the basic components of Schopenhauer's philosophical' ideas. He thought that through a negation of the Will, mystics and creative artists, particularly musicians, could become aware of and express the most profound truths about the fundamental nature of being and becoming. The Will proceeded from desire to temporary satisfaction and thence to renewed desire; and the only escape from the vicious circle was a kind of Buddhist renunciation of desire.[27]

Schopenhauer maintained that experience testifies to the way in which the world is pervaded by pain and destruction, while religion and philosophy try to construct justifications for the universe which will show that pain and destruction have not the last word and in so doing they themselves testify to the force of the Cosmic Will, which has as its aim the continuing of existence on any terms. Schopenhauer explains religion as the human expression of this desire for continued existence. Were we totally certain of our survival after death, or of our extinction at death, religion would be functionless. Moreover, it is not only in our anxiety to continue existing that we exhibit ourselves as manifestations of Will. We also do so in the way that we devote ourselves to continuing the species; sexual passion overrides all our impulses to avoid suffering and responsibility. Yet the pleasures of passionate love are momentary and vanishing

---

26 Newman, Ernest, *The Life of Richard Wagner*, Vol.2, New York, Alfred A Knopf, 1966. 486-488.

27 Schopenhauer, A., *The World as Will and Idea*, Vol. III (trans, Haldane, R.B. and Kemp, J.) Routledgeand Kegan Paul Ltd, London, 1948. 300803

compared with the troubles it brings upon us. We may rationalise our pursuit of various ends and claim to find good in achieving them; the truth is we are what we are constituted by the blind strivings of Will and our thinking cannot alter anything about us.

So seriously does Schopenhauer take this that he treats the entire personality as given from the outset. What we are essentially is Will, unalterable Will. No experience, no reflection, no learning, can alter what we are. One's character is fixed, one's motives are determined. It follows that traditional morality and traditional moral philosophy are founded on a mistake, the mistake of supposing that moral precepts can alter conduct, whether our own or that of others. What, then, can moral philosophy do? It can explain the moral valuations which we do in fact make by an analysis of human nature. If we carry through such an analysis we discover three basic motives in human nature. The first is self-interest On this Schopenhauer has little to say. The second, however, is the fruit of acute observation. It is malice. Schopenhauer observed, as perhaps no previous philosopher or psychologist had done, the gratuitous character of malice. We do not harm others only when and in order that we may benefit ourselves. And when others undergo misfortunes our pleasure in their misfortunes is unconnected with any thought of our own self-interest. It is pure pleasure. For man is the only animal which causes pain to others without any further purpose than just to cause it. Other animals never do it except to satisfy their hunger, or in the rage of combat.[28] The appalling record of human life, of the suffering and infliction of pain, is relieved only when the third motive, sympathy or compassion appears. To feel compassion is to put oneself imaginatively in the place of the sufferer and to alter one's actions appropriately either by desisting from what would have caused pain or by devoting oneself to its relief. But the exhibiting of compassion has yet a further significance. In a moment of compassion we extinguish self-will. We cease to strive for our own existence, we are relieved from the burden of individuality and we cease to be the playing of Will. The same relief is granted to us in the contemplation of works of art and in the Life of a Christ or a Buddha we find a systematic disciplining of self and exercising of compassion in which Self-hood and striving approach the goal of final extinction.

---

28 Schopenhauer, A., *The World as Will and Idea*, Vol. III (trans., Haldane, R.B. and Kemp, J.) Routledge and Kegan Paul Ltd., London, 1948. 315-317

Thus Schopenhauer's message is in the end an injunction to return to the sources of Buddhist teaching.

Wagner adopted and changed what he thought he could use from these ideas, which are sharply displayed in the symbolic notions of his *Tristan* poem. There is the conception of opposites: "Day" and "Night", "Love" and "Hate", "Life" and "Death". For Tristan and Isolde, from the beginning of Act Two, "Day" represents the outer world of ostentatious vanity, avarice, desire and illusion. Each act of *Tristan und Isolde* has a distinct musical atmosphere. Death hangs over the first act; the second act takes place amidst the scents of a glorious summer night; the bleak sea and burning sun of the third act lead into Tristan's inner suffering. In each there is an elemental climax: the drinking of atonement, the extinguishing of a flaming torch, the final embrace; and the third climax contains the music of both the others. This sequence suggests that the actions of the characters are predestined.

At this point Wagner contemplated introducing *Parsifal*, the traveller in search of the Holy Grail, into the Third Act of *Tristan*, so that the self-repudiating mystical knight might encounter the self-anguished lovesick knight. As Millington states of *Parsifal*: "In addition to these Christian and pagan sources, Wagner was strongly influenced both by Buddhism and by the philosopher Schopenhauer many of whose ideas are closely related to oriental thought."[29] Although the "renouncing one" Was, on second thought, saved for a drama of his own, not written until twenty years later, the twin conception of *Tristan* and *Parsifal* is evident in the musical affinity between the works. Wagner saw fit to equip his final music drama with Dresden Amens and pseudomedieval chantings. That sort of religiosity is absent in *Tristan*. Indeed two thirds of *Parsifal* invokes the extreme chromaticism of *Tristan*, freely indulged in again after the predominantly diatonic *Meistersinger* and the completion of *The Ring*.[30] In Wagner's *Parsifal* there is a distinctive mixture of Buddhist and Christian symbolism, for which the initial written outline was undertaken in 1857.[31]

Schopenhauer's morality was a strict one: human emotions and cravings are essentially evil; and suffering, the inevitable fact of life,

---

29 Millington, B. *The Wagner Compendium*, Dent, London, 1992. 307

30 Zuckerman, E. *The First Hundred Years of Wagner's Tristan*, Columbia University Press, New York,1964. 25

31 Millington, B. *The Wagner Compendium*, Dent, London, 1992. 15

is prolonged indefinitely by the act of procreation which is in itself, according to Schopenhauer, an act infected by wickedness and sinfulness. Wagner accepted only part of Schopenhauer's philosophy; he thought his own ideas were an important addition. Wagner intended to enlighten Schopenhauer of his thoughts in a letter he neither finished nor despatched.

With the idea of redemption, the inherent notions involved in *Lohengrin*, *Tannhäuser* and *Der fliegende Holländer* can be linked, if salvation is seen as a means of transformation through self-development and self-revelation. In addition, Schopenhauer's conviction in the inherent uselessness and nothingness of the human's state of being and his support of the repudiation of the "will to live", as the single freeing agent from the remorseless continuation of enduring grief, is contained in *Tristan und Isolde*. The redemption looked for by the eternal lovers is found in the losing of their own individual identities. This is the significance of their longing for the unconsciousness of death and it is also the basis of the music-drama's metaphors: "day" is avoided because it depicts the external material World perceived by the senses; "night" is gladly greeted because it is the sphere of inner consciousness, the utmost reality. There is arguably therefore no real inconsistency in the basic ideas of *Tristan* and Wagner's understanding of Schopenhauer. However, Zuckerman scornfully takes a different view, especially in relation to Wagner's letter to Liszt of 16 December 1854 espousing Arthur Schopenhauer whose philosophy he had discovered that autumn:

> *Wagner's private meditations on Schopenhauer seem like studies for the text of Tristan without the rhyme; and it is fitting that the letter which includes this prose-poem about Nirvana also contains Wagner's first reference to his plans to write his musical memorial to death in love. Despite his protestations, in no sense of the word has Wagner's "will" to be denied. Bernard Shaw notes how in consecutive letters to the same correspondent, Wagner could preach the renunciation of the will to live and, with equal enthusiasm, describe his undertaking of a most beneficial course of hydrotherapy.*[32]

Zuckerman omits to mention that, from the point at which Wagner first discovered Schopenhauer's philosophy until the time of his

---

[32] Zuckerman, E., *The First Hundred Years of Wagner's Tristan*, Columbia University Press, New York,1964. 4

death, Wagner's opinion was one of wholehearted indebtedness to the philosopher.

There has seldom been so fertile a connection between one great thinker and another when the two were in dissimilar areas of activity. When one considers Plato and Aristotle, Goethe and Schiller or even Marx and Engels, we are contemplating in each example one human being of exceptionally high intellectual ability who was helped to develop to the ultimate height of his powers by another in the same sphere. This was not dissimilar to the connection that Schopenhauer had with Kant. Schopenhauer was not a creative musician; but if *Tristan und Isolde* comprises some of the very finest art ever to have come from inside the human mind, it is to some extent because its creator was directly sustained in its writing by a complementary person of exceptional intellectual ability in a different sphere of activity whose task, as Thomas Mann stated, "freed his music from bondage and gave it courage to be itself." [33]

The link between "the will to die" being the only ultimate satisfaction and Wagner's ideas about "love and death" are a contentious augmentation of Schopenhauer's philosophy. It is apparent to Wagner that in death the human-being has progressed beyond carnal love and has gone beyond material desire—the only desire therefore, is the ultimate union with God. Wagner sees procreation as an important part of the process of reincarnation and being ultimately at one with God. This fundamental idea is apparent through Wagner's interpretation of the *Tristan* myth, particularly in the music of the Love-death or Liebestod.

This chapter has placed Wagner's interpretation of the *Tristan* myth in a philosophical and historical context. This gives us a better understanding of the background to Messiaen's compositions in relation to the overall aim of the book. We have seen that Wagner concentrated the story by expanding episodes and reducing the number of characters involved. In a similar way we have observed that Messiaen through the exclusion of minor incidents in the myth threw new light on metaphysical as well as sexual ideas of love. In Chapters Six to Eight we explore Messiaen's *Tristan* trilogy works in the light of this chapter and develop these ideas further.

---

33 Mann, T. *Essays of Three Decades*, (trans. H.T. Lowe-Porter) Secker and Warburg, London, 1942. 330

6

MESSIAEN'S TRISTAN TRILOGY
PART 1: *HARAWI*

Having explored Wagner's use of myth in Chapter Five, Chapter Six will now look at how Messiaen learnt from and adapted Wagner's interpretation of the *Tristan* myth. It will also show how Messiaen applied his own technique and philosophy, drawing on and incorporating his own texts, poems and ideas derived from Debussy's *Pelléas et Mélisande*.

Dramatically and emotionally, *Harawi* is not a problem song-cycle. It has none of *Cinq Rechants* false climaxes, uncertainties of mood or moral ambiguities. Opening, like *Cinq Rechants*, with a running scena in which the heroine is trying to escape, it proceeds through satisfactorily designed stages, creating (out of a number of contemporary elements) its own genre round it as it goes, to a triumphant final song, which is the climax of both the drama and the love-story and at the same time a solemn manifesto of moral and social principles.

Neither is there the smallest doubt what the manifesto asserts. According to Hall, the secret cult of the Love-death, into which the heroine is initiated, is blatantly intended as a symbol of the secret love of *Tristan and Isolde*, in which Messiaen and Richard Wagner had both been interested.

The sense in which *Harawi* really is a problem song-cycle is twofold. First there is a technical difficulty about the poems. Internal evidence shows that the song-cycle is the beginning of an original Eastern version of the story very different from the final result; in other words, the myth was radically changed and the new ending was attached to the old tale. The second difficulty is not so much a difficulty as a blindness. The entire character of the *Tristan* myth has been misconceived. *Harawi* has simply been placed in the wrong genre mistaken for a "fairy-tale". The misconception has two sources: failure to make an informed conjecture, based on a knowledge of Wagnerian operatic thought, about what the medieval *Tristan* myth was like; and failure actually to read the *Tristan* myth, which has long been known as one of Wagner's sources. When these two new clues are explored, not only does *Harawi* turn out to be something far removed from a "fairy-tale", but its poems yield up a precise metaphorical meaning.

In *Harawi* the lovers launch into an intense duet, a true love-death, a liebestod; although we only ever hear Piroutcha and the piano. As Rostand states, "The green dove is a sacred Mayan animal and called the beloved in that folklore."[1] Human love and affection are commemorated in this song-cycle eliciting the fatal loves of the youthful Peruvian girl, Piroutcha. Peru is here in the melodic ideas, in expressions from the Quetchua language, in the imitation of natural sounds and in fact in an entire system of traditional stories of representations and colours. The word "*harawi*" signifies in the Quetchua language, which was spoken by the inhabitants of Peru before the conquistadors arrived and still is to this day, a poem of passion and death. It is of the same kind that we discover in our own literary tradition, from *Romeo and Juliet* to *Tristan und Isolde*. The music and text of Messiaen changes the desire of the lovers, lifting it to the magnitude of the World and the universe. Messiaen states "that it is an irresistible love and powerful passion which results in the death of the two lovers: it is reminiscent of *Tristan* and Isolde, Isolde's name is Piroutcha".[2]

Harawi was written in 1945. It is divided into twelve songs. It has two love themes, which are very melodious, that one often hears in the course of the song-cycle. "One finds rhythmic canons—some of which are retrogradable—the rhythmic canon adds up to a quarter of the length."[3] As Messiaen states, the work is tonal, modal, polymodal and atonal. The principal mode is mode 2^1. Messiaen's second mode is the octatonic scale.

Messiaen's poem is written in a very unusual and concentrated style, compared with his previous works. There are many places where a

---

[1] Rostand, C., *Olivier Messiaen*, Ventadour, 1957, Chapter 6. 35-36 "la colombe verte est animal sacré maya et désignait la bien-aimée dans ce folklore."

[2] Messiaen, O. *Traité de Rythme, de Couleur, et d'Ornithologie* (1949-1992) Book 3, Leduc, Paris, 1996, 279. "Il s'agit d'un amour irrésistible et profondément passionné, qui va jusqu'à la mort des deux amants: comme dans l'histoire de *Tristan* et Yseult. Ici, l'Yseult s'appelle "Piroutcha" - (Piruča)."

[3] Messiaen, O. *Traité de Rythme, de Couleur, et d'Ornithologie* (1949-1992) Book 3, Leduc, Paris, 1996. 279

normal poet would prefer to amplify phrases to give precise definition to the emotions, but which in the songs are left very much to the expressive power of the piano.

Piroutcha often projects her words in sustained tones creating long melodic lines, with few notes against the many in the piano. There are unusual psychological and philosophical qualities in the poem, of unending fascination for discussion. Piroutcha's attitude to death is a case in point. Piroutcha has often courted death, which holds no fear for her.

In "La ville qui dormait, toi", the first song, which is in the key of G major, the only criterion is the effectiveness of the young Peruvian girl's capture by the youth.[4] Whether Piroutcha succumbs, only she can know. When Piroutcha admits she has succumbed, she afterwards inclines to think there is, after all, more merit in chastity. In a state of wretchedness, Piroutcha guesses that the youth offers her fulfilment, which she would gladly accept. She greets him in "Bonjour toi, colombe verte" to show her desire. There is a parallel here with Act One of Wagner's *Tristan und Isolde* when Tristan, in a state of wretchedness, guesses that Isolde offers him poison as atonement, and he gladly accepts it. Isolde has to snatch the cup from Tristan to ensure her desired share.

In all probability it is lust which lies at the root of Piroutcha's desire. Even this is not wholly wrong-headed. It is a muddled apprehension of her feelings toward the youth. Messiaen shows that *Harawi* depends not on patiently and intellectually thinking up ideas but on the ideas coming up of their own accord. We ought not to confuse the irrational, unconscious origin and impulse of *Harawi* with its conscious working out. The greater, the most emotionally effective, composition is that which achieves the most rigorously—indeed, ruthlessly—logical and intelligent working out of a germ which the conscious intellect and will can neither create nor justify.

In the third song, "Montagnes", which contains canons and retrograde rhythmic canons, Piroutcha describes how she has already experienced death, experiencing "black on black", but she has returned

---

4 Messiaen, O. *Traité de Rythme, de Couleur, et d'Ornithologie* (1949-1992) Book 3, Leduc, Paris, 1996. 282

to the Day-light world for the youth.⁵ This is reminiscent of Act 3 of Wagner's opera, when *Tristan* describes how he has already experienced death, "hearing its door crash behind him", but he has returned to the Daylight world for Isolde.

A similar overlapping can be found in the comparison between Messiaen and Debussy, in "Montagnes". Both composers are dramatists, but only Debussyian tragedy mixes romantic with tragic and artificial convention with piercingly real psychology, which are the constituents of the atmosphere of *Pelléas et Mélisande*. Debussyian tragedy at the pitch of *Pelléas* Messiaen never attempted. Like *Pelléas*, "Montagnes" is one of the world's imperfect masterpieces; again like *Pelléas*, it is, thanks to the nature of its symbolic material, an eternal enigma.

In "Doundou tchil", Messiaen reduced the material of the myth, so that he could concentrate on the two main characters. With a continuity unique in song writing, he fully explored their emotional situation, and the song progresses towards a major musical and dramatical climax. This song is in E major and employs mode 2^1 particularly in the central section. Apart from the lovers, no other characters appear in relation to the situation, but Messiaen's characterisation for both Piroutcha and the youth is equally brilliant.⁶ There are distinctive musical styles for the devoted youth and the sad introspective Piroutcha. The contrasts between the dramatic elements are always vivid.

Although "Doundou tchil" sets itself such a resolutely earthly paradise, its principal event takes place in the heavens, but not in heaven. The return of the youth and Piroutcha, now welded into one life, from the darkness of "Montagnes" is crowned by yet a further climax and a yet more powerful application of the theme of coming to light. Piroutcha admits she and the youth are defeated and have come under the spell of "the dance of the stars"; whereupon the youth expands this metaphor by proclaiming, "Piroutcha, there you are, oh my all my own".⁷ This manifestation of the stars is in every sense the final climax of the song;

---

5 Messiaen, O. *Traité de Rythme, de Couleur, et d'Ornithologie* (1949-1992) Book 3, Leduc, Paris, 1996. 285-286; Messiaen, O., *Harawi*, Movement 3, Leduc, Paris, 1945. 18. "Noir sur noir".

6 Messiaen, O. *Traité de Rythme, de Couleur, et d'Ornithologie* (1949-1992) Book 3, Leduc, Paris, 1996. 288-289

7 Messiaen, O., *Harawi*, Leduc, Paris, 1945. 22 and 25. "la danse des étoiles" and "te voilà, ô mon à-moi ".

for by a metaphor of shining simplicity it is the revelation of the mysteries which the youth has laboured through the darkness to attain.

If we are talking about universal, presumably we do not mean some least common denominator of universal appeal, but the capacity to create universes seemingly as wide and as deep as the real universe. Messiaen creates no universes. His magnificent and moving "Doundou tchil" is a failure, though an immortal failure, for the very reason that it does not realise a single character, let alone circumscribe a universe in which they all live and are inter-related. Each of Messiaen's songs is its own cosmos, as vivid and self- sufficient as the cosmoi created by Debussy's major compositions. This is music setting up as extra life, as the biological activity of the human imagination. The shape, proportions and progression of "Doundou tchil" constitute the shape of a certain experience; a narrative which, in the objective world, has never taken place.

Nevertheless, if "L'amour de Piroutcha", which is in G major, is any guide to its ritual, the two lovers chose to include the mystery visit to the life after death in their own initiation ceremony.[8] Why and in what sense they did so is answered, perhaps, by Messiaen. His "Cut off my head doundou tchil" rationalises utterly the whole *Tristan* myth.[9] That, however, was a myth none of Messiaen's contemporaries was in danger of exploring. Since it had long before been driven out by a more potent and detailed work, that of *Pelléas et Mélisande*, which had set aside the underground region exclusively for the wicked dead, who were no longer allowed to dwell even next door to the good, and which had elaborated the punishments inflicted on the bad souls with all the dwelling exactitude of a sadistic fantasy.

With "L'amour de Piroutcha" Messiaen must, if he is to obtain his licence to print, deal circumspectly; and indeed he is careful to choose an exotic setting which almost avoids a direct clash with *Pelléas*. But he need not scruple to attack the superstitious fringe beliefs which were in fact older than Christianity and had no central doctrinal sanction in Roman Catholic theology; these he does attack, and perhaps other beliefs under cover of them, in a song which precedes Piroutcha's initiation but is closely connected to it.

---

8 Messiaen, O. *Traité de Rythme, de Couleur, et d'Ornithologie* (1949-1992) Book 3, Leduc, Paris, 1996 290-291

9 Messiaen, O., *Harawi*, Fifth Movement, Leduc, Paris, 1945. 30 "Coupez moi la tête, doundou tchil".

Piroutcha's almost hysterical cry begins the song "Répétition planétaire" which culminates in the approach of death; the song is atonal, with a tonic of A.[10] Piroutcha's singing is more abandoned still and reaches a momentous climax at the "Planet eats as it turns", which she identifies with the light of day itself.[11] The striding bass phrase represents death's approach. The lovers' terror is represented by the fff markings in the score, an indication of the extreme care with which Messiaen wrote the dynamics.[12] Climaxes are conceived over a relatively short span; although death's arrival is the loudest climax, the extinguishing of life has a musical significance which will resonate more significantly in the later movements.

In Messiaen's "Repetition planétaire", the song has aped not the appearance reality has to the composer's eyes but the self-sufficiency of reality. If the spiritual reality is transcendent, then it is transcendent in Messiaen, too; if it is not, then it is not. Messiaen's supreme excellence lies in the fact that, although he does not fall short of reality, in which case we could not ask the question about his cosmos, he does not tell us the answer, any more than reality does. With Messiaen, we have to agree that the spiritual is transcendent in the world of reality outside music before we can, on those grounds, agree to his claim to supremacy.

In "Adieu" there is a phrase in E-flat major on the principal theme of *Harawi* (resembling "Bonjour toi, colombe verte", "L'escalier redit, gestes du soleil" and "Dans le noir"), the song is in E-flat major and uses mode 2^1.[13]

Messiaen's "Adieu" naturally makes its heroine's green dove a virtuous creature, and when he comes to its posthumous trial Messiaen takes the opportunity to have a eulogy pronounced in which he can detail his conception of a just symbol of love, Good green dove was lenient; it told the truth but did not give away secrets. However, the gist of "Syllabes" is not as plain as it could be but the song represents the secrecy of Piroutcha.

---

10 Messiaen, O. *Traité de Rythme, de Couleur, et d'Ornithologie* (1949-1992) Book 3, Leduc, Paris, 1996 292-294

11 Messiaen, O., *Harawi*, Sixth Movement, Leduc, Paris, 1945. 46. "Planète mange en tournant".

12 Messiaen, O., *Harawi*, Sixth Movement, Leduc, Paris, 1945. fff markings pages 34, 36, 37 and 47

13 Messiaen, O. *Traité de Rythme, de Couleur, et d'Ornithologie* (1949-1992) Book 3, Leduc, Paris, 1996. 295-296

It is composed in G major with a tonic B.[14] Messiaen must have been at pains not to reveal too much, and yet he must have taken care to make his symbolic representation exact and obvious enough to be picked out. Messiaen states that the form consists of the following:

i. Refrain (p.55)
ii. 1st couplet (pp. 56 to 58)
iii. Refrain (p.59)
iv. 2nd couplet (p.59, 3'11 system p.63)
v. Refrain (p.63)
vi. Magic syllable (p.65)
vii. Repeat of the magic syllable (p. 66, 2nd system)
viii. Coda on the magic syllable (p.68, 3rd system to the end)

(Messiaen, Traité, Book 3, p.299)

Piroutcha tragically describes how she now sets her mind on mystical love; the words "Of the sky, of the water of time, the staircase of time", nature is the source of this inspired passage, which returns six times in various guises, anticipating the essence of the song to come, "L'escalier redit, gestes du soleil".[15]

In "L'escalier redit, gestes du soleil" Messiaen's beautifully lucid and forceful artistic intelligence is exercised on the perfect Working out of his images; it is in E-flat major and uses mode 2^1.[16] But the images themselves are unlikely to have been found by just working through the possible permutations of notes. The climax of "its eye is deserted", page 71, or "like death", page 75, takes us by surprise because of its originality. In "L'escalier redit, gestes du soleil" one of the clearest applications of strophes in Messiaen's music occurs. In the first strophe the principal climax, at "its eye is deserted", page 71, lies approximately at the centre of the first period (after 5 bars out of a total of 13).[17] If this example lacks immediately obvious symmetry, the second strophe is less ambiguous,

---

14 Messiaen, O. *Traité de Rythme, de Couleur, et d'Ornithologie* (1949-1992) Book 3, Leduc, Paris, 1996. 299-300

15 Messiaen, O. *Harawi*, Ninth Movement, Leduc, Paris, 1945. 70-71. "Du ciel, de l'eau, du temps, l'escalier du temps".

16 Messiaen, O. *Traité de Rythme, de Couleur, et d'Ornithologie* (1949-1992) Book 3, Leduc, Paris, 1996 304-306

17 Messiaen, O., *Harawi*, Leduc, Paris, 1945. P. 71 "Son oeil est désert".

with a sharply focused principal climax on "like death", page 75, again placed directly in the centre of the second period.[18] All these aspects of Messiaen's composition reflect his interest in nature and particularly the symmetry of nature.

The strophes on pages 84-86 of "Amour, oiseau d'étoile", which is in F-sharp major, illustrate Messiaen's more fluid concept of tension and dynamics.[19] Connected with this is the introduction of undulating dynamic shapes that follow a more independent course, for example the song of the chaffinch in bar 2.

The outcome is dramatic: the sudden "dhenki" rhythmic canons also provide a fulfilment of anticipatory musical events and sequences.

The Star bird motif assumes the poetic qualities it will later have, particularly when played by the piano. The soprano C sharp evokes the radiant image of Piroutcha with which the youth was so impressed. The repeated quaver and dotted crotchet in the first bars are reminiscent of the motif that expressed Piroutcha's modesty in the first song, to which the chromatically ascending piano chords add a gentle quality. A wealth of contrasting motifs show Piroutcha's fluctuating emotions of love and reproach. She recalls the intensity of her hatred and her suffering, "Your head upside down under the sky".[20] The only end to this deception seemed to her to be to draw the youth into death with her; the closeness of love and death is expressed profoundly by the next song, "Katchikatchi les étoiles", and in the writing that transfigures the underlying harmonies of death. The song uses mode 2^1 and the two keys of E-flat major and C major.[21]

The vocal line in the eleventh song is particularly important because it anticipates the mood of existence between time and space which the lovers will inhabit. The youth can now appreciate the true glory of Piroutcha, rather than the empty brilliance of which he had previously talked so much. A stretto-like passage, piling motif upon motif, leads into Piroutcha's sad fury at giving herself to the youth, "fury of

---

18 Messiaen, O., *Harawi*, Leduc, Paris, 1945. p. 75 "comme la mort".

19 Messiaen, O. *Traité de Rythme, de Couleur, et d'Ornithologie* (1949-1992) Book 3, Leduc, Paris, 1996. 307

20 Messiaen, O., *Harawi*, Tenth Movement, Leduc, Paris, 1945. 85. "Ta tête à l'envers sous le ciel".

21 Messiaen, O. *Traité de Rythme, de Couleur, et d'Ornithologie* (1949-1992) Book 3, Leduc, Paris, 1996. 310

the clock at absent murder".[22] The shape of the music may be grasped through listening to the short passacaglia-type soprano motif at the line "Katchikatchi les étoiles". A simple statement sums up the musical landscape just as the semiquaver chords in the piano at, "The electrons, ants, arrows, silence of two" indicates that the lovers are now fully initiated into the mysteries of the night.[23] The composition draws us in to the experience with them. It is fascinating to see how Messiaen repeats "Katchikatchi, the stars make them jump" then "dance".[24] As Piroutcha bleakly sings, "The spiral nebulae, hands of my hair"; we sense that we pass through "the rowdy rainbow space of time".[25] The chromatic harmony of the crucial new motif is in keeping with the more intricate style of the musical language that has developed.

In "Katchikatchi les étoiles", driven to the point of madness by pain, longing and despair, the joy of reuniting with the youth finally unhinges Piroutcha's mind but her rash action proves fatal and she dies in the youth's arms. This section of Messiaen's poem reverses Wagner's ideas where, near the end of the opera, Tristan's joy of reuniting with Isolde finally unhinges his mind, and he flings off his bandages; he is convinced he no longer needs them, now that Isolde has come to heal the wound, but the rash action proves fatal, and Tristan dies in Isolde's arms.

Messiaen's *Harawi* vividly conveys both Piroutcha's wild joy, and then, in very moving transitions to quieter, slower music, the life ebbing out of her. Piroutcha sings, finally, not of her grief but of her vision of a transfigured youth, in a form free of all sorrow and suffering, smiling with the joy of love, in a spiritual realm where she is to join him. It would be difficult to imagine anything more directly inspired from Wagner's *Tristan und Isolde* than Messiaen's complicated symbolic poem.

In the eleventh song the dramatic event has moved from the background to the foreground. An example is the antecedent in bar 1 and the consequence in bar 2 and the five subsequent variations. Accordingly

---

22 Messiaen, O., *Harawi*, Movement 11, Leduc, Paris, 1945. 92. "Rire ionisé fureur d'horloge an meutre absent".

23 Messiaen, O., *Harawi*, Movement 11, Leduc, Paris, 1945. 90. Les électrons, fourmis, flèches le silence en deux".

24 Messiaen, O., *Harawi*, Movement 11, Leduc, Paris, 1945. pp. 88-89. "Katchikatchi, les étoiles, faites les sauter," and "Katchikatchi, les étoiles, faites les danser."

25 Messiaen, O., *Harawi*, Movement 11, Leduc, Paris, 1945. pp. 90-91. "Les nébuleuses spirales, mains de mes cheveux" and "Di la tez l'espace arc en ciel tapageur du temps."

there is little to resolve except the modified theme based on the Peruvian "Kaswa" dance.

A poetic transition fuels the brutality of the music at "Cut off my head" with more than a hint of the danger in the background.[26] The rhythmic throb becomes the basis of the Whole final section.

In "Dans le noir" the principal theme coincides with rhythmic canons on the piano; the first period follows a dynamic course independent of the rhythmic canon. The twelfth song is in E-flat major and again uses mode 2^1, the conclusion consists of polymodal rhythmic canons.[27] The first and second periods show symmetrical tendencies connected to octatonic and E-flat cadences. On page 99, the fff suddenly highlights the grand cry, "My love, my breath."[28] "Dans le noir" is an invocation to the night to envelop the lovers, and release them from the World. The voice and piano intertwine with each other and Piroutcha's theme loudly proclaims "My love, my breath".[29] All the Words of the last line from "Dans le noir" prove to be an exact parallel of the first line of "La ville qui dormait, toi", with the "toi" missing.

Piroutcha's voice is heard singing a long-drawn-out melody "Very far away, very low, very far", like a soul lost in the night.[30] A tonal centre seems to be reached as the soprano sings the final G, where muted piano adds a note of warning; this passage is the most beautiful passage in *Harawi*. It is as though we hear the warning sounds of the outer world through veils of quiet rapture.

Messiaen's text is a philosophical discussion, couched in tender expressions of love, about day and death, about the nature of their love. The piano's link to Piroutcha is memorable for its frenzy and stillness. As the text speaks of boundless realms of rapture, the music seems to create wider and wider spaces of ecstasy. The lovers abandon themselves with phrases that build up to a climactic surge. The song "L'amour de Piroutcha", after a sudden ppp, is cruelly interrupted by the young girl

---

26 Messiaen, O., *Harawi*, Movement ll, Leduc, Paris, 1945. 92. "Coupez ma téte".

27 Messiaen, O., *Traité de Rythme, de Couleur, et d'Ornithologie* (1949-1992) Book 3, Leduc, Paris, 1996. 313-3 15

28 Messiaen, O., *Harawi*, Leduc, Paris, 1945. 99. "Mon amour, mon souffle!"

29 Messiaen, O., *Harawi*, Movement 12, Leduc, Paris, 1945. 99. "Mon amour, mon souffle!"

30 Messiaen, O., *Harawi*, Movement 12, Leduc, Paris, 1945. 100. "Très loin, tout bas, très loin"

singing the youth's part with the words "Cut off my head, doundou tchil".³¹ The outer world has encroached. The youth drops his guard in the sudden realisation that death alone will release him from life. Piroutcha, in the fifth movement, also saw death as a solution to the intolerable prospect of life.

Harawi is, after all, concerned with the invisible, interior lives of Piroutcha and her lover; lives which had found no entirely satisfactory expression in literature until Messiaen claimed them in poetry and music. For Messiaen, feeling enshrined in music is the whole truth; everything else, all action, even that between the lovers, is error and delusion. The ruling tension is between the rival realms of darkness and light. This polarity is symbolic, in the widest sense; the entire composition is a hymn to the Night, although even here Piroutcha and her lover fail to find erotic fulfilment and must seek nirvana in a mystic union beyond death.

Messiaen's text draws upon the exalted exemplary status of the lovers, and on the highly wrought interchanging structures and paradoxes which the medieval poet uses to superb effect. Messiaen employed them as a dramatic and poetic vehicle for his brand of metaphysics, and as a means of exploring the symbolic fascination with the unity of love and death.

But Messiaen's text also displays an uncompromising moral realism and a clear insight into the dissembling hypocrisy of society, where the youth can exploit the ambiguities of language to his own advantage until he is ultimately trapped by them himself. Messiaen has retained and adapted something of this in his first song. Piroutcha's narration of how the youth tricked her into being his bride establishes a tone of sarcasm and deep irony. The youth confronted with her demand for "atonement", can only reply in obscure verbal paradoxes and dark enigmas which tax the powers of listeners and translators alike. Even an audience which can hear the sung text can scarcely be expected to grasp, on a first hearing, the repeated exchanges and the sense of the lines:

> *The water will rise about our heads,*
> *Guardian sun.*
> *Fire will eat our breath.*
> *Philtre with two voices.*
> *Our looks from one end to the other*

---

31 Messiaen, O., *Harawi*, Movement 5, Leduc, Paris, 1945. 30. "Coupe moi la tête, doundou tchil".

Seen by death.[32]

What the youth is refusing to say here is soon spoken when the potion sweeps all inhibitions away; but the piano score has already told us what it was, expressing the dramatic movement on a level the verbal text cannot reach.

Messiaen's poem, judged purely as poetry, is not of the first rank; but it fulfils its purpose completely. The lines are short and very forceful, but they do not offer much resistance to the ebb and flow of the long sentence units. The combination of unifying factors such as alliteration, rhyme and assonance with antithetical figures such as paradox and contrast suggests a linking across the line divisions.

> *I wait in the green, starred with love.*
> *It is so easy to be dead.*[33]

In the ecstasy of the lovers' worship of the night, there is a warning. As the lovers draw ever closer, the effect of the rhymes becomes incantatory: "Death is here, my green dove / Death is here, my limpid pearl / Death is here."[34]

Messiaen's art forces us to attend to the text. In *Harawi* the heroine is heard reflecting on the title of the Work in which she figures. The title *Harawi, Song of Love and Death*, "and", a word which joins together love and death, but which in the very act of joining together demonstrates clearly the condition of separation. Therefore the protagonists' constant need to name that self which they seek to transcend. Messiaen's text is therefore not merely a pretext for music: language is the only possible medium for expressing essential forces in the drama, just as the music articulates elements which are beyond the limits of what language can say.

---

32 Messiaen, O., *Harawi*, Movement 9, Leduc, Paris, 1945. pp. 77-78 "L'eau de-pas-se-ra nos têtes, Soleil gardien, Le feu mange-ra nos souffles, Philtre a' deux voix. Nos re-gards d'un bout a l'autre Vus par la mort".

33 Messiaen, O., *Harawi*, Movement 9, Leduc, Paris, 1945. 74. "J 'attends dans le verte, étoilé d'amour. C'est si simple d'être mort".

34 Messiaen, O., *Harawi*, Movement 9, Leduc, Paris, 1945. 76-77. "La mort est là, ma colombe verte, La mort est là, ma perle limpide. La mort est là".

The Impact of Wagner

The impact of Wagner and Debussy is clearly evident in this Work. The fulfilment which the youth offers Piroutcha is mirrored in Act One of Wagner's *Tristan und Isolde*. In "Bonjour toi, colombe verte" the chords in the piano in bar 6 are clearly inspired by Debussy. Piroutcha's description of experiencing death and her return to the Daylight world is derived from Wagner's *Tristan*. In Messiaen's eleventh song he reverses Wagner's idea of *Tristan*'s premature death. Messiaen's complicated symbolic poem is evidently inspired from Wagner's *Tristan und Isolde*. Wagner reduced the *Tristan* myth text but Messiaen, in *Harawi*, reduced it further, investigating in greater depth the psychological and philosophical impact of the myth on his two lovers.

Love in *Harawi* works miracles, but natural ones; the initiation is allegorical of the transformation love works in human psychology when it is set free from fear. Debussy's *Pelléas* almost points the lesson that love cannot work miracles except through natural processes, which include reasoning and morality. Just as Piroutcha prays to love and in the end her prayer is granted but through an imbroglio of natural means, so the last act of *Pelléas* opens with the words in which the doctor, before undertaking to save Mélisande, reassures Golaud that he must not feel responsible for her death: "So it is not you that killed her, my noble lord. Do not distress yourself so much."[35] Love's answer seems to be given but it is a disappointing one. Piroutcha reveals another and natural sense in which love really does work miracles. In their captivity, she and the youth make just the journey through the darkness of death which *Pelléas* and *Mélisande* undertake in the opera, and, like the lovers, Piroutcha and the youth emerge having vanquished the fear of death through the power of love. In the end it is again the power of love, worked on by reason and bent towards a redemptive philosophy, which impels the youth to grant the freedom Piroutcha could not force from him. This analogy with *Pelléas et Mélisande* has helped place *Harawi* in the context of Messiaen's relationship with the *Tristan* myth. Example 1 and 2.

---

35 Debussy, C., *Pelléas et Mélisande*, Durand, Paris, 1902. 367. "Ce n'est donc pas vous qui l'avez tuée, mon bon seigneur; ne vous désolez pas ainsin…"

Example 1: The Movements *Harawi (Chant d'amour et de mort)*

1. "La ville qui dormait, toi"
2. "Bonjour toi, colombe verte"
3. "Montagnes"
4. "Doundou tchil"
5. "L'amour de Piroutcha"
6. "Répétition planétaire"
7. "Adieu"
8. "Syllabes"
9. "L'escalier redit, gestes du soleil"
10. "Amour, oiseau d'étoile"
11. "Katchikatchi les étoiles"
12. "Dans le noir"

Example 2: *Harawi (Song of Love and Death)*

1. The town which was sleeping, you

The town which was sleeping, you,
My hand on your heart, by you,
The dead of night the seat, you,
The double violet, you,
The motionless eye, without unravelling your look, me.

2. Hello you, green dove

Hello you, green dove,
Return from the sky.
Hello you, limpid pearl,
Departure from the Water,
Chained star,
Shared shadow,
You, of flower, of fruit, of sky and of Water,

Song of the birds,
Hello,
Of Water.

3. **Mountains**

   Red violet, black on black,
   Useless ancient black ray,
   Mountain, listen to vertigo's solar chaos,
   The stone, kneeling, carries its black masters,
   In their tight cowls the firs rush towards the darkness,
   Chasm hurled everywhere in the vertigo,
   Black on black.

4. **Doundou Tchil**

   Doundou tchil, etc,
   Piroutcha there you are, oh my all-my-own,
   The dance of the stars, doundou tchil,
   Piroutcha there you are, oh my all-my-own,
   Mirror of the familiar bird, doundou tchil,
   Rainbow, my breath, my echo,
   Your look has returned, tchil, tchil,
   Piroutcha, there you are, oh my all-my-own,
   My fruit, lightweight in the light, doundou,
   Toungou, toungou, mapa, nama,
   Mapa, nama, mapa, kahipipas,
   Toungou, toungou, mapa, nama,
   Mapa, nama, mapa, mahipipas,
   Piroutcha there you are, oh my all-my-own,
   The dance of the stars, doundou tchil, etc.

5. **Piroutcha's love**

   "Toungou, ahi, toungou, toungou, cradle, you,
   My cinder of light, cradle your little one in your green arms,
   Piroutcha, your little cinder, for you,
   "Your eye all the skies, doundou tchil"
   Cut my head off, doundou tchil,
   Our breath, our breath, blue and gold,

Ahi! Ahi!
Red, black, mauve chains, love, death,
"Toungou, ahi, toungou, tomigou, etc."

6. **Rehearsal of the planets**

Ahi! Ahi! Ahi! Ahi!
Mapa, nama, mapa nama lila, tchil, etc.
Mapa nama lila, mika, pampahika,
Ahi! Oh Oh Oh, etc,
Straddle a black cry,
Black echo of time,
Cry from from before the earth at any time,
Black echo of time,
Spiral staircase,
Whirlwind,
Red Star,
Whirlwind,
Planet eats as it turns,
Tchil, tchil, etc.

7. **Adieu**

Adieu you, green dove,
Saddened angel,
Adieu you, limpid pearl,
Guardian sun,
You, of night, of fruit, of sky, of day,
Wing of love,
Adieu you, new light,
Philtre with two voices,
Chained star,
Shared shadow,
In my hand my fruit of sky, of day,
Distant with love,
Adieu you, my sky of earth,
Adieu you, weeping desert,
Mirror without breath of love,
Of flower, of night, of fruit, of sky, of day,

Forever.

8. **Syllables**

   Dove, green dove,
   The figure five to you,
   The double violet will double,
   Very far away, very low,
   Oh oh my sky you bloom,
   Piroutcha mia!
   Oh oh let us unfold from the sky,
   Piroutcha mia!
   Oh oh let us bloom from the water,
   Piroutcha mia!
   Kahipipas, mahipipas,
   Pia, pia, pia.
   Doundou tchil, etc.
   Pipaskahi, pipasmahi,
   Pipas, pipas, etc.

9. **The staircase repeats, gestures of the sun**

   It no longer speaks, the staircase smiles,
   Each step towards the South,
   Of the sky, of the water, of time the staircase of time,
   Its eye is deserted, light in secret,
   Bright stone and bright sun.
   Of the water, of time, of the sky, the staircase of the sky,
   My little cinder you are here, your temples green, mauve, on some water,
   Like death,
   The eye of the water,
   The staircase repeats, gestures of the sun,
   Colour of new silence,
   Of the water, of time, of the sky, the staircase of the sky,
   I wait in the green, starred with love,
   It is so easy to be dead,
   Of time, of the sky, of the water, the staircase of the water,
   My little cinder you are here, your temples green, mauve, on

some time
Like death.
The eye of time,
Of the sky, of the water, of time,
Your eye present and breathing.
Of the water, of time, of the sky,
The heart of the mad clock,
Death is here, my green dove,
Death is here, my limpid pearl,
Death is here,
We sleep far from time in your look,
I am dead,
The water will rise above our heads, guardian sun,
Fire will eat our breath,
Philtre with two voices.
Our looks from one end to the other
Seen by death.
Let us invent the love of the world
To seek us, to weep for us,
To dream of us, to find us,
Of the sky, of the water, of time, your heart beating,
My fruit, my share of the darkness, you are here, you,
Love, joy!
Silence is dead, embrace time,
The sun with joyful cries,
Of time, of the sky, of the water, the staircase of the water,
Joyfulness blossoms in the arms of the sky,
Fan in the shape of bird song,
Of the sky, of the water, of time, the staircase of time,
My little cinder you are here, your temples green, mauve, on some sky,
Like death,
The eye of the sky.

10. **Star bird Love**

   Star bird,
   Your eye which sings,
   Towards the stars,
   Your head upside clown under the sky,
   Your star eye,
   Falling chains,
   Towards the stars,
   Shortest route from the shadow to the sky,
   All of the star birds,
   Far from the scene my hands are singing.
   Star, increased silence of the sky.
   My hands, your eye, your neck, the sky.

11. **Katchikatchi the stars**

   Katchikatchi the stars, make them jump,
   Katchikatchi the stars, make them dance,
   Katchikatchi the atoms, make them jump,
   Katchikatchi the atoms, make them dance.
   The spiral nebulae, hands of my hair.
   The electrons, ants, arrows, silence of two.
   Alpha Centauri,
   Betelgeuse, Aldebaran,
   Swell the rowdy rainbow space of time,
   Ionised laugh fury of the clock at absent murder,
   Cut off my head, its figure rolls in blood!
   Tou, ahi! Mané mani,
   Rolls in blood, etc.

12. **In the darkness**

   In the darkness, green dove,
   In the darkness, limpid pearl,
   In the darkness, my fruit of the sky, of day,
   Distant with love,
   My love, my breath!
   Dove, green dove,
   The figure five to you,

The double violet will double,
Very far away, very low,
Very far away, very low, very far,
The town which was sleeping.

Translation by J.P. Travell

7

MESSIAEN'S TRISTAN TRILOGY PART 2: *TURANGALÎLA*

INTRODUCTION

The word *"Turangalîla"* comes from two Sanskrit Words. "Turanga" means "time", "rhythm", "movement" and "Lila" is variously used to describe the play of divine action on the cosmos. As Barrett states, "the play of creation, of destruction and reconstruction, the play of life and death."[1] Messiaen first came across the word *"Turangalîla"* in 1935, when, in a French encyclopaedia, he found it in a list of 120 Indian rhythms, compiled in the thirteenth century by an Indian scholar called Sarngadeva.[2] Most of the rhythms are ametric, some are non-retrogradable, others contain units that expand or contract. The *Turangalîla* rhythm a contracting one: two dotted semi-quavers are followed by two semi-quavers—3 : 3 : 2 : 2. The list was of importance to Messiaen for two important musical and literary reasons: first because it placed at his disposal an invaluable reservoir of additive rhythms, a fact that immediately became apparent in his nine meditations for organ, *La Nativité du Seigneur* (1935), and the nine *Poèmes pour Mi* for soprano and piano or orchestra (1936-7); and second because all 120 rhythms have Sanskrit names, and some of the titles had cosmic overtones which were of significance to him in *Turangalîla*.

The *Turangalîla-Symphonie* is a vast, ten-movement work for piano, ondes martenot (an electronic keyboard instrument capable of sustaining notes and producing glissandi) and orchestra. Messiaen called it a love song, a hymn to joy—love that is fatal, irresistible, transcending everything, suppressing everything outside itself; joy that is superhuman,

---

1 Barrett, N., "Hymn of love", Broadcasting and the Arts, The Listener, 18" August 1977. 213

2 Hook, J. L., "Rhythm in the Music of Messiaen: an Algebraic Study and an Application in the *Turangalîla-Symphonie*", *Music Theory Spectrum*, V20. Part 1, 1998. 98

overflowing, blinding, unlimited.³ The "love" music is nearly always east in floating additive rhythms and played by the highly mellifluous ondes martenot, the "joy" music in corporeal rhythms with, as often as not, a strong, swinging beat. The exultant fifth movement that ends the first half, "Joie du sang des étoiles" ("Joy of the blood of the stars"), is one of the best illustrations of the vast counterpoint of rhythms pervading the work.

"Joie du sang des étoiles" is not the most complex section in the symphony, but it contains what Messiaen calls "personnages rythmiques". As Hook states:

> *Messiaen himself used the term "rhythmic characters" (personnages rythmiques) to describe the elements of these constructions, reflecting his conviction that each rhythm has its own "personality" and that the character of the whole passage is strongly influenced by the characters of the individual rhythms.*⁴

The whole of the "Joie du sang des étoiles" is based on a theme in thirds and nearly always played on the trombones fortissimo, which is first heard at the very beginning of the symphony. Messiaen calls it the "statue theme" because it evokes the oppressive, "terrifying brutality of old Mexican monuments".⁵

The "personnages rythmiques" occur in two passages in the central section of the movement, and Messiaen describes them in this way:

> *Let us imagine a stage on which we place three characters. The first acts; he even acts brutally by striking the second. The second person is "acted" (upon), since his actions are dominated by those of the first character. Finally, the third character is present at the conflict and remains inactive. If we transfer this analogy into the realm of rhythm, we obtain three rhythmic groups: in the first the durations are always increasing—this is the attacking character; in the second*

---

3 Messiaen, O., *Traité de Rythme, de Couleur, et d'Ornithologie*, Book II, Leduc, Paris, 1995. 151

4 Hook, J.L., "Rhythm in the Music of Messiaen: an Algebraic Study and an Application in the *Turangalîla-Symphonie*", *Music Theory Spectrum* Vol. 20, Part 1, 1998. 99. Also see Messiaen, Music and Colour, 70-71, (Hook, footnote 13).

5 Barrett, N., "Hymn of Love", Broadcasting and the Arts, The Listener, 18th August 1977. 213

the durations decrease—this is the character who is attacked; and in the third the durations do not change—this is the immobile character.[6]

Messiaen's purpose in "Joie du sang des étoiles" was not to create something explicitly dramatic, but to attain a symmetry which would symbolise the physical union of the two lovers, one balancing the other in perfect harmony. What is interesting is that the third rhythmic character, far from being the one who stands aside and never changes, is in a state of constant transformation. It is this character who is the real actor, and who eventually brings about the perfect symmetry.

In the first episode shaped by the "personnages rythmiques" the augmenting rhythm of the "attacking character" is produced by the addition of a semiquaver to each of its durations at successive occurrences (4:1:4, 5:2:5, 6:3:6, 7:4:7), the diminishing rhythm of the "character attacked" by the successive subtraction of a semiquaver (8:4:8, 7:3:7, 6:2:6, 5:1:5). The "observer" begins with the set of durations 1:2:2:2:1:2, but thereafter the pattern is varied, sometimes beyond recognition. In the second episode, which happens about thirty seconds after the first is completed, all three rhythmic characters appear, with mirror images of themselves running alongside them. This means that even the haphazard patterns of the "observer" have become symmetric. Since the "observer" initiates the addition of the retrogrades, and not the "attacking character", who took the lead in the first episode, the "observer" must get all the credit for the overall symmetry and balance.

Shortly before the first performance of the *Turangalîla-Symphonie* in 1949, Messiaen composed a short piece for piano called *Mode de valeurs et d'intensites*. It had a profound influence on the thinking of the young up-and-coming composers of the day, for it appeared to defy the whole of tradition and open up the possibility of making a completely fresh start in music. According to Hall, the piece had no melody, harmony, pulse or discernible rhythm. It appeared to be nothing but a series of random single notes. Stockhausen likened it to looking at stars twinkling haphazardly in the sky at night, Boulez to his experimental period, in the best sense of the term.[7] As far as Messiaen was concerned it was probably an exercise in the art of making music out of material that

---

6 Johnson, R.S., *Messiaen*, Dent, London, 1989. 35-36. also quoted in Samuel, C., Messiaen, Pierre Belfond, Paris, 1967. 72. (Johnson footnote 3, p.39).

7 Boulez, P., *Orientations*, ed. Cooper, M., Faber and Faber, Ltd., London, 1990. 412

was absolutely fixed. It was the kind of exercise composition teachers give their students to test their imagination and ingenuity. He took thirty-six pitches, twenty-four durations, twelve types of attack (staccato, tenuto, various kinds of accents) and seven dynamic markings (ranging from ppp to fff) and arranged them into three descending scales that overlap with one another.[8] A glance at the score reveals that he applied his musical skills, learnt from the *Tristan* trilogy compositions, with all the imagination and ingenuity he would have expected from the best of his students. Each scale makes as convincing a line as is possible in the circumstances, and the three lines work together to produce good counterpoint. However, as we have seen in the *Turangalîla-Symphonie* the ear cannot pick up what the eye can see. For those who heard the work at Darmstadt, the annual summer school devoted to discussing and playing the advanced music of the day, its appeal was due to the impression it gave, resembling the lovers' feelings for each other in the *Turangalîla-Symphonie*, of being wholly untouched by human volition.

Messiaen: *Turangalîla*

Not quite eleven years after Messiaen's death in 1992 we can appreciate his *Turangalîla Symphonie* in terms of two stylistic periods: the Works from *Le Banquet céleste* (1928), to *Harawi* (1945), in which he learned his métier and matured his personal musical language, and those composed afterwards, his supreme masterpieces *Cinq Rechants* (1949), *Catalogue d'Oiseaux* (1956-8), *Chronochromie* (1960), and *Livre du Saint Sacrement* (1984). Curiously, if not surprisingly, Messiaen had decided on all these later subjects before *Harawi* was completed; he had only to resolve in which order to set them to music.

Creative compulsion, destined that he would not attempt those last three until he had worked himself into the new language of his *Cinq Rechants*.

He had read Gottfried von Strasburg's poetic narration of the *Tristan* story between 1945 and 1948. In 1945 his artistic attention was taken up with a song cycle about the death of Piroutcha, which effectively set other projects aside. *Harawi* which gradually evolved into twelve songs, each lasting for approximately two minutes consumed his energy

---

8 Johnson, R.S, *Messiaen*, Dent, London, 1989 105-106

until 1945, and 1948 In 1945 his artistic attention was taken up with a song cycle about the death of Piroutcha, when his interest in Wagner brought the *Tristan* material back to mind. Here was the great love, such as Wagner never experienced; a love not to be fulfilled in life, but only consummated in death together, lover and beloved.

In June 1946 he wrote down his first musical ideas for the *Turangalîla-Symphonie*, and by the end of the year the subject had so much taken possession of him that he had to devote his whole mind to the symphony. Messiaen found Wagner's *Tristan und Isolde* more than cogent: it possessed his being, despite being dedicated to Schopenhauer's teaching that mankind must value death as the only self-fulfilling response to the frustration and emptiness of life on earth. Hence the attraction of *Tristan und Isolde* a saga of perfect love, pledged in terms of a suicide pact, and fulfilled by union in death, first his then hers, The fatal love affair of Tristan and Isolde in Wagner's opera impelled Messiaen to a new, more sophisticated musical vocabulary of love, which had to be realised in the composition of *Turangalîla*.

Messiaen wrote the music for *Turangalîla* between 1946 and 1948. The first performance took place on 2nd December 1949, at the behest of Serge Koussevitzky.[9] By 1950 *Turangalîla* was acknowledged as one of the most revolutionary musical compositions since Beethoven's Ninth Symphony, a verdict that no musician today has thought fit to question. Its only rival to date is Stravinsky's *The Rite of Spring*. As Malcolm Williamson states:

> *No voice cried in the wilderness announcing that in the 1950s a genius would appear whose music denied that Bartok, Webern and Stravinsky had ever existed. How could the critic explain that here was a fully-grown giant figure, at one and the same time a poised classicist, and a romantic whose overt tastelessness—by current ideas of taste at least—would have made Massenet or Gounod blush? While one army of composers was straining to push Schoenbergian formulae to further extremes, Messiaen showed that a key was not simply something to unlock the door that Webern closed; and while another anny was trying pathetically to outwit Stravinsky's rhythmic and metric ingenuities, Messiaen invented stillness in music.*[10]

---

9 Johnson, R.S. *Messiaen*, Dent, London, 1989. 82

10 Williamson, M., "*Turangalîla* is a Mighty Stillness", *The Listener* 3 April, 1969. 469

The first two cyclic themes of the "Introduction" are known as the "statue theme" and the "flower theme".[11]

No longer considered harmonic anomalies, let alone an affront, they are instantly recognized. The "Introduction", resembling Wagner's "Prelude" to *Tristan und Isolde*, evokes the strange, unwelcome, frustrated, yet blissful growth of love in the minds and bodies of Tristan and Isolde. The "Développement de l'amour" shows the first fulfilment of that love as Isolde feels her life slip away to join *Tristan*, in spirit, outside the confines of earthly existence. The "Introduction" and the "Développement de l'amour" can be perceived, like the "Prelude" and "Liebestod" of Wagner's opera, as some of the most languorous moments in the history of music.

A complete performance of Messiaen's *Turangalîla-Symphonie* explores every aspect of the drama with unprecedented depth and cogency. Yet of narrative there is none, of operatic artificiality there is very little (the love-potion is the symbol of a real human experience that words cannot describe, though music does). Nevertheless, it is ceaselessly eventful, eternally compelling, and as original now as it was fifty four years ago.

The "statue theme" at the opening of the "Introduction" is a watershed in the course of musical history, Crucial though the tonality of the opening bars may be for the subsequent development of compositional techniques, it does not represent experiment for its own sake: it is not a doctrinaire pronouncement that conventional harmony is henceforth anathema. For Messiaen this was the only means of expressing what had never been expressed in music before, a means to which he never returned in subsequent works. The "Introduction" opens with two overlapping themes. The "flower theme" turns in on itself, the "statue theme" strives upwards, seeking a resolution that does not come. The ensuing symbolic drama, its conflicts and their ultimate solution are generated out of the tension of these opening bars. The "Introduction" does not encompass the whole interiorised drama and thus render what follows superfluous but in it is prefigured the synthesis which must be achieved before a final point of rest can be reached.

The "Joie du sang des étoiles" is a further development in human terms of the situation presented in the "Introduction" in musical terms. The lovers symbolically meet despite the dangers that encompass

---

11 Johnson, R. S., *Messiaen*, Dent, London, 1989, 83

them and they gradually come to understand, through the music alone, that there is total incompatibility between the realm of Day, Life and temporal values, and their love, which is identified with the forces of Night, Death, Truth and Eternity. Messiaen indirectly reminds us that in Wagner's Love Duet Brangaene's warning goes unheeded but not unheard. For the lovers, Brangaene's admonition "Night soon gives Way to Day" provides further impetus to their defiance of the hostile elements and deeper commitment to their dedication to Night.

The "Développement de l'amour" opens with the music which has become associated with Tristan and Isolde's dedication to Night. Their love has now assumed cosmic qualities and is no longer capable of earthly fulfilment. Isolde's physical death, now inevitable, is a transfiguration. Only now can the musical tensions of the opening bars of the symphony look to the point of rest towards which they have been striving.

Movements in *Turangalîla*

"Introduction"—first movement. Here as in the whole work we notice the evocative, almost hypnotic power of figures or elements repeated twice. The "statue theme" is gradually abstracted into its dotted opening motive, symbolic of scale and authority. In doing so it entwines itself with the "flower theme" and already forecasts the future of the lovers, and thus tells us that Tristan is in love with Isolde. The triplets in the piano solo, figure 11, p.15, suggest the murmurs of the forest and are strongly reminiscent of *Boris Godunov* (accompaniment to Pimen's narrative). They also remind us of the "Interlude" in *Debussy's Pelléas et Mélisande.*

"Chant d'amour 1"—second movement. During the couplet refrain form of this movement we hear the fascinating sounds of a "nature orchestra", which conjures above all a seascape. Contrasts of shadow and light, of the dark woods and the bright sea, show the unique skill of the tone painter, especially at the sudden change of the second element played by the ondes martenot. The theme of the two lovers is plainly exposed. See Example 3. Example 4 *Turangalîla*, figure 4, p.38, shows the theme of the two lovers.

All the important structural events are involved here and by comparison with the "Introduction", the tonal structure of "Chant d'amour I" shows an enormous advance in subtlety. How easily Messiaen now moves within the tonal framework is indicated by the skill with which he handles the movement's points of resolution. After a short coda "Chant d'amour I" comes to rest on an f-sharp.

Two different aspects are evoked—earthly love and tender love. The refrain is in F-sharp major. The two contrasting elements of love are depicted from figure 4 and the first is a rapid passionate motif on the trumpets. From figure 5 the second element is depicted by a slow tender motif. There are a series of chords which are reminiscent of the lovers in *Harawi* ("Adieu" and "Syllabes") from the first bar of figure 4. The coda begins at figure 40 and closes the movement.

"*Turangalîla* I"—third movement. There are strong contrasts between clarinets, ondes martenot, bassoon, trombones and double basses in this movement. There is an unusual rhythmic blend of the oboe theme alternating with the clarinet.

We can observe the expressive use of solo woodwind and horn phrases in "*Turangalîla* I" and the non-retrogradable rhythmic climax of the coda. There is a strong parallel with Act 3 of Wagner's *Tristan und Isolde* with the contrast between strings and violins and the unusual blend of solo cello and horn for the melody of the first statement, then alternating solo clarinet, oboe and horn for the second statement. Overjoyed at signs of life sweeping cello glissandi settle into a more formal passage. The rhythmic complexity of the music anticipates the last movement of *Cinq Rechants* and has a firm uncomplicated directness. The independent rhythmic structure leads to quieter reminiscences.[12] The self-torturing quality of agony is expressed in music not heard since the first movement.

During the 3rd section at figures 4 and 5 the first theme is accompanied by a double rhythmic movement. The rhythmic augmentation of the horns and the woodwind are on an ostinato of 4 chords—rhythmic diminution of the 2nd violins and cellos, on another ostinato of 4 chords. The horns and the woodwind follow two lines of alternate figures, each line gives a long chromaticism.

4th section—figure 6 towards the middle of the first section played by a solo double bass, a pizzicato passage descends chromatically from the middle to the end. The rhythm and melody are disassociated; the retrograde canon is only rhythmic, the two melodic lines stay entirely different.

---

12 Messiaen, O. *Traité de Rythme, de Couleur, et d'Ornithologie* (1949-1992) Book II, Leduc, Paris, 1995. 159-160

5th section—figure 8. The theme of the gamelan, piano and celesta is repeated by the woodwind. The ostinato of the "personnages rythmiques" continues on the woodblock and maracas.

6th section—figure 13. A silence separates us from the preceding sounds. Coda. Resembling Debussy a re-exposition is replaced by several brief allusions to previous ideas and recapitulates the entire piece.

"Chant d' amour II" -fourth movement. The subdued unrest of the orchestral introduction forecasts forthcoming conflicts.

The orchestra depicts the merry atmosphere of the lovers but it sounds quite artificial and unreal, worlds away from the reality of the coming tragedy. The composer has succeeded perfectly in rendering this dialectic opposition.

This movement consists of two trios which are superimposed on the scherzo. In the bridge there is "Klangfarbenmelodie" and bars 4, 5 and 6 are in Mode 2^1. Within this movement Messiaen has created a simultaneous re-exposition of all the themes with separate entrances. We hear birdsong, four rhythms and the "statue theme" played on the trombone. The tonal balances remain excellent for the style, and the sumptuous sounds of the score, unique. In the first and second sections of the "Chant d'amour II", for example, there is frequent use of varied tone colours, often subtly blended, for either answered or dovetailed phrases in most of the main themes.

The fourth movement has a distinctive musical language, with its special harmonic and orchestral colouring. In its use of chromatic linear writing, its instrumental polyphony, free treatment of discords for such periods that the ear finally accepts them almost as concords. Compared with Messiaen's earlier compositions, there is an increased use of brass and horns, which are regarded more as part of the woodwind group. They have solo passages throughout and distinctive use is also made of muted horn notes and chords. There is an expressive balance between the ondes martenot and orchestra in a continuous but often free line and in the transitions between sections and dramatic moods. The shifting emotions of love are potently expressed through the shifting harmonies and orchestra textures, in a small handful of themes continually developed on a symphonic scale. The result is something far more, however, than a symphonic poem. The ebb and flow of extended passages in different tempi and conveying different moods resembles the motion of the stars, which unites and separates *Tristan* and Isolde. The tragic element of the "love-theme" is often conveyed by the darker timbres of piano and celesta, in their upward ascent and chromatic descent. There are important passages for the piano. The orchestral textures show vividly imagined detail in every bar, and increase in variety and polyphonic complexity, throughout this movement.

"Joie du sang des étoiles"—fifth movement. Now follows possibly the most powerful movement in the whole symphony. It describes Tristan and Isolde's love and suffering with aching accents worthy of Wagner's *Parsifal* and shows two extensive climaxes in the two phrases of the opening theme: the first the "statue theme"; the second the "love theme". Isolde's short-lived happiness blossoms on Tristan's ruins. During the "Joie du sang des étoiles", which heightens the excitement of what has gone before, the tempo is motivated by the emotion represented. For example, the turmoil of the movement drives on passionately; the ecstatic intensity of the main theme is then eased. The triumphant return of the "statue-theme", in the last 19 bars, is established in a passage of rapture which transforms the union of Tristan and Isolde. Although the music is overwhelming, it follows the usual ternary form of a scherzo: the transformation of the "statue-theme" is notable. The crescendo in wind and brass and the hyper-active string figuration gives the movement a very full texture.[13]

As quiet passages materialise, Tristan and Isolde explore their mutual love. If this is omitted one loses not only a very important dimension of the work but also some of its most fascinating music. The opening theme can be interpreted, once again, as Tristan's passionate plaint against the day—fiery with violin semi-quaver passages and a quickened form of the "statue-theme". The "love-theme" reply is more tender. The cadences of each section sum up several themes and prepare the subsequent passage. The music often passes into quieter regions in flat keys associated with the night.

Messiaen states that, "the allure is sublime...all true loves know that the flesh is terrible, beautiful and separated, when it is the flesh of Tristan, when it is the flesh of Isolt. The union of true love is a transformation.

---

13 Messiaen, O., *Turangalîla-Symphonie*, Durand, Paris, 1948. p.100

The cosmic character of the carnal union is expressed here by a hymn of life to movement, to joy, it is a long and frenetic dance of joy.[14]

"Jardin du sommeil d'amour"—sixth movement. Messiaen states that, "the two lovers are wrapped up in the sleep of love. The two lovers are wrapped up in themselves. The journey is for two. The garden that they travel is called *Tristan*, and the garden that they travel is called *Yseult*. The garden is full of shadow and of light, of plants and of new flowers, of clear and melodic birds who sing of love.[15] The old legend of *Tristan* and *Yseult*, speaks of the songs of birds. Tristan, as a youth enjoyed the art of imitating the songs of the forest birds, imitating the golden oriole, the blue tit and the nightingale. The piano solo represents the songs of the birds. There is an onomatopoeic: tio, tio, tio, which represents the nightingale.

The sixth movement consists of only 65 bars and the only instruments employed are flute, clarinet, percussion, gamelan, ondes martenot, piano and strings. The form of the movement is—a, a^1, ba^2, coda.

The four sections of this movement offer subtle contrast. Again the music impresses us through its slower rhythm. The flute symbolically underlines the events with relentless insistence. There is a diminuendo in the coda, interrupted by silences and the splendid, heart-rending catharsis of the whole movement is brought about at the end by the harmonies of the woodwind section.

"*Turangalîla* II"—seventh movement. From the moment the movement begins the nervous pulse of the piano solo sets in and its effect is all the stronger after so much slower and static music. Tristan and Isolde's powerless rage lives on in the dark chaos of the violent music with its

---

14 Messiaen, O. *Traité de Rythme, de Couleur, et d'Ornithologie* (1949-1992) Book 2, Leduc, Paris, 1995. 235. Ce titre aux allures surréalists sublimise la passion charnelle. Tous les vrais amants savent que la chair est terrible, belle, et séparée, quand elle est la chair de *Tristan*, quand elle est la chair d'Yseult … L'union des vrais amants est une transformation, une transformation a l'échelle mondiale … Ce caractere cosmique de l'union charnelle est exprimé ici par un hymn à la vie, au mouvement, à la joie. C'est une longue et frénétique danse de joie!

15 Messiaen, O. *Traité de Rythme, de Couleur, et d'Ornithologie* (1949-1992) Book 2, Leduc, Paris, 1995. 275. Les deux amants sont enfermés dans le sommeil de l'amour. Les deux amants sont enfermés en eux-mêmes. Un paysage est sorti d'eux. Le jardin qui les entoure s'appelle *Tristan*, le jardin qui les entoure s'appelle Yseult. Ce jardin est plein d'ombres et de lumières, dc plantes et de fleurs nouvelles, d'oiseaux clairs et mélodieux qui chantent l'amour.

relentless fortissimo, unlike the preceding movement. In *"Turangalîla* II" it may be observed how Messiaen uses the separate phrases to form bridges between sections. The "theme d'accords" introduces a sensation of enlargement before the lively sound of the tam tam. It is then, with the piano cadenza that the main theme follows. We hear again the two juxtaposed episodes, the retrograde form music, and that of the 3rd episode. The music of Tristan and Isolde's embrace eases in momentum with a converging passage in the ondes martenot and trombones. The climax of life and death occurs when this passage appears in retrograde form. The rhythm is spun out almost into timelessness as the first episode is superimposed on the main theme, the woodwind taking up phrases where the cor anglais leaves off.[16]

The movement is fundamental to the psychological explanation for phrases in the *Turangalîla-Symphonie* which Messiaen did not pursue. It is a moment of vigour, the percussion section rushed and frenzied. The oboe and clarinet take up the melody alternately. It seems that it is intolerable longing which prevents Tristan and Isolde from dying.

The final statement with its arresting orchestration brings two rhythmic structures together for the first time. In the strength of the music can be felt the progress that *Turangalîla* has made in the voyage of Tristan and Isolde's self-discovery.

Here we discover the threatening elements in the symphony—the elements of death and of suffering, as in the seventh movement, which Messiaen informs us were suggested by *The Pit and the Pendulum* by Edgar Allan Poe.[17] This movement stands in bleak and forceful contrast to its predecessor—"Jardin du sommeil d'amour".

"Développement de l'amour"—eighth movement. The mixture of intensity as well as delicacy which Messiaen found in Debussy's *Pelléas* are reflected in this movement. The more intimately one knows it, the more one tends to remember, not so much its initial emotional impact, as the refinement of so many passages, culminating in one of the most exquisite movements of interwoven melodies. In this movement its recapitulation of the passionate "love-theme" transforms it into something calmer, slower and more truly mystical.

---

16 Messiaen, O., *Turangalîla-Symphonie*, Durand, Paris, 1948. 103

17 Messiaen, O. *Traité de Rythme, de Couleur, et d'Ornithologie* (1949-1992) Book 2, Leduc, Paris, 1995, 297. "dans le célèbre come d'Edgar Poë : le puits et le pendule".

This piece is based on the harmonic use of all the cyclic themes and the movement concerns eternal love. In the "Introduction" at figure 2 there is a small tutti, consisting of 2 oboes, cor anglais, 2 clarinets, 2 bassoons, 1st and 3rd horns, a cornet, 4 1st violins, 4 2nd violins, 4 violas and 6 cellos, which play the "theme d'accords" in a new presentation.

The development begins in the principal key of the symphony, F-sharp major. At figure 12, there is a repetition of three chords in E major. There is a second development of the "love theme" which starts in D major at figure 27.

A recapitulation is then signalled at the loudest fortissimo in the movement. This is followed by a piano cadenza which looks back to the opening section of the movement. The "Développement de l'amour" ends with a seven bar coda which encompasses references to all the themes.

With this movement we pass into different vein. It is of intriguing ingenuity, and although Messiaen's predilection for Debussy's *Pelléas* is in evidence, the content is intensely personal, reflective and vibrant: it is valid symphonic material and should be regarded as such. Both design and instrumentation display the touch of a composer pre-eminent in his craft. Pianissimo timpani, horns, lower strings and woodwind introduce a 2/4 "Bien modéré"—evident in woodwind, piano and double basses—of pastoral quality. The cyclic themes are introduced in varied style and mood—passionate, sombre, mysterious, with a cantabile passage rich yet biting. The movement progresses in lighter vein and passes through a plethora of time-signatures which never distort the flow. Climactic moments are few; the themes subtly combined, orchestrated and developed, creating tension tempered with elegiac wistfulness. The climax proper reintroduces the gentle reflection of the opening.

An enchanting Modéré, p. 290, in which the use of woodwind is notable and two bars of woodwind and strings precipitate an endearing figure for the clarinets. Chattering violins take up the idea at figure 11, until brief reinforcement from the horns and the piano. The repetition of oboe and trumpet add enchantment to this rhythmical section. The music is enriched with celesta and percussion and the movement concludes with a restatement of the piano figure, a few bars of strings, woodwind, timpani and pizzicato bass.

Like the text of the *Tristan* myth, the music glides from one thought into the next in a process of continuous development. As Messiaen states, "the summit of all the *Turangalîla* music the intensity of the orchestration and the spiritual intensity of the feeling of love. The spiritual summit is like the transfiguration through love at the end of the "death of Isolde", like the redemption through love at the "death of Brünnhilde" in Richard Wagner. Like all the lyrical effusions which end a Work of some importance".[18]

"*Turangalîla* III"—ninth movement. Variations are made on the opening theme and are joined simultaneously by the now omnipresent "gamelan". The music is extended by the woodwind with difficult phrases. Perhaps the most intriguing passage of all is where a fourth variation is added to the texture of the music.[19] It intensifies with the depiction of pain and finds a tragic release in the crescendo at the finale.[20]

The fourth variation contains inverted elements of the music already associated with suffering and longing. It begins with emotionally powerful effect in the woodwind and brass which swells from mezzofoxte to fortissimo whilst the harmony changes underneath.[21] In addition the piano leads to the most shattering of four climaxes within this section.

This movement is divided into three sections, 1st section: antecedent, 4 bars—consequent, 4 bars. 2nd section: 2 fragments of 2 bars antecedent and consequent. 3rd section: 4 bars. In the 2nd section there is "Klangfarbenmelodie". From figure 3 to figure 5 is the 1st variation. The theme enters with the reprise of the piano and gamelan (celesta and glockenspiel). The 2nd variation starts at figure 6. 1st period (antecedent only)—2nd period: 1st fragment with antecedent and consequent—reprise of the 1st period (consequent only). At figure 7 the third period begins. At figure 12, the progression is finished utilising the modes 2^1, 1^2, 2^1 and 3^1. The theme is augmented—2nd fragment of the 2nd period with changes of register. At figure there is a new transformation of the theme. There are

---

18 Messiaen, O. *Traité de Rythme, de Couleur, et d'Ornithologie* (1949-1992) Book 2, Leduc, Paris, 1995. 321-322. C'est ici le sommet de touts la *Turangalîla-Symphonie*. Le sommet d'intensité matérielle de l'orchestration, le sommet d'intensité spirituelle du sentiment d'amour. Comme pour la Transfiguration par l'amour à la fin de la "Mort d'Isolde", comme pour la Redemption par l'amour à la fin de la "Mort de Brünnhilde", dans Richard Wagner, comme pour toutes les effusions lyriques qui terminent une oeuvre de quelque importance.

19 Messiaen, O., *Turangalîla -Symphonie*, Durand, Paris, 1948. 358

20 Messiaen, O., *Turangalîla-Symphonie*, Durand, Paris, 1948. 358-363

21 Messiaen, O., *Turangalîla -Symphonie*, Durand, Paris, 1948. 363

four simultaneous presentations of the theme by figure 10. "*Turangalîla III*" consists of a set of variations on the theme, announced at the start of the movement, each being superimposed on its predecessor until the movement comes to a sudden end at its most complicated point.

"Final"—tenth movement. In the last movement more themes from the past return and the symphony's jubilation is expressed finally in sonata form. It is the beginning of another parallel; through fragments of the "love-theme", the music reaches its climax with the first subject now played fortissimo, punctuated by the triplets of the trumpets and timpani. From this climax comes a heightened and shortened recapitulation as the fever increases and draws us back yet again to the idea of love and death. The "love theme" recurs and fades away to a seemingly timeless suspension, as it appeared in the "Jardin du sommeil d'amour". The falling fourths resume the "love-theme" for the last time. Thus the climax connects the sixth and last movements.

Although the music in the "Final" is a repetition of the sixth movement music in shorter form, the new melodic line creates the impression of a new composition. The comparative gentleness evoked here by the orchestra is "all revealing". Only just before the climax—continually interrupted in the tenth movement—does the "love theme" become a statement. The theme has already been the source of important climaxes in the symphony. Resembling Wagner's *Tristan und Isolde* the long winding-down of the final bars matches the long circling build-up that has preceded them. The "love theme" comes to rest; the tones of the celesta and piano, formerly so all pervading, are significantly absent from the final seven bars. The climax of the Transfiguration has veered between the four cyclic themes in such a way as to leave not a little ambiguity as to which should carry the greater weight; it is one of the enigmas of *Turangalîla* that such questions may never be finally resolved. The 1st theme is a fanfare of brass. It is written in f-sharp major and uses mode 2^1. The 1st period: antecedent, consequent (mode 2^1). The second period begins at figure 1. Figure 6 Development. Section 1 – 1st theme is in G major.

Section 2 11: 2nd theme "love-theme" is in F major, antecedent. Section 3—figure 14. 1st theme is in D major. Section 4. Figure 15. The 1st theme is in B major. Section 5, figure 20 uses Modes 2^1 and 2^2. Figure 24, return of the 1st theme in F-sharp major using mode 2. Figure 27 1st period, antecedent and consequent. At figure 29: the 2nd theme with the antecedent of the 2nd period of the "love-theme". At figure 33, large cascade of chords ascending and descending in the different sections of the orchestra. The Woodwind uses modes 2^1 and 2^3. The piano uses mode 3^1 and at the seventh bar of figure 33, the brass employs mode 6^2. At figure 34 the apotheosis of the "love-theme" is reminiscent of the "Jardin du sommeil d'amour". This is followed by the Coda.

Thus Messiaen brings this tumultuous Work to a conclusion. Every emotion has been explored from love, fear, expectancy and terror to ecstasy. We are left in no doubt that Tristan and Isolde have experienced love and death on a cosmic scale and that the literary sources of the *Tristan* myth have penetrated the very heart of the *Turangalîla* music. We have seen that other literary sources from Shakespeare to Edgar Allan Poe have inspired the work, Whilst the influence of Wagner and Debussy have always been present. Messiaen's *Turangalîla-Symphonie* is truly eclectic, borrowing not only from Western myth and musical styles but also from the exotic, the eastern through its rhythms, and Sanskrit for its title. Messiaen has taken Wagner's *Tristan und Isolde* and reinterpreted it by looking at the interior lives of the lovers, infusing and amalgamating his unique score with ideas derived from Debussy, Stravinsky, Mussorgsky, Berg and Verdi.

The Human Tragedy in *Turangalîla*

The more man knows about himself, his origins and his place in the universe, the more inclined he becomes to take a tragic view of life; and the twentieth century has brought a vast increase in that knowledge. Love, fear, expectancy, and terror are no substitutes for tragedy, but rather different facets of that tragic sense of life, which every increase in our knowledge seems to impose inexorably. The reason for this lies in the fact that while our knowledge increases yearly, our understanding of ourselves and our place in the universe diminishes. We are overwhelmed simultaneously by the inconceivable vastness of the universe and the contradictions and complexities of the individual personality. These complexities are reflected in the stark oppositions conveyed in *Turangalîla*.

The great tragic writers have been those most richly endowed with what used to be called common-sense—the instinctive belief that, in spite of all appearances to the contrary, life is, indeed must be, worth living.

Men themselves on the whole are more remarkable for the recurrent flashes of good in their character and behaviour than for their ludicrous limitations or their downright vices. One of the last great writers whose view of humanity was dominated by this untroubled sanity and common sense was Maeterlinck, who died in 1949. The very greatness of Dickens lies in the fact that he combined an overwhelming sense of life's ultimate goodness with a very clear awareness of the Schattenseite (shady side) of human existence.[22] By what can only be a coincidence, both the supreme tragic masterpieces of the twentieth century's repertory—*Debussy's Pelléas et Mélisande* and Messiaen's *Turangalîla-Symphonie*—are marked, however faintly, not by the veins of tragedy that recur in Shakespeare's tragedies but by the suspicion—it is no more—that human existence is in some sense itself an illusion. In *Turangalîla*, the final Transfiguration may well reflect the thought of the composer, but it scarcely overshadows the work. Far more serious, both in their placing and in their reflection on the character of Tristan and Isolde are the cyclic themes, and thereby hangs *Turangalîla*.

In 1946 Messiaen was looking for a subject which would provide him with the greatest possible contrast to the *Visions de l'Amen* and *Vingt Regards sur la' Enfant-Jesus* compositions on which he had been working. With the thoroughness and the inclination to philosophical generalisation that were characteristic of him, Messiaen very soon penetrated beneath the surface of the facts and events of Gottfried's *Tristan* to the ideas inherent in formulating and preserving the rules of his art. That he was

---

22 Dickens, Charles (1812-80) British novelist Son of a naval clerk, he worked in a blacking factory when his father was imprisoned for debt and later as a solicitor's clerk and court reporter. He began his writing career by contributing to popular magazines, achieving sudden fame with *The Pickwick Papers* (1837), which he followed with *Oliver Twist* (1838) and *Nicholas Nickleby* (1839) and the very successful *Old Curiosity Shop* (1840-41); like all his novels, these first appeared in monthly instalments. In the 1840s he travelled abroad, visiting America in 1842, and founded (1846) the liberal Daily News and two weekly miscellanies. *David Copperfield* (1849-50) was a strongly autobiographical work, portraying Dickens' father as the feckless Mr Micawber. His later novels from *Bleak House* (1853) to the incomplete *Edwin Drood* (1870), were increasingly pessimistic in tone; *Great Expectations* (1860-61) and *Our Mutual Friends* (1864-65) in their depiction of the destructive powers of money and ambition, develop most fully Dickens' radical view of society. Dickens' marriage was an unhappy one and in 1856 he and his wife agreed to separate. He formed a relationship with Ellen Ternan, a young actress. In 1858 he began his famous public readings from his work, the strain of which hastened his death. *The Macmillan Encyclopedia*, London and Basingstoke, 1981. 364.

fascinated by the poetic inventiveness and tragedy displayed by Wagner is shown by the titles with which he gave his *Turangalîla-Symphonie*. The fact that any academy of the arts must inevitably imply conservatism and may therefore eventually favour the pedant at the expense of the true artist is exemplified in the figure of Messiaen. At an early stage of any art, the formulation of rules is almost a necessity, but such rules may outlive their usefulness. They may eventually be applied not to promote the ait they were designed to serve, but to shackle its free development in new forms. It was a cardinal point in Messiaen's creed (as it had been earlier in Schoenberg's) that the opposition to his music came from the pedantry and conservatism of many listeners rather than from professional musicians. As Armfelt states:

> *Messiaen's music demands an extraordinary intensity of response; and each piece demands entire acceptance. It has the quality of a statement rather than an argument or question. It is a statement expressed emphatically and intensely. The critical listener is disturbed by this. He wants to question the validity of the statement; he regards music as an argument. But Messiaen's music seems not to allow this: it demands all or nothing. Indeed it seems to demand all. That is why it has often provoked such violent reactions. Many listeners, while admitting the expression to be forceful, have found it hard to cope with a music so extreme in its emotive demands.[23]*

The position of Tristan in Messiaen's *Turangalîla* was at first ambiguous. Tristan was the hero of a poem, *Tristan*, by the medieval poet Gottfried von Strassburg. Wagner's opera *Tristan und Isolde* was based on this work, which Wagner certainly knew without being tempted to plagiarism. The development of Tristan's character in Messiaen's mind seems to have taken place between the writing of *Harawi* and the completion of *Turangalîla* as it stands—that is to say, between 1945 and 1948. During this time, *Tristan* not only increased in importance but also changed in character. What was eventually to become a philosophical work concerned with illusion (Wahn) in human affairs was originally a lament derived from the *Tristan* myth and the writings of Béclard d'Harcourt.[24]

---

23 Armfelt, N., "Emotion in the Music of Messiaen", *The Musical Times*, November 1965. 856

24 Johnson, R.S., *Messiaen*, Dent, London, 1989. 79. Also see Goléa, A., *Rencontres avec Olivier Messiaen*, Julliard, 1960. 149 (Johnson, footnote 3, p.100)

In *Turangalîla* we have traces of this purely aesthetic concern in the lack of narrative, which comes strangely, in a sense, from the much more deeply troubled Piroutcha of the "Wahn" song cycle *Harawi*.

In no other composition of Messiaen's before *Turangalîla* are the musical worlds of the characters so clearly distinguished by rhythm and orchestral colours as well as by melodic and harmonic constraints. Most unmistakable are the four-square rhythms, fanfare-like melodies, and harmony of the lovers themselves. There are also the unmistakable dance and leaping rhythms and short plastic phrases of the surreal aspect of the stars and the universe. Both the scene and the era are evoked by Messiaen's use of a dramatic style cleverly suggesting, though never imitating, that of Richard Wagner. Of the four main cyclic themes, the first (the "statue theme") is used, as it were—simply as a dramatic property in the opening and subsequent movements. The "flower theme" is, by contrast, a historical reference, an art form chosen as the symbol of purity. In the "love theme" we have something approaching in music to the neo-medievalism of Wagner, with Rossetti and the pre-Raphaelite Brotherhood in the near distance. The romantic idealisation of the "thème d'accords" recalls the medievalism of the Romantic poets, such as Eichendorff, Arnim and Brentano.[25] It also recalls English sensibilities, the social utopianism of William Morris and John Ruskin. Morris and Ruskin would have relished the birdsong on the piano, the garden emanating from the lovers and the plants and new flowers.

In Tristan's symbolic exchanges with Isolde ("Jardin du sommeil d'amour"), Messiaen showed in its highest form his ability to create an illusion of dialogue. Its natural rhythms and phrase-shapes seem to spring like obbligato voices from the symphonic counterpoint in which the orchestra develops deeper ideas. Occasionally *Turangalîla* sounds a tragic note that is familiar from *Harawi* or Wagner's *Tristan und Isolde*, as

---

25 Eichendorff Josef, Freiherr von (1788-1857) German Romantic writer. He studied at Heidelberg and Berlin, where he became involved in the Romantic movement, and rose high in the Prussian civil service. His lyrical nature poems were set by many composers. His best-known novel is Memoirs of a Good-for-Nothing (1826). *The Macmillan Encyclopedia*, London and Basingstoke, 1981. 399. Brentano, Clemens (1778-1842) German writer, a member of the Heidelberg School of Romantic Writers. With Achim von Arnim he published the influential folksong collection, *Des Knaben Wunderhorn* (1805-08). Emotionally unstable in early life, he became a Roman Catholic in 1817, and for six years was a monk. *The Macmillan Encyclopedia*, London and Basingstoke, 1981. 184.

when the "statue theme" of the *"Turangalîla"* movements burst out.[26] His other movements, however, resemble nothing else in Wagner's own music. In them melody takes on a totally new and wholly convincing life. The "flower theme" suggests the saddest, as well as one of the most felicitously drawn of Messiaen's cyclic themes. Isolde is by no means simply the sad lover. At her first symbolic appearance, in the "Chant d'amour I", there is an implied spontaneous and unmistakable interest in Tristan which quite overrides the strict conventions of the day in matters concerning the relationship between the sexes. In fact, spontaneity is the strongest trait in the music. Indeed one feels that, had Tristan not appeared on the scene, Isolde might well have been content to many Mark. As it is, the tender, half-flirtatious nature of the relationship between Isolde and Tristan finds exquisite, yet always natural expression in the long, flowing lines and gently swaying rhythm of the "flower theme". When the same material recurs in "Chant d'amour II", Messiaen unites the "flower theme" with the "statute theme" and it does not imply the same old flirtatious note. For after the lovers' acknowledgement of their mutual love in the "Joie du sang des étoiles", Isolde symbolically loses all tentative timidity and becomes determined to transform her love. In the "Jardin du sommeil d'amour" there is a breathlessness in the music, long, rapturous phrases which clearly recall for a moment the world of Isolde. When Brangaene's warning cuts off their retreat, the lovers' ignore her completely. It is the orchestra which gives expression to what is really happening in the lovers' minds beneath the commonplace reality of the world. Once again it is to memories of *Tristan* that Messiaen turns, only a *Tristan* with the tragic overtones arising from the sense of guilt and betrayal.

Tristan, so alive in his relationship to his fellow Knights and his devotion to Mark, gives the impression of being very much the pursued rather than the pursuer in his relationship with Isolde. The maternal element in Isolde's love for him is in any case evident in Gottfried's original account; we only have to think of her healing his wounds and nursing him back to health. Messiaen's music with its strong character and rhythmical complexity suggests a healthy, open-hearted youth. The very complicated rhythmic patterns of the "Joie du sang des étoiles" has the character of a bright boy's boasting of his knowledge.

---

26 Johnson, R.S., *Messiaen*, Dent, London, 1989. 88

Messiaen's "Chant d'amour" music has all the mellow warmth and sense of generous ease that also characterises Isolde. But the self-questioning and philosophising of Isolde is quite outside Tristan's character. The florid variations in *"Turangalîla* III" not only contribute to the element of parody in the Work as a whole, but also add another sense of tragedy to the doomed lovers. Isolde is marked from the first by the protective, paternal tone of this music, though she at first gets more paternal discipline than paternal affection. In the mosaic of motives Woven into the variations in *"Turangalîla* III", Messiaen enables *the listener* to follow Tristan's thoughts as they range over the events of the past; the infinitely coloured tâlas sealing his conclusion in favour of death. It is an entirely different Tristan that symbolises the theme of human tragedy in the "Final" and it is impossible to find any valid argument against his existential melancholy. Certainly Tristan's discomfiture with the events of the *Tristan* myth are in themselves sufficient to cause such a mood. Once again *the listener* is soon to follow the course of his thoughts from the events of the preceding movement to the conclusion of the "Final". There remains Isolde, the character upon whom Messiaen concentrated a long accumulated store of admiration. In Isolde, as in Piroutcha (in *Harawi*), there appears no delight in hurting and humiliating the heroine; this was one of the most amiable traits in Messiaen's character. Isolde's fate is sealed and Messiaen steps outside the great tradition of tragedy and comes much closer to calamity. No great tragic writer must get involved with any of his characters; the great tragic writers are observers and not engaged in the arena. That is the difference between Messiaen's Isolde and Wagner's Isolde, and it is the difference between a woman compounded of his creator's aversions and a living, breathing human being. If the figure of Isolde is something of an anomaly in the tragedy, this is the only shadow on a score which many would regard as Messiaen's finest achievement.

Conclusion

One might say the legend is the symbol of all great loves and for all the great love poems in literature or in music, but to me, only the myth of m seemed worthy of attention; in no way did I wish to rework Wagner's *Tristan und Isolde* or Debussy's *Pelléas*, to mention only the two greatest "Tristans" in music.[27]

Messiaen stated this in conversation with Claude Samuel in 1964, but the symphony which eventually emerged was more than a "symbol of great love". It became one of the landmarks of cultural history and Messiaen explores all the conscious and unconscious aspects of love. By excluding all incidental episodes from the myth, Messiaen concentrates on the souls of the lovers, illuminating metaphysical as well as erotic aspects of love. This illumination comes from the unique style of his orchestral music, which evokes, powerfully as well as sensitively, every shade of emotion in the lovers, ranging from mockery pride and despair, to sublime ecstasy. Messiaen's musical inspiration, like Wagner and Debussy before him, reached its supreme peak, which he may have equalled in parts of later works, but never surpassed.

An examination of the contents of Gottfried's *Tristan* will show at once how Messiaen rejected the exhaustive details of the poem, which like Wagner before him, an historical poet is obliged to employ so as to clarify the outward developments of his plot, to the detriment of a lucid exposition of its inner motives, Messiaen trusted himself to the latter alone. Life and death, the whole meaning and existence of the outer world, here hang on nothing but the inner thoughts of Tristan and Isolde.

The opposition of the values of love and death offers a glimmer of orchestral possibility which would allow something to be shown as well as heard. *Turangalîla* enshrines symbolic confrontations between reason and instinct and between light and darkness. What Messiaen wanted was to interiorise Wagner's *Tristan*, and nothing suited him better than *Turangalîla* and the other two works in the *Tristan* trilogy.

It is incredible that Messiaen was able to infuse everything that he created with meaning. In Chapter Six We discussed issues pertaining to

---

[27] Samuel, C., *Olivier Messiaen* Music and Colour, trans, E. Thomas Glasgow, Amadeus Press, Portland, Oregon, 1994. 30.

the drama and in this chapter we have considered many, aspects of the meaning in the music. We have seen that the *Tristan* myth is used in many ways throughout *Turangalîla*; sometimes in harmony with the story (for example, at the first occurrence of the "Chant d'amour" movements), and sometimes in contradiction with the story (for example, through the lack of narrative). We have seen how quintessential the *Tristan* myth is to *Turangalîla*, so it is not surprising that the story tells us so much about the state of the lovers' souls, for example, the level of their absolution. This chapter has shown that a fascinating relationship exists between myth and music in Tristan and Isolde's respective roles in *Turangalîla*.

8

MESSIAEN'S TRISTAN TRILOGY PART 3 : *CINQ RECHANTS*

Cinq Rechants is the third and last section of Messiaen's *Tristan* trilogy and comprises five rechants or refrains for a group of mixed voices. The work, which finishes Messiaen's compositions on the topic of love as experienced by Tristan and Isolde, is relatively short, almost twenty minutes in duration, and therefore the briefest of the three compositions which make up the *Tristan* trilogy. According to Hall, the purpose of the initial work, *Harawi*, is to present the composer's new way of treating and examining the *Tristan* myth in music. The *Turangalîla-Symphonie* is the most far-reaching in its treatment of mythical and musical ideas, while the concluding *Cinq Rechants* brings to an end the entire *Tristan* trilogy. Employing a poem which is hard to understand and occasionally almost incomprehensible, *Cinq Rechants* unites broken words with musical structure and form in an integrated way. Language and disjointed ideas discover their place in the unified composition of Messiaen, who painstakingly mixes together music and ideas in his treatment of an original love tale.

The narrative in *Cinq Rechants*, and in the whole of the *Tristan* trilogy, basically differentiates Messiaen's from Wagner's attitude to the topic. Resembling Hellenistic drama, Wagner represents myths by means of human action. His individuals are governed by the rules of time and continuity, even though their deeds may have a non-earthly or immortal meaning. Messiaen, however, transports the *Tristan* myth from the actual world of individual feelings into a surrealistic world.[1] Words are dislocated fragments that the couplet-refrain structures cause to appear two or even three times, broken off abruptly while the second soprano is halfway through a syllable.

---

1 Johnson, R.S., *Messiaen*, London, Dent, 1979. 78

The form which the composer makes use of in *Cinq Rechants* relies on the form discovered in Claude le Jeune's couplet--refrain alternation in the group of songs entitled *Le Printemps*.² The characteristic quality of *Cinq Rechants* in the clearest of any of the three works which make up the *Tristan* trilogy, with sustained portions of unison composition followed by sections of up to five-part harmony. Occasionally the make-up of the songs extends to employ eight or even twelve part harmony which, because the composer specifically indicates a group of singers consisting of twelve voices, signifies that in a relatively small number of instances there will be a single voice to a section. Unspecified uttered voice effects, for example the sounds "tk tk" sung to make resonant sounds, are also present, and the composer's intricate rhythmic patterns are an omni-present feature.

However, the total result is one of shining beauty.

Allowing that the form and structure are clear, the text is not immediately obvious. The French syllables are generally in the common vocabulary, although the rules connecting words are frequently ignored and the style is one of immense disjunction. The language is of extreme mystery even to a listener who has understood much of the obscurity existing in the extraordinary and tormenting words of *Harawi*. In addition to the obscure quality of the French words, we meet the artificial text which the composer has created from Sanskrit words together with the improvised Sanskrit sounds, making words which are not accessible to the usual conventions of grammar. Certain meanings can be the topic of conjecture, but little certainty is possible. As Messiaen states,

> *"The syllables are chosen for their softness or their violence of attack, for their aptitude in stressing the musical rhythms. They enable the easy combination of the four orders: phonetic (timbres), dynamic (intensities), kinetic (accents) and quantitative (values)."*³

In this way, the difficulties of decoding Messiaen's intention in the poems which make up his text for *Cinq Rechants* is greater than any met in explaining the twelve movements of *Harawi* and infinitely more difficult than in comprehending the composer's plan for the *Turangalîla-Symphonie*.

---

2 Johnson, R.S., *Messiaen*, London, Dent, 1979. 95

3 Quoted in Johnson, R.S., *Messiaen* Dent, London, 1989. 94; See also p.100 footnote 17. "Messiaen's note on the work for the Philips recording (ABL 3400)".

Messiaen feels forced to turn to a secret language suitable for his inner reflections and emotions. Messiaen chooses his artificial Sanskrit language and he reawakens the dream-like effects which infused *Harawi*. Nevertheless, the text of *Cinq Rechants* on occasions goes further than irrational fantasies in its disjunction and moves towards Cubist art, which attempts to reduce natural forms to their fundamental geometric shape, through painting and verse.

The composer's indebtedness to the art and verse of Surrealism is already known and it is a debt which is plainly shown in this last work of the Tristan trilogy. It is apparent that the representation of Tristan and Isolde placed in a capsule in the crystal ball is derived from the canvas of the artist Hieronymus Bosch, who is the fifteenth-century painter most highly regarded by the Surrealists.[4] The other artist whose ideas reverberate through *Cinq Rechants* in the symbol of *Tristan* and Isolde moving through the air into the universe is Marc Chagall, not a strict Surrealist but one whose art, resembling that of the Surrealists, resides in the sphere of illusion and the fantasy world.[5] In the text of *Cinq Rechants* there is once more the brining together of opposites or even the idea of that which is not possible; such as page 19, which contains the conflicting representations of "octopus of light", injuring, crushing, becoming red and "my caress".[6]

At this point each idea strikes against the next without connection. Messiaen's regard for Andre Breton appears pertinent here and describes the words from *Cinq Rechants* quoted above with its extraordinary but striking phrases. From a linguistic point of view it seems that the most significant effect of all upon the composer's poems may be the writing of Pierre Reverdy, whose verse is also distinguished by the virtual absence of rational connections, whereas Reverdy, a solitary mystic, has frequently been referred to as a poet of Surrealism, his verse could fittingly be

---

[4] Piper, D., *Art and Artists*, Mitchell Beazley, London, 1981. 30 "Bosch's work took on a second life in the early 20th century, when it was seen as a precursor of Surrealism and suitable for Psychoanalysis."

[5] Gombrich, E.H., *The Story of Art, Phiaidon*, Oxford, 1987. 470 "Marc Chagall (1887-1985) did not allow his acquaintance with modern experiments to blot out his childhood memories. His paintings of village scenes and types, such as his musician who has become one with his instrument, succeed in preserving something of the zest and childlike wonder of real folk art."

[6] Messiaen, O., *Cinq Rechants*, Salabert, Paris, 1949. Movement III 19 "pieuvre de lumiere"; "ma caresse".

described as Cubist because of the way in which it is assembled, almost in the style of a collage or photomontage.[7]

Messiaen's *Harawi* consisted of a certain amount of disconnection, particularly in "L'escalier redit, gestes du soleil" in which "Of the water, of time, of the sky, the staircase of the sky" was unexpectedly slipped in elliptically and mysteriously.[8] Now in *Cinq Rechants* virtually each line of verse is, resembling Reverdy's poetry, portrayed by ellipsis and mystery.

The most important mythological ingredients for *Cinq Rechants* are again taken from the *Tristan* myth, and, as anticipated, stress is fixed on the idea of the "love-death". In *Cinq Rechants* Messiaen draws together both events and characters from the myth. Messiaen identifies Brangaene as the friend of Isolde, in the initial words of the first song. Brangaene is the person who had performed the task of the night guard of the alba or morning song in Wagner's *Tristan und Isolde*. Isolde in person becomes visible, here seemingly as in the *Turangalîla-Symphonie*, to be compared with the sorceress Vivian. Tristan is depicted as the rower of love in the fifth refrain; so we remember that it was Tristan who was responsible for transporting Isolde to Cornwall, where she was to be married to King Mark, and in the course of the journey they fell disastrously in love. There is, in addition, one more journey which Isolde submits herself to when she is conveyed to what the composer has described as Tristan's "wond'rous crystal castle" in Brittany.[9] As we may predict, the love potion is apparent, strangely changed to "philtres", which, "are drunk this night".[10]

Lastly there is the garden of flowers, which had been seen as a flowery bank in *Harawi* and had shaped the creative impulse for the whole of the "Jardin du sommeil d'amour" in the *Turangalîla-Symphonie*. Of most significance, however, is Messiaen's paring down of all accounts of the myth to an even smaller group of events, rendering his poetic interpretation more economical than the libretto of Wagner's *Tristan und Isolde*. Nevertheless each separate section of the myth which Messiaen selects

---

7 Balakian, A., *Surrealism: The Road to the Absolute*, Dutton, New York, 1970. 103

8 Messiaen, O., *Harawi*, Leduc, Paris, 1945. 73 Movement IX, "De l'eau, du temps, du ciel, l'escalier du ciel".

9 Messiaen, O., record jacket notes by Messiaen for *Cinq Rechants* (Musical Heritage Society, MHS 1 187)

10 Messiaen, O., *Cinq Rechants*, Salabert, Paris, 1949. 29 Movement III, "philtres sont bus ce soir".

is vitally important, because collectively these portions constitute the mythological core around which *Cinq Rechants* is built.

In *Cinq Rechants* we can see the relation to Wagner's *Tristan und Isolde*. We are fully prepared for the first appearance of Brangaene's warning from the tower to the lovers, for it is anticipated by a distinctive introduction which lasts for approximately forty-five seconds. When Messiaen's introduction starts we are aware that a significant event is imminent, for there are abrupt changes in the tonal centre, rhythmic momentum and dynamic level.

Tension is maintained throughout the introduction itself by the reduction of dynamic surge and repetition of leading phrases (for example, "la li la li la", bar 1). Eventually, we hear the warning, which sweeps up the octaves just descended by the introduction:

"*Les amoureux s'envolent*
Brangien dans l'espace tu souffle."
"*the lovers fly away Brangäne you breathe in space.*"

The essence of the myth of *Tristan* and Isolde, most applicable to *Cinq Rechants* is the lovers' concern only for each other and their heedlessness of Brangaene's warning of approaching dawn. In the third couplet, the effect is continued and increased by a long crescendo. Unfolding itself like a tonal rapier in a twelve-part canon it reaches a climactic collective scream, reminiscent of Wagner's unpitched vocal cries, before receding into a gentle supple and caressing coda. Examples of non-pitched vocal sound are found in all of Wagner's stage works from *Der fliegende Holländer* (1843) onwards.[11]

Whilst Messiaen in this work reduces the *Tristan* myth to its basic essentials, he also makes more of it through passing references and allusions to different mythical themes and literary people. Vivian has already been referred to by Messiaen in the third movement, p.21, but later in the context of the text of the fifth movement, p.37, her significance for his comprehension of existence, love and death is more completely revealed.[12] Vivian, named so by Tennyson in his *Idylls of the King* but called Nimue in Malory's *Morte d'Arthur*, acquired Merlin's magic by controlling

---

11 Freidheim, P., "Wagner and the Aesthetics of the Scream" *Nineteenth Century Music*. Volume VII, Number l, Summer 1983, 64

12 Messiaen, O., *Cinq Rechants*, Salabert, Paris, 1949. Movement III. 21 and 37

his love and, becoming herself a sorceress, directed the magic against her master, whom she places under a boulder. Vivian in this way becomes a part of the far-reaching pattern of symbols of enclosure and freedom, and she in addition may be connected in an unknown way with the mysterious powers possessed by Isolde, who has an almost supernatural capacity to heal.

Different mythical or literary figures who appear in the poetic figurative language of *Cinq Rechants* are derived from origins which are more distant. One is the early Greek traveller *Orpheus* who "finds his heart in death", whereas another is Perseus, who kills the feared Medusa.[13] One more is the scoundrel Bluebeard, Whose final bride in Maeterlinck's play, flees from the confinement of her husband's fortified mansion.[14] Maeterlinck's drama may have been known to Messiaen through Dukas' opera *Ardiane et Barbe Bleue*, in which the heroine's name holds a slight suggestion of that Ariadne who explained the puzzle of the Minotaur's maze, thereby rescuing her lover, Theseus, who then left her. To this extent the representations of love, death, imprisonment and freedom are all reinforced by these allusions.

In addition, it can be observed that the poems of *Cinq Rechants* consist of more symbols which are not easily identifiable in connection to origin or subject. There are, for instance, the "four lizards".[15] These reptiles, may involve a passing reference to the Hieronymus Bosch painting Earthly Paradise, which depicts a group of lizards near the centre. Next there is the strange "octopus of light" or the "octopus with the golden tentacles".[16]

Even this could perhaps be inspired by the identical picture by Bosch, who has depicted a curious vegetable-like structure with bony tentacles. The mollusc-like animal in the picture is drawing a number of lovers into its mouth.

Resembling *Harawi* and the *Turangalîla-Symphonie*, *Cinq Rechants* contains Messiaen's preoccupation with the recurrent idea of Time. Possibly

---

13 Messiaen, O., *Cinq Rechants*, Salabert, Paris, 1949. 2-3, Movement I "L'explorateur Orphée trouve son coeur dans la mort".

14 Maeterlinck, M., *Sister Beatrice and Ardiane and Barbe Bleue*, trans. Miall, B, George Allen and Sons, London, Mcmviii. 183-186

15 Messiaen, O., *Cinq Rechants*, Salabert, Paris, 1949. 10, Movement II, "quatre lézards".

16 Messiaen, O., *Cinq Rechants*, Salabert, Paris, 1949. Movement III, "pieuvre de lumière" p.19; Movement V, "pieuvre aux tenfacules d'or", 38

even more emphasis is placed on the idea that time can be surpassed. For *Tristan* and Isolde, time is outside the material universe and yet is attainable to them in all of its forms—bygone, existing and future. As the text of the fifth movement, ignoring the rules of syntax, states, "your eyes voyage into the past".[17]

Although *Cinq Rechants* can be seen as travelling towards and then away from the sensual completion of its third rechant, its mood is more that of ritual prayer, possibly a liturgy of desire. The five rechants, the *Turangalîla* love-song in E major, and the ultimate prayer all come to repose on an unadorned tritone.

In this way, expectations, fears and hopes are exposed in words and sound.

In this concluding work of the *Tristan* trilogy even more diffuse than the idea of Time is the notion of Space and the Universe, since the initial words of the first poem are, "the lovers fly away, Brangaene you breathe in space".[18] Tristan and Isolde moving through the air into space denotes that their love is so expansive that it extends beyond the limits of the World. Different representations of Space Within the Words of *Cinq Rechants* comprise of enclosure for example, "my prison of love", "circle of day(light)", "castle", "the grotto", and, possibly most important of all, the crystal capsule in which the lovers are shut in Hieronymus Bosch's painting Earthly Paradise.[19]

The areas of enclosure are skilfully counterpoised against representations of expansion; in this way implying that although there is a restricting element to love, its expansive powers also exist.

The composer's apparently self-contradictory insistence on the representations of freedom and openness, and simultaneously of confined spaces, concealment and possibly claustrophobia, influences all five texts of *Cinq Rechants* to an unexpected degree. In the initial movement, Tristan and Isolde take off into space, as explained above; also mentioned is

---

17 Messiaen, O., *Cinq Rechants*, Salabert, Paris, 1949, Movement V. 36, "tes yeux voyagent dans le passé"

18 Messiaen, O., *Cinq Rechants*, Salabert, Paris, 1949. Movement I, 1 "les amoureux s'envolent Brangien dans l'espace tu souffles". Also see Johnson, R.S., Messiaen, Dent, London, 1989. 95

19 Messiaen, O., *Cinq Rechants*, Salabert, Paris, 1949. Movement III, "ma prison d'amour". p15; Movement V, "cerele du jour" p.46; Movement I, "chateau" p.3 and Movement V, "grotte" p.43

Bluebeard's seventh door, which involves some danger in opening, but some compensations as well. In the second movement, the fan is not only closed but also opened and is therefore a reminder of the musical "fan" from *Turangalîla* with its connections with fear taken from 'Edgar Allen Poe's *The Pit and the Pendulum*.[20] The third movement portrays not only a prison of desire, but also a new extensive landscape. In the text of the fourth movement, the bunch of flowers is untied, released from confinement, set free but there are pink Wooden shutters for windows depicted which can enclose. In the final movement of *Cinq Rechants*, stretched out arms, a representation of freedom, are placed next to the closed garden.

The two opposed characteristics of the representations of "open" and "closed" as used in *Cinq Rechants* are given very perceptive treatment by Messiaen. His phenomenological work initially discusses the quality of being open and the emotion of high elation and hugeness that is often characteristic of the poetic experience. The enlargement of love for the composer brings a state of being free earlier attained only in a portion of "Katchikatchi les étoiles", of *Harawi* and in "Joie du sang des étoiles" and "Final" of the *Turangalîla-Symphonie*. There are still parts which cause distress in *Cinq Rechants*, but these are subjugated to the security of enclosure and even beyond that, to the release of moving through the air into space.

The musical ides with which the composer chooses to enfold his mythological poems again has many origins. Messiaen might well be influenced by the basic pattern of the Middle Ages rondeau with its recurrent refrain. Nevertheless, it should be apparent that Messiaen's form is nearer to the couplet-refrain form of Claude le Jeune than to the numerous rondeaux of the Middle Ages.

Messiaen does recognise some effect from Middle Ages song. In particular, he cites the love songs of Jaufré Rudel and a dawn song by the medieval wandering composer of love poems and songs Folquet de Marseilles. In spite of the fact that Messiaen does not speak of the most well-known morning song, Guiraut de Bornelh's *Reis glorios*, it seems apparent that opinions and feelings made known in the words of that song give us an understanding of Messiaen's complete *Tristan* trilogy.[21]

---

20 Johnson, R.S., *Messiaen*, Dent, London, 1989. 92
21 Gennrich, F., (ed) *Troubadours, Trouvéres, Minnesang and Meistersang*, Arno Vulk, Cologne, 1960. 14

In *Reis glorios*, the medieval composer starts with a devout greeting to the Lord, but quickly begins his prayers for and his anxieties about the fellow-traveller who has been paying attention to a lady (probably another Knight's wife) before the night descended. Folquet de Marseilles's *Vers Dieu* consists of some similar religious outcries, but directed to the Virgin Mary. This song appears to be an entirely spiritual one, because it worships God and the Blessed Virgin, not at any time speaking of any sexual love. Nevertheless, the general characteristics of Folquet de Marseilles's song is similar to that of secular medieval composers' song. It is apparent that the boundary between the genuinely devout song and the erotic song is a very narrow one. There is no uncertainty about the intention behind Jaufré Rudel's love song, *Languan li jorn son lonc en may*. In this poem, Rudel candidly concedes that the poet desires his far away love.[22] This song speaks of the woman's own room and her garden; in this way we perceive once again how widespread are the metaphors of enclosure, especially of the garden, in poems of the Middle Ages. We also understand how Messiaen is indeed indebted to the medieval narrative poetic tradition, for his own reshaping of the *Tristan* myth depends upon the corresponding categories of observation and representation that were explored by the French poets of the Middle Ages.

Musical similarities between medieval composers of love songs and Messiaen's melodic technique would be more difficult to establish, because Messiaen's melodies so frequently make use of dissonant intervals, for example, the tritone and often have a larger scope than the melodies of the Middle Ages with their comfortable voice range. Possibly an unerring rhythmic or melodic pliability discovered in certain linear parts of the chants may be connected to the rhythms and melodies discovered in more unrestrained arrangements of medieval song. In addition, each individual phrase of the medieval composer's song is fixed skilfully to the next much as one portion of a jigsaw puzzle fits into the space adjoining another; accordingly Messiaen's additive technique of connecting phrases to each other appears in agreement with the troubadour's equally cumulative and additive procedures.

Robert Sherlaw Johnson contends that the Peruvian "yaravi" or "*harawi*", which Messiaen drew upon for his initial *Tristan* trilogy composition *Harawi*, supplies one of the starting points for his melodic

---

22 Wilhelm, I., (trans. and ed.) *Seven Troubadours*, University Park, Pennsylvania State University Press, 1970. 90-91

inspiration in *Cinq Rechants*.²³ Unlike the straightforward manner in which the ancient South American tunes were adopted for *Harawi* with actual melodies being made use of and changed by Messiaen, there is no such obvious borrowing in *Cinq Rechants*. No direct connection between Peruvian melody and *Cinq Rechants* may be established, in comparison with *Harawi*, which consists of definite Peruvian tunes that have been filtered through the prism of Messiaen's musical techniques. However, what *Harawi* and *Cinq Rechants* do share, as well as the mythical central core of the *Tristan* myth, is Messiaen's musical techniques, which makes use of the rising and descending tritone; intervals outside the diatonic scale; far-reaching dissonant leaps and added and non-retrogradable rhythms.

In *Cinq Rechants*, Messiaen sets out to merge together poetry, music and myth. Its component parts, like that of *Harawi*, certainly rely on the interplay of music and text. The five rechants add new aspects to our comprehension of the interaction of music and myth. The first rechant starts with the freedom of space, the confinement of claustrophobia, disunion and death; however, in spite of the three darker subjects, there seems to be no actual sensation of tragedy cast by the initial rechant. The theme of being free is repeated near the end of the poem and accordingly seems to establish the predominant mood of the piece. Whatever threatening and evil elements are present, these appear to be neatly counterpoised by more joyful ideas.

The balance of freedom and enclosure becomes visible once again in the second rechant, represented by the fan being opened and closed. Shadow and laughter are both present, while the solo flue sound is placed next to the cold-blooded lizards. In the third rechant, the magic potion with its connection with love and death is the guiding factor and there is also the repetition of entrapment or even dread of confined spaces in the second allusion to the Bosch painting: "My prison of love made of light air".²⁴ The mysterious reference to the octopus is discovered in this rechant. The fourth rechant also balances open-closed metaphors and light-dark imagery.

The last rechant combines all the threads of flower melody, octopus, lizard, enclosure—freedom and love-death. Medusa, the terrible

---

23 Johnson, R.S., *Messiaen*, Dent, London, 1989. 95

24 Messiaen, O., *Cinq Rechants*, Salabert, Paris, 1949. Movement III, 15, "ma prison d'amour faite d'air léger".

feminine figure whose snake-covered head was cut off by Perseus is introduced into the couplet of the rechant. Once more we are reminded of "L'amour de Piroutcha" and "Katchikatchi les étoiles" in *Harawi* and the agonized cry "Cut off my head!".[25] The terror is now removed and all the frightening images of the previous compositions in the *Tristan* trilogy as well as *Cinq Rechants* are laid to rest.

It has been useful to examine the way in which Messiaen treated the subject matter in *Cinq Rechants* and interpreted fundamental aspects of the *Tristan* myth. Chapter Eight has shown how the origins of the myth have been developed through the ideas of troubadour song, surrealism and open/closed metaphors. This chapter has looked at the way in which Messiaen changed the emphasis of the myth through a representational reinterpretation which avoids conventional narrative, yet relies heavily on vocal effects, conflicting representations, mythical literary figures and lack of chronology.

---

25 Messiaen, O., *Harawi*, Leduc, Paris, 1945. 30. Movement V, "L'amour de Piroutcha", "Coupe-moi la tête".

9

Conclusion

Gottfried von Strassburg lived in an age when story-telling was a competitive art. In her book on Gottfried, Goldschmidt Kunzer makes us aware of Gottfried's talent in this art. He kept the audience's attention with cliff-hangers, he showed the expected respect for his original sources, and he fought the constant battle of keeping his listener's goodwill. As Goldschmidt Kunzer states,

> "By holding all the conflicting elements within the epic—good and evil, weakness and strength, bravery and cowardice, friendship and treachery, passion and deceit, religious terms and classical metaphors—in a state of ironic balance, the author, through his narrative, creates a unified though many-faceted structure, based on a consistent point of view."[1]

Messiaen also lived in an age of competitive art, but that is where the similarity ends. Messiaen did not remain true to his original source, as illustrated in Chapters Six, Seven and Eight. The *Tristan* trilogy's intensity is enough to keep the audience's attention, without the aid of cliff-hangers, and it seems that Messiaen was little concerned about causing offence to those who follow Gottfried's philosophy.

However, Messiaen's imagination was awakened by Gottfried's tale. He saw in it the beginnings of something powerful, and meditated upon it at considerable length. The years between his first reading of *Tristan* and his completion of the *Tristan* trilogy are full of significant events, and the gradual evolution of his philosophy. We have discussed a few philosophical issues in Chapter Five; for example, the influence of Schopenhauer and Buddhism, and Messiaen's stance towards Christianity. The integration of music and poetry was also an important philosophical development of Messiaen's during this time period; in Chapter Six

---

1 Goldschmidt Kunzer, R., *The Tristan of Gottfried von Strassburg An Ironic Perspective*, University of California Press, Berkeley, Los Angeles, London, 1973. 197

we briefly considered the interaction of Piroutcha With the drama of *Tristan*.

Messiaen's Piroutcha is a complex character. The amount of meaning she embodies is far-reaching. As an object of the youth's desire she contains the pagan/Christian conflict which has lived and grown for two millennia. She holds the whispered associations with female sexuality which have existed for many millennia. As the dark-eyed heathen, she encapsulates the threat to a pure race, which had been perceived as a real social problem in Wagner's time.

We have previously drawn attention to the remarkable frequency with which operas and music-dramas treat profoundly theological themes.[2] In some cases, such works simply reflect contemporary theological thinking; but in others, especially in the case of works Written by composers, such as Debussy, who stand on the periphery or even outside a particular faith tradition, they can become a medium for novel theological exploration.

In addressing Messiaen's *Tristan* myth from a literary perspective, we should note the composer's own religious sensibilities. His early music included many religious works: these were obviously intended for church performance. He was certainly a conventional believer. Some of his views and attitudes to belief may be inferred from his *Turangalîla-Symphonie*, a huge and powerful work designed for the concert hall rather than for liturgical use. This work portrays the nation's faith not on a religious basis but on a moral one which calls God to Witness.

Essentially a Christian, he appears to have kept such understandings of God as he had deliberately specific and defined, whilst yet being prepared to elaborate imaginatively upon them when his artistic conscience prompted him to do so.

It is nevertheless noteworthy that many overtly theological themes course through the pages of Messiaen's *Tristan* trilogy. Those which we have seen emerging consistently centre upon two foci: sin, guilt and expiation, and death and resurrection.

Sin, guilt and transcendence form an obvious part of the plot of *Harawi* We have also detected intimations of a theme which will grow in importance in the latter *Tristan* trilogy works: that of death and resurrection. As Piroutcha faces the eternal finality of death in "Dans le noir" there is a crescendo in the piano, and the song cycle looks set to end on

---

2 Green, J., "Vast, unfathomable, proud": some theological thoughts on the creator God and opera", *Theology*, vol. XCIX (1996), p.194

a note of doom and despair amid Piroutcha's shattered hopes. However, from the depths of hopelessness there wells up a blaze of hope. Love, it appears, can triumph over all adversity and bring good out of evil. Death is not a hopeless end: it can be transcended.

Some of Messiaen's works from *Livre du Saint Sacrement* (1984) onwards carry the process of subverting chord-complexes to their full conclusion, by ultimately defying any line and largely avoiding the predominating texture. "Les ténèbres" eschews obvious individual pitches almost completely, and the chords are less dependent on them than earlier works. This does not disprove the relevance of individual notes in chords in earlier works; it merely reflects that some of the late compositions explore a very different idiom—particularly with the lack of voice-leading. When chord-complexes are clearly present, as in *Livre du Saint Sacrement*, one only experiences a succession of varying sound textures. Sometimes other technical devices are involved, such as complex monody. A line consisting of continually changing coloration remains: the last of all Messiaen's organ works, the *Livre du Saint Sacrement* begins and ends with worship, reaching a climactic point in the fifteenth movement "La joie de la grace", after fourteen of its total of eighteen movements.

To examine those aspects of Messiaen's late style properly would require another thesis. But the idea can be summarised briefly by stating that Messiaen, continuing his constant progression away from the musically obvious, occasionally moved away from any expectations that might be involved in following the process of not subverting chord-complexes to their full conclusion—avoiding the expected modification of timbre just as his earlier compositions develop by forestalling the sound of the resonance notes. When chord-complexes are partly present, as in *"Adoro te"* and *"La Source de Vie"*, they could simply set in motion musical relationships that can then be prolonged and expanded in different ways.

It can be added that if Messiaen was not aware of subverting chord-complexes to their full conclusion, the unconscious perception accountable first of all for developing them with such exact logic would later have had to avoid completely, and still unconsciously, the possibility of such occurrences in a certain number of the late compositions. This would make a fascinating topic for further study.

Bibliography

Abbate, C.	*Analyzing Opera: Verdi and Wagner*, University of California, 1989.
Abbate, C.	*Unsung Voices: Operatic Musical Narrative in the Nineteenth Century*, Princeton University Press, 1991.
Abravanel, C.	*Claude Debussy: A Bibliography*, Detroit Studies in Music, Bibliography 29, Detroit: Information Coordinators, 1974.
Adam, J.	*Mes premières ames littéraires et politique*, Girod, Paris, 1904.
Adorno, T.	*Versuch über Wagner*, 1952, Trans. R. Livingstone, *In search of Wagner*, NLB, London, 1981.
Aiken, H.D.	*The Age of Ideology*, The New American Library, New York, 1962.
Apollinaire, Guillaume	*Apollinaire on Art: Essays and Reviews* 1902-1918, Trans. Susan Suleiman, Ed. Leroy C. Breunig, Viking Press, New York, 1972.
Apollinaire, Guillaume	*Ouevres complètes*, 4.vols., Ed. Michel Décaudin, Balland and Lecat, Paris, 1965-66.
Auric, Georges	*Quand j'étais là*, B. Grasset, Paris, 1979.
Barth, H., Mack, D., and Voss, E.,	*Wagner: a Documentary Study*, Thames and Hudson, London, 1975.
Baudelaire, Charles	*Baudelaire as a Literary Critic*, Trans. and Ed. Lois Boe Hyslop and Francis E. Hyslop, University Park: Pennsylvania State University Press, 1964.
Baudelaire, Charles	*Correspondance générale*, 4 vols., Paris, 1947-48.

Baudelaire, Charles	"Les fleurs du mal", Paris, 1968, in *Baudelaire: Selected Poems*, Harmondsworth, Penguin, London, 1980.
Beckett, Lucy	*Richard Wagner: Parsifal*, Cambridge University Press, Cambridge, 1981.
Bédier, J.	*Le Roman de Tristan et Iseult*, Paris, 1918, The Romance of Tristan and Iseult, translated by Hillaire Belloc and Paul Rosenfeld, Garden City, N.Y., 1956; reprinted New York, n.d.
Bekker, Paul	*Neue Musik*, E. Reiss, Berlin, 1920.
Berlioz, Hector	*Mémoires*, Trans. and Ed. David Cairns, Knopf, New York, 1969.
Berlioz, Hector	*Mémoires*, 2 vols, Ed. Pierre Citron, Girod, Paris, 1969.
Berne	*Folie Tristan*, Ed. Joseph Bédier, *Les deux poèms de la folie Tristan. Société des anciens textes français*, No.LIV, Paris, 1907.
Berne	*Folie Tristan de Berne*, Ed. Ernest Hoepffner, 2nd ed., Paris, 1949.
Béroul	*Le Roman de Tristan par Béroul*, Ed. E. Muret, Société des anciens textes français, No.LI1, Paris, 1903.
Béroul	Les classiques français du moyen âge, revised by L.M. Defourkes, Paris, 1947.
Béroul	*The Romance of Tristan by Béroul*, Ed. A. Ewert, Oxford, 1953.
Billy, André	*L'époque contemporain*, Tallandier, Paris, 1956.

Black, M.	"The Literary Background" in *The Wagner Companion*, Eds. P. Burbridge and R. Sutton, New York, 1979.
Boulez, P.	*Notes of an Apprenticeship*, Ed. and Trans. H. Weinstock, New York, 1968.
Boulez, P.	*Boulez on Music Today*, Trans. Susan Bradshaw and Richard Rodney Bennett, Faber, London, 1971.
Boretz, Benjamin and Edward T. Cone, Eds.	*Perspectives on Schoenberg and Stravinsky*, Norton, New York, 1972.
Brereton, G.	*An Introduction to the French Poets*, 2nd ed., Methuen, London, 1973.
Bromwich, R.	*Trioedd Ynys Prydein - The Welsh Triads in Arthurian Literature in the Middle Ages*, Ed. R.S. Loomis, Oxford University Press, London, 1959.
Campbell, S.L.	*The Second Empire Revisited*, New Brunswick, N.J., 1978.
Carney, J.P.	*Studies in Irish Literature and History*, University of Dublin, 1955.
Chalupl, René	*Ravel au miroir de ses lettres*, R. Laffont, Paris, 1956.
Champfleury	*Grandes figures d'hier et d'aujourd'hui: Balzac. Gérard de Nerval, Wagner, Courbet*, Paris, 1861.
Champfleury	*Richard Wagner*, Paris, 1860.
Clark, T.J.	*Gustave Courbet and the 2nd French Republic 1848-1851*, Greenwich, Conn., 1973.
Claudin, G.	*Mes Souvenirs: Les boulevards de 1840-1870*, Paris, 1884.

Cocteau, Jean	*Cocteau's World*, Trans. and Ed. Margaret Crosland, Dodd Mead, New York, 1972.
Cocteau, Jean	*Oeuvres complètes de Jean Cocteau*, 11 vols., Marguerat, Geneva, 1950.
Collaer, Paul	*A History of Modern Music*, Grosset and Dunlap, New York, 1991.
Cooper, Martin	*French Music from the Death of Berlioz to the Death of Fauré*, Oxford University Press, London, 1961.
Cooper, Martin	*French Music*, Oxford University Press, London, 1974.
Cortot, A.	*La musique française de piano*, 2nd ed., Leduc, Paris, 1948.
Dansette, A.	*Le Boulangisme, 1886-1890*, Paris, 1938.
Debussy, Claude	*Debussy on Music*, Trans. and Ed. Richard Langham Smith, Intro. and Coll. François Lesure, Knopf, New York, 1977.
Debussy, Claude	*Lettres de Claude Debussy à son editeur*, Durand, Paris, 1927.
Debussy, Claude	*Lettres inédités à André Caplet*, Editions du Rocher, Pans, 1957.
Decaux, A.	*Offenbach: Roi du Second Empire*, Durand, Paris, 1958.
Demuth, Norman	*Ravel*, Dent, London, 1947.
Dietschy, M.	*La passion de Claude Debussy*, Neuchâtel: La Baconnière, 1962.
Digeon, Claude	*La crise allemande de la pensée française*, Presses universitaires de France, Paris, 1959.

Donington, R.	*Wagner's Ring and its Symbols*, Faber, London, 1974.
Drumont, E.	*Richard Wagner jugé en France*, Paris, 1887.
Duranty, E.	*Caractéristique des oeuvres de M. Champfleury*, Paris, 1859.
Duval, E.	*Téodor de Wyzewa: Critic without a Country*, Geneva, 1961.
Eisner, S.	*The Tristan Legend. A Study in Sources*, Illinois University Press, 1969.
Ferrante, J.M.	*The Conflict of Love and Honor. The Medieval Tristan Legend in France, Germany and Italy*, Mouton, Paris, 1973.
Field, G.C.	*Evangelist of Race: The Germanic Vision of Houston. Stewart, Chamberlain*, New York, 1981.
Fiorentino, P.A.	*Comédies et comédiens: Feuilletons*, 2 vols., Paris, 1866.
Flaubert, G.	*Madame Bovary*, Paris, 1936, Penguin, Harmondsworth, Middlesex 1987.
Gasperini, A.	*La nouvelle allemagne musicale: Richard Wagner*, Paris, 1866.
Georges-Michel, Michel	Les peintres que j'ai connus, A. Fayard, Paris, 1954.
Gilman, L.	*Debussy's "Pelléas et Mélisande": A Guide to the Opera*, Schirmer, New York, 1907.
Goléa, A.	*Rencontres avec Olivier Messiaen*, Julliard, Paris, 1960.

Gorce, Pierre de la	*Histoire du Second Empire*, 7 vols., Girod, Paris, 1894-1905.
Gregor Dellin, M.	*Richard Wagner*, London, 1983.
Griffiths, P.	*A Concise History of Avant-Garde Music from Debussy to Boulez*, Oxford University Press, New York, 1978.
Gut, S.	*Le Groupe Jeune France*, Ventadour, Paris, 1977.
Halbreich, H.	*Olivier Messiaen*, Fayard/SACEM, Paris, 1980.
Hamlyn, R.	*Schopenhauer*, Macmillan, London, 1989.
Happold, F.C.	*Religious Faith and Twentieth-Century Man*, Penguin, Middlesex, 1986.
Happold, F.C.	*Mysticism, A Study and An Anthology*, Penguin, Middlesex, 1983.
Hatto, S.T.	*Gottfried von Strassburg*, Penguin, Middlesex, 1980.
Hegermann-Lindencrone, Lille de	*In the Courts of Memory 1858-1875*, Schirmer, New York, 1912.
Hoepffner, E.	*The Breton Lais in Arthurian Literature in the Middle Ages*, Ed. R.S. Loomis, Oxford University Press, London, 1959.
Hoepffner, E.	*Les Lais de Marie de France*, Mouton, Paris, 1955.
Hodier, A.	*Since Debussy*, Trans. Burch, N., New York, 1975.
Holloway, Robin	*Debussy and Wagner*, Eulenburg, London, 1979.
Huysmans, Joris-Karl	*Oeuvres complètes*, 18 vols., G. Crès et Cie., Paris, 1926.
d'Indy, Vincent	*La Schola Cantorum en 1925*, Blond and Gay, Paris, 1927.

Jackson, K.H.	*Language and History in Early Britain*, Edinburgh University Press, Edinburgh, 1953.
Jackson, K.H.	*The Arthur of History in Arthurian Literature in the Middle Ages*, Ed. R.S. Loomis, Oxford University Press, London, 1959.
Jackson, W.T.H.	*Gottfried von Strassburg in Arthurian Literature in the Middle Ages*, Ed. RS. Loomis, Oxford University Press, London, 1959.
Jacobs, R.L.	*Three Wagner Essays* (trans), Eulenburg, London, 1979.
Jarocinski, S.	*Debussy: Impressionism and Symbolism*, translated from the French by Rollo Myers, Eulenburg Books, London, 1976.
Johnson, R.S.	*Messiaen*, Dent, London, 1989.
Jullien, A.	*Richard Wagner: Sa vie et ses oeuvres*, Durand, Paris, 1886.
Kapp, J. (Ed.)	*Richard Wagner an Mathilde und Otto Wesendonck: Tagebuchblältter und Briefe*, Leipzig, 1915.
Kellet, E.F.	*A Short History of Religions*, Penguin, Middlesex 1982.
Kerman, J.	*Opera as Drama*, California University Press, New York, 1956.
Kerman, J.	*Opera as Drama (Opera as Symphonic Poem)*, Faber, London, 1990.
Kloss, E. (Ed.)	*Briefwechsel zwischen Wagner und Liszt*, 2 vols., Leipzig, 1910.

Kohler, J.	*Nietzsche on Wagner: Lessons in Subjugation*, Yale University Press, 1998.
Lalo, Charles	*Esquisse d'une esthétique musicale scientifique*, F. Alcan, Paris, 1908.
Larousse, P.	Grand dictionnaire universel du XIX siècle, 15 vols., Paris, 1866-1876.
Leroy, M.	*Les prémieres amis français de Wagner*, Durand, Paris, 1925.
Lesure, François	"Debussy et le XVIe siècle", *Hans Albrecht in Memoriam*, Ed. W. Prennecke and M. Masse, Kassel: Bärenreiter, 1962.
Levin, D.	*R. Wagner, Fritz Lang and the Nibelungen*, Princeton University Press, 1998.
Little, Roger	*Guillaume Apollinaire*, Athlone Press, London, 1976.
Lockspeiser, Edward	*Debussy et Edgar Poe*, Editions du Rocher, Monaco 1961.
Lockspeiser, Edward	*Debussy, his Life and Mind*, Vol. 1 (1962), Vol.2 (1965), Cassel, London; Macmillan, New York, 1987.
Lockspeiser, Edward	*Debussy*, J.M. Dent, London, 1980.
Loomis, R.S., Ed.	*Arthurian Literature in the Middle Ages*, Oxford University Press, London, 1959.
Loomis, R.S., Ed.	*A Bibliography of Tristan Scholarship after 1911*, appended to 2nd edition of G. Schoepperle's *Tristan and Isolt*, New York University Press, New York, 1959.

Loomis, R.S., Ed.	*Problems of the Tristan Legend*, Romania, LIII, 1927.
Mach, G.	*Gustave Courbet*, Schirmer, New York, 1951.
Machlis, J.	*Introduction to Contemporary Music*, 2nd ed., New York, 1979.
Mahler, Alma	*And the Bridge is Love*, in collaboration with E.B. Ashton, Harcourt, Brace, New York, 1958.
Mahler, Alma	*Gustav Mahler. Memories and Letters*, Viking Press, New York, 1969.
Mallarmé, Stephane	*Stephane Mallarmé: Selected Prose. Poems, Essays and Letters*, Trans. and Ed. Bradford Cook, John Hopkins Press, Baltimore, 1956.
Mallory, Thomas	*Le Morte d'Arthur*, Intro. by J. Rhys, Everyman's Library Nos. 45 and 46, 2 vols., New York and London, 1906; reprinted 1941.
Mari, P.	*Olivier Messiaen: l'Homme et son Oeuvre*, Seghers, Paris, 1965.
Marie de France	*Le Chèvrefeuil*, Ed. Ernest Hoepffner, *Lais*, Strasbourg, 1921.
Marie de France	*Le Chèvrefeuil*, Ed. Karl Warnke, *Die Lais der Marie de France*, 3rd ed., Halle, 1925, pp. 181-85.
Marie de France	*Le Chèvrefeuil*, Ed. A. Ewert, *Lais*, Oxford, 1944, pp. 123-26.
Mascaro, J.	*The Upanishads*, Penguin, London, 1987.
Maudais, Camille	*L'art independent français*, La Renaissance du livre, Paris, 1919.
Maynial, E.	*L'époque réaliste*, Durand, Paris, 1931.

McClatchie, S.	*Analyzing Wagner's Operas. Alfred Lorenz and German Nationalist Ideology*, Rochester University Press, 1998.
Messiaen, Olivier	*Lecture in Brussels (Conférence de Bruxelles)*, a lecture on aspects of rhythm and nature in music, Leduc, Paris, 1958.
Messiaen, Olivier	*Technique de mon langage musical*, Vol.1, Alphonse Leduc et Cie., Paris, 1942.
Messiaen, Olivier	*Technique de mon langage musical*, Vol.2, Leduc, Paris, 1944.
Messiaen, Olivier	*Traité de Rythme. de Couleur. et d'Ornithologie*, Torne I, Leduc, Paris, 1994.
Messiaen, Olivier	*Traité de Rythme. de Couleur. et d'Ornithologie*, Tome II, Leduc, Paris, 1995.
Messiaen, Olivier	*Traité de Rythme. de Couleur. et d'Ornithologie*, Tome III, Leduc, Paris, 1996.
Messiaen, Olivier	*Traité de Rythme. de Couleur, et d'Ornithologie*, Tome IV, Leduc, Paris, 1997.
Millington, B.	*Wagner (The Master Musicians)*, Dent, London, 1984.
Millington, B.	*The Wagner Compendium*, Dent, London, 1992.
Millington, B.	*Richard Wagner, Dent, London, 1992.*
Mitchell, Allan	*The German Influence in France after 1870. The Formation of the Third Republic*, Chapel Hill: University of North Carolina Press, 1979.

Moréas, Jean	*Cent soixante-treize lettres de Jean Moréas à Raymond de la Tailhede et à divers corresponddants*, Ed. Robert A Jouanny, Paris : Lettres modernes, 1968.
Muller and Wapnewski (Trans. Deathridge)	*Tristan: The Wagner Handbook*, Harvard, 1992.
Myers, Rollo	*Modern Music*, Dutton, New York, 1923.
Myers, Rollo	*Modern French Music from Fauré to Boulez*, Praeger, New York, 1971.
Nerval, Gérard de	*Lorely: Souvenirs d'Allemagne*, Girod, Paris, 1852.
Newman, E.	*Life of Richard Wagner 1859-1866*, Vol.3, New York, 1933.
Newstead, H.	*Bran the Blessed in Arthurian Romance*, New York University Press, 1939.
Nattiez, J.J.	*Orientations*, Macmillan, London, 1986.
Nichols, Roger	*Debussy*, Cambridge University Press, Cambridge, 1972.
Nichols, Roger	*Debussy*, Oxford University Press, London, 1973.
Nichols, Roger	*Ravel*, Dent, London, 1977.
Nichols, Roger	*Olivier Messiaen*, Oxford University Press, London, 1986.
Nichols, Roger	*The Life of Debussy*, Cambridge, Cambridge University Press, 1998.
Nietszsche, F.	*Ecce Homo (Behold the Man)*, Trans. Kaufmann, Munich, 1956.

von Oberge, Eilhart	*Tristant*, Ed. Fran Lichtenstein, *Quellen und Forschungen zur Sprach - und Kulturgeschichte*, Vol. XIX, Strasbourg, 1877.
von Oberge, Eilhart	*Tristrant*, Ed. K. Wagner, *Reinische Beiträge*, Vol.V, Bonn, 1924.
von Oberge, Eilhart	*Tristrant*, Synopsized by Gertrude Schoepperle, *Tristan and Isolt: A Study of the Sources of the Romance*, 2 vols., Frankfurt and London, 1913; reprinted New York, 1959, 1, 11-65.
Orenstein, Arbie	*Ravel Man and Musician*, Columbia University Press, New York, 1975.
Orledge, R.	*Debussy and the Theatre*, Cambridge University Press, Cambridge, 1982.
Ostini, K.	*Bayreuther Festblätter in Wort und Bild*, Munich, 1884.
Périer, A.	*Messiaen*, Seuil, Paris, 1979.
Polidori, F.L. (Ed)	*La Tavola Ritonda*, Collezione di opere inedite o rare, VIII, Bologna, 1864.
Peyser, J.	*The New Music*, New York, 1971.
Pichois, C. (Ed.)	*Propos sur Baudelaire*, Paris, 1957.
Proust, M.	*A la recherche du temps perdu.*, 3 vols., Edition Pléiade, Paris, 1954.
Reverdy, M.	*L'Oeuvre pour orchestre d'Olivier Messiaen*, Leduc, Paris, 1988.
Rostand, C.	*Olivier Messiaen*, Oxford University Press, Oxford, 1986.

Routh, Francis	*Contemporary Music. an Introduction*, 2 vols., Dover Publications, New York, 1988.
Roy, J.A.	*Histoire du Jockey Club de Paris*, Paris, 1958.
Royer, A.	*Histoire de l'opéra*, Paris, 1875.
Rudorff, Raymond	*The Belle Epoque, Paris in the Nineties*, Hamilton, London, 1972.
Sadie, S.	*New Grove Dictionary of Opera*, Putnam, London, 1992.
Saintou, P.	*The Life of Richard Wagner*, 4 vols., Schirmer, New York, 1946.
Salzmann, Eric	*Twentieth-Century Music: An Introduction*, 2nd ed., Prentice-Hall, Englewood Cliffs, N.J., 1974.
Samuel, Claude	*Entretiens avec Olivier Messiaen*, Editions Pierre Belfond, Paris, 1967.
Samuel, Claude	*Olivier Messiaen. Music and Colour Conversations with Claude Samuel*, Trans. E. Thomas Glasgow, Amadeus Press, Portland, Orego, 1994.
Satie, Eric	*Ecrits*, Ed. Ornella Volta, Editions champ libre, Paris, 1977.
Schweizer, K.	*Olivier Messiaen Turangalîla–Symphonie*, Munich, Meisterwerke der Music, Heft 32, Wilhelm Fink Verlag, 1982.
Schoepperle, G.	*Tristan and Isolt: A Study of the Sources of the Romance*, 2 vols., Frankfurt and London, 1913; reprinted New York University Press, 1959.
Schuré,	*Le drame musical*, 2 vols., Paris, 1886.
Searle, H.	*The Music of Liszt*, Dent, London, 1975.

Snodgrass, J.	*A History of Philosophy and Religion in Germany*, Victor Gollancz Ltd., London, 1989.
Steegmuller, Francis	*Cocteau*, Macmillan, New York, 1970.
von Strassburg, Gottfried	*Tristran und Isolde*, Ed. and Trans. Wilhelm Hertz, *Tristan und Isolde von Gottfried von Strassburg*, 3rd ed., Stuttgart and Berlin, 1901.
von Strassburg, Gottfried	*Tristram und Isolt*, Ed. F. Ranke, Berlin, 1930.
von Strassburg, Gottfried	*Tristram und Isolt*, Ed. A. Closs, 2nd rev. ed., Oxford, 1947.
von Strassburg, Gottfried	*Tristram und Isolt*, Trans. A.T. Hatto, *Gottfried von Strassburg, Tristan with the Surviving Fragments of the Tristan of Thomas*, Harmondsworth, Middlesex and Baltimore, 1960.
Sutton, Denys	*André Derain*, Phaidon Press, London, 1959.
Symons, A.	*The Symbolist Movement in Literature*, New York, 1958.
Szabolesi, J.	*The Twilight of Ferenc Liszt*, London, 1959.
Thomas of Britain	*Die nordische und die englische Version der Tristansage*, 2 vols., Trans. Brother Robert of Norway, Heilbronn, 1882.
Thomas of Britain	*Le Roman de Tristan par Thomas*, Ed. Joseph Bédier, Société des anciens textes français, No.LIII, 2 vols, Paris, 1902-5.
Thomas of Britain	*Fragments du Tristan de Thomas*, Ed. B.H. Wind, Leiden, 1950.
Thomas of Britain	*The Romance of Tristram and Ysolt*, Ed. and Trans. Robert Sherman Loomis, rev. ed. New York, 1951.

Thomas of Britain	*Gottfried von Strassburg. Tristan with the Surviving Fragments of the Tristan of Thomas*, Trans. A.T. Hatto, Harmondsworth, Middlesex and Baltimore, 1960.
Tienot, Yvonne	*Chabrier par lui-même et par ses intimes*, H. Lemoine, Paris, 1965.
Tiersot, J. (Ed)	*Lettres françaises de Richard Wagner*, Durand, Paris, 1935.
Tour, M. de la	*Mémoires de Louise Méritte-Viardot*, Girod, Paris, 1922.
Toye, F.	*Rossini: A Study in Tragi-Comedy*, Macmillan, London, 1934.
Prose *Tristan*	*Le roman en prose de Tristan*, Ed. E. Löseth, Paris, 1891.
Oxford Folie *Tristan*	*Folie Tristan d'Oxford*, Ed. Ernest Hoepffner, 2nd ed., Paris, 1943.
Sir *Tristrem*	Die nordische und die englische version der Tristan-sage, Ed. Eugen Kölbing, 2 vols., Heilbronn, 1882.
Ystoria *Tristan*	*The Romance of Tristran and Ysolt*, Ed. and Trans. Roger Sherman Loomis, rev. ed., New York, 1951, xxi-xxvi.
Vallas, Léon	*Claude Debussy, his Life and Works*, Trans. Maire and Grace O'Brien, Oxford University Press, London, 1933, repr., Dover, New York, 1973.
Vier, I.	*La comtesse d'Agoult et son temps*, Paris, 1963.
Vinaver, E.	*Etudes sur le Tristan en prose. les sources. les manuscrits, bibliographie critique*, Mouton, Paris, 1925.

Vinaver, E.	*The Tale of the Death of King Arthur by Sir Thomas Malory*, Oxford University Press, London, 1955.
Vinaver, E.	*Sir Thomas Malory. Arthurian Literature in the Middle Ages*, Oxford University Press, London, 1959.
Vinaver, E.	*The Prose Tristan. Arthurian Literature in the Middle Ages*, Oxford University Press, London, 1959.
Wagner, C.	*Cosima Wagner's Diaries*, Trans. G. Skelton, 2 vols., London, 1978-80.
Wagner, R.	*Tristan und Isolde*, Breitkopf and Härtel, Wiesbaden, 1865.
Wagner, R.	*Gesammette Schriften*, Leipzig, 1887.
Wagner, R.	*Richard Wagner's Prose Works*, Ed. and Trans. W.A. Ellis, 8 vols., London, 1892-9.
Wagner, R.	*Parsifal* (vocal score), Trans. Margaret H. Glyn, Mainz, B. Schott's Söhne, 1902.
Wagner, R.	*Gesammette Schriften und Dichtungen von Richard Wagner*, 10 vols., Peters, Leipzig, 1907.
Wagner, R.	*Mein Leben*, Eulenburg, Munich, 1963.
Wagner, R.	*Wagner Writes from Paris. Stories, Essays and Articles by the Young Composer*, Ed. and Trans. R. Jacobs and G. Skelton, London, 1973.
Wagner, R.	*Richard Wagner: Stories and Essays*, Ed. C. Osborne, London, 1973.

Wagner, R.	*Wagner on Music and Drama: A Compendium of R. Wagner's Prose Works*, Eds. Goldman, Albert and Sprinchorn, Evert eds., New York, 1964, repr. 1977.
Wagner, R.	*Three Wagner Essays*, Trans. and Ed. R. Jacobs, *Music of the Future, On Conducting and On Performing Beethoven's Ninth Symphony*, Eulenburg, London, 1979.
Wagner, R.	*The Diary of Richard Wagner 1865-1882: The Brown Book*, translated and annotated by Bergfeld and Bird, Victor Gollancz Ltd, London, 1980.
Wagner, R.	*My Life*, Trans. of 1976 edn. A. Gray, Ed. M. Whittall, Cambridge University Press, Cambridge, 1983.
Walker, A. (Ed)	*Franz Liszt*, Barrie and Jenkins, London, 1970.
Waterhouse, E.S.	*The Philosophical Approach to Religion*, Epworth Press, London, 1983.
Waumsley, S.	*The Organ Music of Olivier Messiaen*, Leduc, Paris, 1968.
Wenk, A.B.	*Debussy and the Poets*, Berkeley, University of California Press, 1976.
Whitehead, F.	The Early Tristan Poems. Arthurian Literature in the Middle Ages, Ed. R.S. Loomis, Oxford University Press, London, 1959.
Zeldin, Theodore	France 1848-1945, 2 vols. Clarendon Press, Oxford, 1973.
Zeldin, Theodore	Emile Ollivier and the Liberal Empire of Napoleon lll, Open University Press, 1963.

Zimmer, H.	Beitrage zur Namenforschung in den altfranz Arthurepen, "Tristan Isolt Marc", Zeitsehrift fur französische Sprach und Litteratur, XIII, 1891.
Zuckerman, E.	The First Hundred Years of Wagner's Tristan, Columbia University Press, New York, 1964.
Zuckerman, E.	Encyclopaedica Biblica; Adam and Charles Black; London; 1973.
Zuckerman, E.	Encyclopaedica Judaica; Keter Publishing House Ltd, Jerusalem; 1971.
Zuckerman, E.	Macmillan Encyclopedia, London and Basingstoke, 1981.

Brochures

Bayreuther Festblätter in Wort und Bild, Munich, 1848.

Stanford French Review 5, 1981, pp 97-106.

L'illustration, 27 June 1857.

Periodicals

Aber, Adolf	"Wohin des Wegs," *Melos*, 16 October, 1920 : 378-84.
Armfelt, N.	"Emotion in the Music of Messiaen," *Musical Times*, November, 1965 : 856.
Auric, Georges	"Du 'Sacré du printemps' à 'Maura *Les nouvelles littéraires*, 6 January, 1923 : 4.
Auric, Georges	"M. Vuillermoz et la musique d'aujourd'hui," *Les nouvelles littéraires*, 10 March, 1923 : 4.
Auric, Georges	"La musique," *Les nouvelles littéraires*, 26 April, 1924: 7.
Auric, Georges	"La musique: quelques maîtres contemporains," *Les écrits nouveux*, March, 1922 : 70-78.
Auric, Georges	"Une oeuvre nouvelle de theatre," *Littérature*, March, 1919: 24.
Banés, Antoine	"Courrier des théâtres," *Le Figaro*, 13 May, 1920: 3.
Bordes, Charles	"Credo d'art", *La tribune de Saint Gervais*, September, 1903: 307.
Bromwich, R,	"Some Remarks on the Celtic Sources of Tristan" The *Transactions of the Honourable Society of Cymmrodorion, Session 1953*, London, 1955 32-60.
Brussel, Robert	"Les concerts", *Le Figaro*, 10 April, 1922: 4.
Burkat, L.	"*Turangalîla-Symphonie*", *Musical Quarterly*, Vol XXXVI April, 1950: 259-68.
Calvocoressi, M.D.	"Debussy and the Leitmotiv, *Musical Times*, 66 1935 695- 97.

Chalupl, René	"Ravel", *Les ecrits nouveaux*, December, 1918 312-19.
Cicore, M.A.	"Mythology as Metaphor, Romantic Irony, a Critical Theory and Wagner's Ring", contribution to the study of *Music and Dance*, No.46, Westport Greenwood 1998.
Drew, D	"Messiaen - a provisional study", *The Score*, December, 1954 8-9.
Dujardin, Edouard	Chronique: fin de saison, M Lamoureux, M d'Indy et Chabrier", *Revue wagnérienne*, 8 April, 1886 97-99.
Dujardin, Edouard	"Chronique (Les wagnéristes)" *Revue wagnérienne* 8 April, 1885 : 57-58.
Evans, A.	"Olivier Messiaen in the Surrealist Context a Bibliography" *Brio*, X1, 1974: 25-35.
Friedheim, P.	"Wagner and the Aesthetics of the Scream" *Nineteenth Century Music* Vol.VII No 1 Summer, 1983 63-70.
Gavoty, Bernard	"Who Are You, Olivier Messiaen?" *Tempo*, 58 Summer, 1961 : 33-36 and 42-48.
Gervais, Françoise	*Etude comparée des langages harmoniques de Fauré et de Debussy*, Diss., Université de Paris, 1951, 2 vols published as special number of *La Revue Musicale*, 1971 272-273.
Goléa, Antoine	"French Music Since 1945", *Musical Quarterly*, 51, January 1965: 22.
Griessle, Felix	"Die Formalen Grundlagen des Bläserquintetts von Arnold Schoenberg", *Musikblatter des Anbruch*, February, 1925 63- 68.

Hahn, Reynaldo	"Les théatres—Les premières", *Excelsior*, 17 May, 1920: 1.
Henry, Leigh	"London Letter", *Chesterian*, January, 1921: 371.
Hirsbrunner, T.	"Zu Debussys und Ravels Mallarmé-Vertonungen" (On the Mallarmé settings of Debussy and Ravel), *Archiv für Musikwissenschaft*, 35, 1978: 81-103.
Hold, T.	"Messiaen's Birds", *Music and Letters*, lii, 1971: 113-22.
Jean-Aubry, Georges	"Claude Debussy", *The Musical Quarterly*, 4.4 (1918): 542-54.
Laloy, Louis	"Le courrier de Paris - La musique - Les ballets russes", *L'Europe nouvelle*, 23 May, 1920: 679-80.
Laloy, Louis	"Wagner et nos musiciens", *La grande revue*, 10 April and 10 May, 1909: 558-66 and 160-164.
Landormy, Paul	"L'état actuel de la musique française", *La revue bleue*, 26 March and 2 April, 1904: 394-97 and 421-26.
Landowska, Wanda	"Bach et ses interprètes. Sur l'interprétation des oeuvres de clavecin de J.S. Bach", *Mercure de France*, 15 November, 1905 : 214-30.
Lessem, Alan	"Schoenberg, Stravinsky and Neo-Classicism : The Issues Re- examined", *The Musical Quarterly*, 68.4 (1982): 541.
Lesure, François	"Claude Debussy after his Centenary", *The Musical Quarterly*, 49.3 (1963): 268.
Mallarmé, Stephane	"Richard Wagner, rêverie d'un poète français", *Revue wagnérienne*, 1, 1885: 195-200.

Meier, M.	"The Court of Justice of the Eumenides and of Götterdämmerung. Further Aspects of Aeschylean Influence on the Work of Richard Wagner", *Die Musik Forschung*, Vol.Li-4, Oct.-Dec. 1998: 409-419.
Mendès, Catulle	"Le jeune prix de Rome et le vieux wagnériste", *Revue wagnérienne*, 8 June, 1885 1 131-35.
Messiaen, Olivier	"Pièce pour le tombeau de Paul Dukas", *Revue Musicale*, 166, 1936.
Messiaen, Olivier	"Le rythme chez Igor Stravinsky", *Revue Musicale*, 191, 1939: 91-92.
Morland, Jacques	"Enquète sur l'influence allemande: VI Musique", *Mercure de France*, January, 1903: 89-110.
Newman, Ernest	"The Present Trend", *Musical Times*, 1 June, 1917: 249.
Oxford *Folie Tristan*	"Les Deux Poèmes de la Folie Tristan", Ed. Joseph Bédier, *Société des anciens textes français. No.LIV*, Paris, 1907.
Scott, Cyril	"The Genius of French Music", *The Musical Times*, 1 October, 1917: 447.
Smalley, R.	"Debussy and Messiaen", *Musical Times*, V, 109, February, 1968: 128-131.
Tiersot, Julien	"Promenades musicales à l'exposition", *Le ménestrel*, 9 June, 1889: 180.
Tiersot, Julien	"Promenades musicales à l'exposition", *Le ménestrel*, 23 June, 1889: 196.
Ystoria *Tristan*	"L'Ystoria Trystan et la question des archétypes", Ed. and Trans. J. Loth, *Revue Celtique*, XXXIV, 1913: 366-96.
Ystoria *Tristan*	*A Welsh Tristan Episode*, Ed. and Trans. Tom Peete Cross, *Studies in Philology*, XVII, 1920: 93-110.

Ystoria *Tristan*	*Trystan ac Esyllt*, Ed. Sir Ifor Williams, *Bulletin of the Board of Celtic Studies*, V, 1930.
Wellesz, Egon	"Die letzten werke Claude Debussys", *Melos*, 16 May, 1920: 166-68.
Wyzewa, Téodore de	"La musique descriptive", *Revue Wagnérienne*, 8 April, 1885: 75-76.

Dissertations

van Appledorn, Mary Jean	*A Stylistic Study of Claude Debussy's Opera Pelléas et Mélisande*, Ph.D. Diss., The University of Rochester, 1966 (Ann Arbor: University Microfilms, 67-1312).
Briscoe, James	"The Compositions of Claude Debussy's Formative Years", Diss., University of North Carolina, 1979.
Fulcher, J.	"Wagner, Courty and Proudhon: Aesthetics of Positivism in France", *Symposium* 33, 1979, pp. 142-152.
Goehr, L.	"The Quest for Voice: on Music, Politics and the Limits of Philosophy", *1997 Ernest Bloch Lectures*, Clarendon Press, Oxford, 1998.
Ringgold, John Robert	*The Linearity of Debussy's Music and its Correspondences with the Symbolist Aesthetic : Developments Before 1908*, Ph.D. Diss., University of Southern California, 1972 (Ann Arbor: University Microfilms, 73-762).
Seraphin, Helmut	*Debussy Kammermusikwerke der mittleren Schaffenzeit*, Diss., Erlangen, 1962, Kassel: Bärenreiter, 1964.

Documents

Denis, M. — *Henri Lerolle et ses amis, suivi de quelques lettres d'amis*, Imprimerie Duranton, Paris, 1932.

Lesure, François, Ed. — *Claude Debussy I Iconographie Musicale*, Editions Minkoff, Geneva: 1975.

Scores

Debussy, C.	*Pelléas et Mélisande*, Editions Durand et Cie., Paris, 1902.
Debussy, C.	*Préludes* pour piano, premier livre, Durand, Paris, 1910.
Debussy, C.	*Préludes* pour piano, deuxième livre, Durand, Paris, 1913.
Debussy, C.	*Pelléas et Mélisande*, full score, Durand, Paris, 1957.
Debussy, C.	*Pelléas et Mélisande*, vocal score, International, New York, 1962.
Debussy, C.	*Pelléas et Mélisande*, study score, International, New York, 1962.
Messiaen, O.	*Préludes*, Durand, Paris, 1929.
Messiaen, O.	*Harawi* ("Chant d'amour et de mort"), Leduc, Paris, 1945.
Messiaen, O.	*Cinq Rechants*, Salabert, Paris, 1948.
Messiaen, O.	*Turangalîla - Symphonie*, Durand, Paris, 1948.
Wagner, R.	*Tristan und Isolde*, Trans. H. and F. Corder, Breitkopf und Härtel, Wiesbaden: 1865.

General Index

Ad nos, ad salutarem undam,   *16, 18, 139*

Adieu,   *100, 108, 110, 122, 139*

Adoro te,   139, 153

Alberich,   19, 139

Allemonde,   53, 139

Amen des étoiles,   *41, 139*

Amour, oiseau d'étoile,   *32, 56–58, 75–76, 96, 99, 102, 104, 106, 108, 120–123, 125–130, 133–135, 137, 139–142, 144–145, 148–149, 181*

Anabaptists,   16, 139

Années de Pèlerinage,   *15, 139*

Antiphon Melodies,   36, 139

Anti-Wagnerism,   23

Archaism,   26, 71, 139

Ardiane et Barbe Bleue,   *139, 144*

Aristotle,   93, 139

Arkel,   49, 51, 53, 139

Arnauld,   86, 139

Artus,   7–8, 139

Attacking Character,   116–117, 139

Awakened One,   87, 139

Bach,   16–18, 139, 176

Bartok,   4, 11–12, 119, 139

Baudelaire,   25, 74, 139, 155–156, 166

Bédier,	7–8, 139, 156, 168, 177
Berg,	130, 139
Berlioz,	5, 48, 139, 156, 158
Béroul,	63–65, 139, 156
Bhavachakra,	88, 140
Bihar,	87, 140
Binary Sentence,	40–41, 140
Birdsong,	36, 123, 133, 140
Bizet,	23, 140
Boris Godunov,	*34, 48, 51, 121, 140*
Bosch,	140–141, 144–145, 148
Boulez,	v, 11–12, 22, 24, 33, 37–38, 117, 140, 157, 160, 165
Bourgeois Drama,	84, 140
Brahms,	16, 140
Brangaene,	73, 81, 121, 134, 140, 142–143, 145
Brentano,	133, 140
Breton,	8, 63, 72, 140–141, 160
Brother Robert,	64, 140, 168
Brünnhilde,	20, 128, 140
Buddha,	7, 28, 87–90, 140
Cantéyodjayâ,	*39, 75, 140*
Catalogue d'Oiseaux,	*8, 118, 140*
Celtic sagas,	22, 140
Chaconne,	19, 140
Chaffinch,	140
Chagall,	140–141

Chant d'amour I,	*121–122, 134, 140*
Chant d'amour II,	*123, 134, 140*
Chants d'amour,	75, 140
Chants de terre et de ciel,	*34, 140*
Charm of Impossibilities,	32, 140
Chausson,	19, 141
Chivalric,	23, 141
Chopin,	13–15, 141
Chrétien de Troyes,	63, 141
Christianity,	22, 27–28, 69, 99, 141, 151
Chronochromie,	*38, 118, 141*
Cinq Rechants,	*ix, ix, 2–3, 5, 13–14, 26–28, 39, 54–55, 57, 59–60, 69, 74–76, 95, 118, 122, 139–146, 148–149, 181*
Claude le Jeune,	26, 28, 59, 140–141, 146
Codice Ponciatichiano,	*65, 141*
Combat de la Mort et de la Vie,	*34, 40*
Comtesse d'Agoult,	15, 141, 169
Consolations,	*15, 141*
Couleurs de la Cité céleste,	*141*
Cubist,	141–142
Dans le noir,	*54, 100, 104, 108, 141, 152*
Danse sacrale,	*9, 28, 38–39, 141*
Dante,	82, 141
Darmstadt,	118, 141
de Bornelh,	141, 146
de Marseilles,	141, 146–147

Debussy,	ix, 1–2, 4–8, 13, 19–20, 23–26, 28–29, 43, 45–54, 60, 95, 98–99, 107, 121, 123, 126–127, 130–131, 136, 141, 152, 155, 158–162, 165–166, 169, 171, 174–177, 179–181
Der fliegende Holländer,	*92, 141, 143*
Des pas sur la neige,	*4, 141*
Développement de l'amour,	*58, 76, 120–121, 126–127, 141*
Dharma,	87, 141
dhenki,	102, 142
Diaghilev,	11–12, 142
Dickens,	131, 142
Die Meistersinger,	*46, 142*
Dieu parmi nous,	*34, 142*
Doundou tchil,	55–56, 98–99, 105, 108–109, 111, 142
Dresden Amens,	91, 142
Dukas,	11, 31, 142, 144, 177
Dupré,	31, 36, 142
Dyptyque,	*34, 142*
Ecce Homo,	82, 142, 165
Ecclesiastical,	27, 142
Edda,	45, 142
Edgar Allan Poe,	25, 126, 130, 142
Eichendorff,	133, 142
Eightfold Path,	88, 142
Eilhart von Oberge,	64
Engels,	93, 142
Enlightenment,	28, 87–88, 142

Episodic Construction,	41, 142
Exposition Universelle,	24, 50, 142
Fauré,	50, 142, 158, 165, 175
Flower Theme,	56, 121, 133–134, 142
Fokine,	12, 142
Four Noble Truths,	88, 142
French prose,	24, 65, 142
Fugue,	16–18, 31, 142
Gamelan,	28, 123, 125, 128, 143
Gautama,	28, 87–88, 143
Geoffrey of Monmouth,	63, 143
German myth,	23, 143
Gesamtkunstwerk,	66, 143
Gide,	74, 143
God,	19, 31–32, 67–68, 71, 86, 89, 93, 143, 147, 152
Goethe,	93, 143
Golaud,	6–7, 50–53, 107, 143
Gottfried,	1–3, 22, 63–72, 74, 76, 79, 118, 131-132, 134, 136, 143, 151, 160–161, 168–169
Gottfried von Strassburg,	22, 64, 67–68, 70–72, 79, 132, 151, 160–161, 168–169
Gounod,	23, 119, 143
Greek metre,	31, 143
Green Dove,	55, 96, 100, 106, 108, 110–113, 143
Gregorian,	52, 143

Haec Dies,	*36, 143*
Hagen,	19, 143
Harawi,	*ix, 2–3, 5, 12–15, 19–20, 25–26, 32, 42, 54–56, 60, 69, 74–76, 95–108, 118, 122, 132–133, 135, 139–144, 146–149, 152, 181*
Harmonic Forms,	31, 143
Hegelianism,	86, 143
Hellenistic,	139, 143
Hindemith,	11–12, 143
Hindu music,	36, 143
Hindu rhythms,	35, 143
Hinduism,	88–89, 143
Holy Grail,	91, 144
Holy Spirit,	32, 144
Hymns to Night,	45, 144
Île de feu II,	*36, 38, 144*
Japanese theatre,	24, 144
Jardin du sommeil d'amour,	*57, 75, 125–126, 129–130, 133–134, 142, 144*
Jâtis,	36, 144
Jeux d'eau,	*8, 13, 144–145*
Joachim,	16, 144
Jung,	21, 144
Kant,	86, 93, 144
Kareol,	53, 72–73, 144
Kashchei,	12, 144

Kaswa,	104, 144
King of Lyonesse,	72, 144
Klangfarbenmelodie,	123, 128, 144
Klingsor,	23, 144
Kontakte,	38, 144
Kundry,	88, 144
Kurwenal,	72–73, 79–80, 144
Kusinagara,	88, 144
Kyrie,	35–36, 144
L'amour de Piroutcha,	32, 99, 104, 108, 144, 149
L'Ascension,	6, 34, 144
L'escalier redit gestes du soleil,	144
L'Evocation des Ancêtres,	144
L'oiseau de Feu,	11, 144
La joie de la grace,	145, 153
La Mer,	53, 145
La Messe de la Pentecôte,	38, 145
La Nativité du Seigneur,	39, 115, 145
La revue musicale,	19, 145, 175
La Source de Vie,	153
La ville qui dormait, toi,	13, 20, 54, 97, 104, 108, 145
Lavignac,	36, 46, 145
Le Banquet céleste,	32, 118, 145
Le Martyre,	47, 52, 145
Le plein minuit le banc,	20, 145
Le Prophète,	16, 145

Le roman de Tristan,	*7, 145, 156, 168*
Le Rossignol,	*12, 145*
Le Sacre du Printemps,	*9–10, 28, 33, 145*
Leibniz,	86, 145
Leitmotiv,	20, 51–52, 145, 174
Les Corps Glorieux,	*31, 34, 36, 145*
Les Jeux d'eau à la Villa d'Este,	13
Les Offrandes oubliées,	*9, 145*
Les Sylphides,	*12, 145*
Les Ténèbres,	*145, 153*
Liadov,	11, 145
Liebestod,	93, 96, 120, 145
Limpid Pearl,	55, 106, 108, 110, 112–113, 145
Liszt,	1, 4, 8, 13–19, 28–29, 81, 85, 92, 145–146, 161, 167–168, 171
Liszt Piano Concerto No.	1, 13
Liszt's Organ Music,	16, 146
Livre du Saint Sacrement,	*118, 146, 153*
Lohengrin,	*46–47, 92, 146*
Love death,	76, 146
Love Potion,	71, 142, 146
Love Theme,	57–58, 76, 124, 127, 129, 133, 146
Love's Transfiguration,	54, 146
Lovedeath,	146
Maeterlinck, ix, ix,	4, 6, 24–25, 49, 131, 144, 146
Mahayana,	28, 88, 146
Mallarmé,	25, 37, 146, 163, 176

Mallatâla,	146
Malory,	143, 146, 170
Marx,	93, 146
Massenet,	23, 119, 146
Mathilde Wesendonck,	80, 83–84, 146
Mayan,	96, 146
Medieval,	3, 8, 19, 45, 66–67, 82, 95, 105, 132, 146–147, 159
Meditations sur le Mystère,	*20, 146*
Mélisande,	1, 5–7, 20, 24, 46–47, 50, 52–54, 60, 95, 98–99, 107, 121, 131, 146, 148, 159, 179, 181
Melot,	24, 51, 58, 73, 79–80, 146
Merseburg Cathedral,	18, 146
Messiaen, v, ix,	1–22, 24–29, 31–43, 45–46, 53–60, 63–64, 67–71, 74–77, 79, 83, 93, 95–107, 115–128, 130–136, 139–149, 151–153, 159–161, 163–167, 171, 174–177, 181
Meyerbeer,	16–17, 23, 146
Mode de Valeurs et d'intensites,	*117*
Modes of limited transposition,	ix, 32, 37, 42, 147
Monodic Theme,	41, 147
Montagnes,	*55, 97–98, 108, 147*
Morold,	70, 72, 147
Morrois Wood,	79, 147
Musiques nocturnes,	*4–5, 147*
Mussorgsky,	48–49, 51, 130, 147
Mystical Experience,	32, 147

nandayantî,	36, 147
Necrophilism,	20, 147
Neoclassicism,	19, 147
NeoHellenic,	147
NeoMedievalism,	147
Nibelung,	19, 147
Nietzsche,	3, 48, 81–83, 147, 162
Nietzsche Contra Wagner,	82, 147
Nightingale,	12, 125, 147
Nirvana,	7, 28, 88–89, 92, 105, 147
Noctuelles,	*8, 147*
NonRetrogradable,	147
NonTheological,	147
Notes of an Apprenticeship,	24, 33, 147, 157
Novalis,	45–46, 147
O sink hernieder Nacht der Liebe,	*57, 147*
Observer,	38, 117, 147
Oiseaux tristes,	*4, 8, 147*
Ondes Martenot,	25, 39, 115–116, 121–123, 125–126, 147
Otto Wesendonck,	84, 148, 161
Paris Conservatory,	31, 33, 36, 148
Parlando,	25, 148
Parsifal,	*4, 7, 46–48, 51, 60, 91, 124, 148, 156, 170*
Parzival,	45, 60, 148
Pelléas et Mélisande,	*1, 5–7, 20, 24, 46–47, 50, 52, 54, 60, 95,*

	98–99, 107, 121, 131, 148, 159, 179, 181
Pentatonic Structure,	52, 148
Personnages Rythmiques,	116–117, 123, 148
Petrushka,	*10, 12, 148*
Piroutcha,	3, 19, 26–27, 32, 42, 53–55, 74, 96–105, 107–109, 111, 118–119, 133, 135, 144, 148–149, 152–153
Pit and the Pendulum,	126, 146, 148
Plainsong,	9, 13, 36, 148
Plato,	21, 86, 93, 148
Poèmes pour Mi,	*5, 33–34, 39, 115, 148*
Polyrhythmic,	9, 148
PreRaphaelite,	148
Proust,	74–76, 148, 166
Quatour pour la fin du Temps,	*37, 148*
Quetchua,	96, 148
Radhula,	87, 148
Râgavardhana,	35, 40, 148
Ramayana,	89, 148
Rationalism,	86–87, 148
Ravel,	4, 8, 148, 157–158, 165–166, 175–176
Regard du temps,	*41, 148*
Reincarnation,	80, 89, 93, 148
Reis glorios,	*146–147, 149*
Répétition planétaire,	*19, 100, 108, 149*
Répons,	*38, 149*

Revue Wagnérienne,	*46, 149, 175–178*
Rhetoric,	71–72, 149
Rhetorical Exaggeration,	49, 149
Rhinemaidens,	20, 149
Rhythmic Canon,	34, 37, 41, 96, 104, 149
Rhythmic Canons,	37, 96–97, 102, 104, 149
Rhythmic Cells,	9, 37–38, 149
Rhythmic characters,	9, 31, 38–39, 42, 116–117, 149
Rhythmic Ostinati,	37, 149
RimskyKorsakov,	149
Ring cycle,	47, 149
Rivalin,	66, 72, 149
Rodrigue de Chimène,	*51, 149*
Roman Catholic Church,	31, 149
Romeo and Juliet,	*82, 96, 149*
Rossetti,	133, 149
Ruskin,	133, 149
SainteBeuve,	149
Salve Regina,	*36, 149*
Samgîtaratnâkara,	149
Sanskrit,	40, 87, 115, 130, 140–141, 149
Scharf markiert,	14, 149
Schattenseite,	131, 149
Schiller,	93, 149
Schopenhauer, ix, ix,	3, 27, 80, 85–87, 89–93, 119, 150–151, 160
Shakespeare,	80, 82, 130–131, 150

Shaw,	92, 150
Siddhartha,	28, 87, 150
Siegfried,	20, 150
Sieglinde,	20, 150
Siegmund,	20, 150
Simhavikridita,	39, 150
Sonetti del Petrarca,	*15, 150*
Spinoza,	86, 150
St. François d'Assise,	*4, 150*
Star bird,	102, 113, 150
Statue theme,	56–57, 116, 120–121, 123–124, 133–134, 150
Stockhausen,	35, 117, 150
Stravinsky,	1, 4, 8–12, 28, 33, 38, 119, 130, 150, 157, 176–177
Suddhodama,	87, 150
Superimposition,	35, 40, 42–43, 150
Surrealism,	3, 5, 21, 141–142, 149–150
Surrealistic,	139, 150
Suspended Tonality,	13, 150
Syllables,	*25, 111, 140, 150*
Symbolic Ideas,	32, 42, 59, 150
Tantris,	72, 150
Tasso,	14, 150
Tavola Ritonda,	*22, 65–66, 150, 166*
Technique de mon langage musical,	*36, 150, 164*
Tennyson,	143, 150

The Divine Comedy,	82, 151
The double violet,	20, 108, 111, 114
The Fire Bird,	*9, 151*
The Rite of Spring,	*9, 119, 151*
The Victors,	89
theme d'Accords,	*126–127, 151*
Theological,	2, 31–32, 42, 65, 76, 151–152
Theravada,	28, 88, 151
Thomas of Britain,	64, 151, 168–169
Traité de Rythme,	*75, 96–102, 104, 116, 122, 125–126, 128, 151, 164*
Transformation Of Themes,	14, 151
Tristan myth,	ix, 1–5, 13, 22–24, 26–29, 31, 43, 45, 54, 59–61, 63–66, 72, 74, 76–77, 79, 81, 93, 95, 99, 107, 127, 130, 132, 135, 137, 139, 142–143, 147–149, 151–152
Tristan und Isolde,	*1–2, 20–21, 25–26, 46–47, 54–56, 58, 60, 74–76, 81–85, 91–93, 96–97, 103, 107, 119–120, 122, 129–130, 132–133, 136, 142–143, 151, 168, 170, 181*
Tristano Riccardiano,	*65, 151*
Tristram's Saga,	64, 151
Trois petites liturgies,	*28, 151*
Turangalîla,	*ix, 2–3, 5, 9, 11–14, 21, 25–28, 35, 37, 39–42, 54, 56–60, 69, 75–76, 115–122, 124–126, 128–137, 139–140, 142, 144–146, 151–152, 167, 174, 181*
Turangalîla,	*ix, 2–3, 5, 9, 11–14, 21, 25–28, 35, 37, 39–42, 54, 56–60, 69, 75–76, 115–122, 124–126, 128–137, 139–140, 142, 144–146, 151–152, 167, 174, 181*

Typologies,	71, 151
Upanishads,	85, 151, 163
Uttar Pradesh,	88, 151
Vaughan Williams,	18, 151
Venus,	83, 151
Verdi,	48, 130, 151, 155
Verlaine,	50, 151
Vers Dieu,	*147, 151*
Vingt Regards,	*31, 41–42, 74, 131, 151*
Visions de l'Amen,	*37, 41, 131, 152*
Volsunga Saga,	45, 152
von Bülow,	82, 152
von Meysenburg,	83, 152
Wagner, ix, ix,	1–8, 15, 19–29, 45–60, 63, 66, 72, 74–77, 79–85, 87–89, 91–93, 95–98, 103, 107, 119–122, 124, 128–130, 132–136, 139, 142–143, 147,152, 155–157, 159–162, 164–167, 169–172, 175–177, 179, 181
Webern,	119, 152
Weimar,	15–18, 152
Wesendonck Lieder,	*57, 152*
William Morris,	133, 152
Winterberger,	17, 152
yaravi,	147, 152
Yasodhara,	87, 152
Yniold,	50, 152
Yseult,	72, 96, 125

www.ingramcontent.com/pod-product-compliance
Lightning Source LLC
Chambersburg PA
CBHW070547170426
43201CB00012B/1745